Militant Islam

the text of this book is printed
on 100% recycled paper

G.H. Jansen

Militant Islam

HARPER & ROW, PUBLISHERS

NEW YORK

Cambridge
Hagerstown
Philadelphia
San Francisco

1817

London
Mexico City
São Paulo
Sydney

297.197

FIRST U.S. EDITION

ISBN: 0-06-012202-1
      0-06-090759-2 pbk

LIBRARY OF CONGRESS CATALOG CARD NUMBER: 79-2623

80 81 82 83 84 10 9 8 7 6 5 4 3

Contents

that she may,
in the years to come, understand –
.this book is for
Marya Elin Jansen
binti Hajja Michael Elin

Acknowledgements

I wish to give thanks to:

Brian Beedham, Foreign Editor of the *Economist*, who started it all by suggesting I write an essay on militant Islam for that publication.

Dr George Georgalides, of Nicosia, who made the further suggestion that the published essay be expanded into a book.

The *Economist*, for giving me the time to write this book.

St Antony's College, Oxford, for providing the place.

The Middle East Centre, of that College, and everybody there, for hospitality, facilities and quiet.

Albert Hourani, especially: intellectual godfather to an entire generation – now almost two – of students of, and writers on, the Middle East; for being infinitely helpful and stimulating, but demanding; a work such as this cannot but fall short of his high and 'judicious' standards, but, I hope, not too far short.

The Librarians of Pusey Hall and the Commonwealth Institute, Oxford.

Doctor Mehdi Teheranian.

Diana Markides, of Nicosia, for the Cromwellian references.

Margaret Ko, of New Marston, for her hard, fast work turning a rather difficult manuscript into legible type.

Martin Wollacott, my colleague of the *Guardian*, for his helpful generosity with books and information.

My wife, Michael, who, by providing it herself, relieved me of worry about the journalistic 'coverage' of my turbulent parish when my back was turned; and for her distracting but encouraging telephone calls; and for everything else.

Prologue

'There is no new thing under the sun,' certainly not in the human domains of religion or politics or of politics-religion. Therefore, 'militant Islam', now so very much in the news, is really no new thing. It has caught the attention of the world merely because several different manifestations of political Islam have emerged, more or less simultaneously, in several Muslim countries. Otherwise there is nothing new in the claim, now being reiterated with varying degrees of insistence and power, that Islam, in countries with Muslim majorities, must be central to every aspect of life, especially politics. The essential nature of Islam requires that such an assertion, and the political pressure it produces, is made on the structure of the Muslim state. What has happened in the past few years is that this Islamic pressure has broken through the weakening structure of several Muslim states, culminating spectacularly in the Iranian uprising led by Muslim men of religion. But this is only the most recent episode in the long history of militant Islam, a history as old as Islam itself. And, in the future, as long as Islam retains any real vitality it will necessarily contain within it elements of political militancy.

Since about 1973, in the aftermath of the Arab–Israel war of that year, it has been gradually borne in on the minds of Western observers that something 'new' was brewing out there in the East, a lowering thunderstorm moving out of Asia. It was, of course, the oil embargo imposed by Muslim countries, with its resultant scarcity of fuel oil, that drove the point home to every single Western citizen through sheer physical discomfort and inconvenience. Since then evidence of a political resurgence of Islam in many Muslim countries, from Morocco to the Philippines, has accumulated with increasing speed. In the Philippines itself, even before 1973, the Muslim minority in the southern islands, the Moros, had been fighting the central government in a prolonged guerrilla war, in which, moreover, they were being helped quite openly by Muslim countries far removed from the area of the South China Sea, like Saudi Arabia and Libya. General Suharto, in Indonesia, was under constant pressure from Muslim political parties to move towards an 'Islamic state' and away from his devotion to Jewanere mysticism. (In Pakistan there has been a continuation of the endless debate on the constitution of an Islamic state and its manifestation in the form of such punishments as the whipping of thieves and wine-bibbers. In neighbouring Afghanistan, Muslim tribesmen have joined battle with the new communist government, and the events in Iran, with the Ayatollah Khomeini and his Islamic state, are too well known to be more than mentioned. To add to Turkey's chronic internal violence Shiah Muslims have started killing Sunni Muslims in the eastern areas, while Muslim politicians do their best to dismantle Ataturk's ramshackle secular state. Even President Sadat and his equally moderate and pro-Western ally President Numeiry of the Sudan have been talking of Islamic constitutions and orthodox Muslim laws. In north Africa, Libya is, of course, an Islamic state, and in Morocco the party of the Muslim Brothers is said to be gaining strength secretly. And at the very heart of the Islamic world, the government of Saudi Arabia, the guardian of the holy places of Islam in Mecca and Medina, amputates and decapitates and prohibits women from using public swimming pools.)

The image that the Western observer could take away from his contemplation of this vast, turbulent unsettled area is one of precarious unease and violence – of strange, bearded men with burning eyes, hieratic figures in robes and turbans, of blood dripping from the stumps of amputated hands and from the striped backs of malefactors, and piles of stones barely concealing the battered bodies of adulterous couples.

But when all is said and done and, more particularly, the gory TV screen has been switched off, what is this Islamic resurgence really about? It is, very tamely, about autonomy, constitutions and legal systems. Why then is militant Islam a matter for alarm and despondency in the West? Why is it that it is almost exclusively the bloody, violent side of the movement that lodges in the Western memory? It is because these latest events are just the recent link in a long, long chain, part of a story of misunderstanding of the Muslim Orient by the Christian Occident that goes back 1500 years. There has been much written recently, in connection with this and similar topics, about the subtle but preponderating role in the relationship between groups of people that is played by 'attitudes', 'images' and 'stereotypes'. The relationship of Christian West to Islamic East is particularly replete with these set patterns. It has not even been a love-hate relationship: from the Western side the attitude to the Muslim East has been first one of fear and, later, of contempt; from the East towards the West there was first hate and then impotent envy mingled with just a little admiration.

Present-day attitudes reach back to and re-awaken atavistic stereotypes. In their more vague form these are the echoes and resonances of such evocative words as 'Moor', 'Turk', 'Arab', 'dervish', 'fuzzy-wuzzy' and 'mad mullah'. The mental pictures evoked are of green banners fluttering over Turkish cavalry galloping into the heart of Europe up along the Danube, of those same green flags flaring over the camel-riding hordes of the Mahdi trying to break the British military square. One of the many books that have been written about this long sad story of East–West misunderstanding begins with the despairing words: 'The earliest Christian reactions to Islam were something like those of much more recent date. The tradition has been continuous and it is still alive.'[1] The continuous tradition does, however, have its stages. In the world of medieval Europe, when Christianity was still alive, the Muslim was the pagan, the fanatical unbeliever who converted churches into mosques. A little later in history the Muslim Turk became a physical threat when in 1683 he laid siege to Vienna, and remained a menacing force in southeastern Europe for another two centuries; after all, the frontier of the Ottoman Empire ran within a few hundred miles of Belgrade until 1912. Even in the Age of Enlightenment the European attitude to Islam remained un-enlightened. Voltaire himself wrote a play entitled *Fanaticism, or the Prophet Mohammed*; a little later on the pictures of licentious Turks lolling in the harem with their odalisques painted by Ingres finally fixed the image of the Muslim as a vicious voluptuary. Later still, in the heyday and then during the long lingering twilight of European empire, Muslims, in many countries, were seen as subversive agitators, involved in vast pan-Islamic plots, culminating in that master-plotter Nasser, who had the temerity to filch the Suez Canal from its rightful owners. In the contemporary world the Arab has been incarnated by the Western cartoonist as the fat oil sheikh who seeks to buy up or bankrupt the West; or as the 'mad mullah' back again, but modernized and mechanized this time, brandishing his submachine gun instead of his lance or scimitar. So, like a complicated palimpsest, the Western image of the 'fanatic Muslim' has layers of religious, political and economic interest. Muslims have, in turn, hurt the West's faith, pride and pocketbook, and they are still at it, more than ever. Ample reason then, it would seem, for the alarm, despondency, even fear, arising in the West from the resurgence of militant Islam.

If it is any comfort, militant Islam today is part of a much wider problem that confronts not just the Muslim, not just Afro–Asia, but the whole of the Third World, the non-Western underdeveloped 'south' of the globe. This is the problem of how to come to terms with the Western way of life that is rapidly becoming the global way of life. Because it is an all-embracing challenge, we find in the East's politico-religious response not just militant Islam, but militant Hinduism (the assassin of Gandhi was a militant Hindu) and militant Buddhism (Ceylon's first prime minister, Solomon West Ridgeway Bandaranaike, was a Buddhist monk). The aggrieved feelings of the Third World have been expressed with brutal bluntness by a youngish, religious Muslim politician: 'Today backward and deprived, we face an economic and military giant with the moral and spiritual scruples of a flea. It is not a pleasant encounter.'[2] (Sadeh al Mahdi, former prime minister of the Sudan.)

And yet, if the West keeps its head and does not allow primitive hatred and fear of Islam to cloud its judgement, there is no real reason why its encounter with militant Islam should be unpleasant. In fact the West should have got used to the encounter with Islam because, since 1500, there has scarcely been any five-year period when Muslims have not been in arms against Europe somewhere in the Muslim world, and usually in more than one country at the same time. Now the arms of militant

Muslims are directed against their own people. However, it must be stated that the militantly Islamic countries could still use the economic power they have recently acquired should the West choose to be hostile.

Why should it? For what is militant Islam up to? It is, for the most part, a sincere attempt by leaders, some of them men of religion, some of them religious laymen for whom religion is a living, vital faith, to re-model their public and private life – politics, economics, law, social *mores* – according to the precepts of their faith. That surely is laudable or at least understandable: after all, Islam is monotheistic, is counted among the 'higher religions' and is universal; its followers number between a fifth and a quarter of the human race. What is wrong with this attempt to square the conduct of public life with the principles of religion? Why should not the attempt be made? It is, as we shall see, a most forbidding enterprise and no very great successes have been achieved anywhere so far. The one encouraging factor for Muslim reformers today is that the attempt is now being made more seriously and intelligently than ever before and in more than one country at the same time. There is strength in numbers, particularly when the number of Muslim countries following the path of militant Islam may quite suddenly be added to, as seems likely.

There are only three possible responses that the non-Westerner can make to the challenge of the West: he can join the West by imitating it; he can turn his back on the West, rejecting it and all its works; or he can, most difficult, try to work out a liveable compromise between his own cultural background and set of values and those of the West. Militant Islam has made the same three responses to the particular type of Western challenges it has had to face.

However, all Muslims, not just the militant ones, have to face a still greater, internal challenge, because for them God is not 'dead'.

Before describing the challenge and response we will first have to say something about the basic elements of the subject and object of the struggle – Islam itself, which lends itself to this confrontation because of the unique nature of one of its constituent elements.

It would, perhaps, be in order to sketch in here the vast

world-wide backdrop against which militant Islam must be placed. There are about 750 million Muslims in the world today to be found in more than seventy countries, and this is to count only the countries where the Muslim population is indigenous. There are of course many countries where there are colonies of Muslim immigrants. Because of these, Islam is now the second largest religion in Europe, with 1.5 million Muslims in Britain, and two conversions a week in Denmark. Islam is as world-wide a faith as Christianity. Adherents are everywhere, but major strength is in certain continents – for Christianity Europe and the Americas, for Islam Asia and Africa. What is striking is that Islam's strength in Africa is rapidly growing. Twenty-five years ago it was estimated that one in 4, perhaps one in 3, Africans was Muslim. In the twenty years before that the number of African Muslims had doubled. So by the early 1980s over half of the population of Africa should be Muslim. This increase is in the area south of the Sahara ('Black Africa'), which makes nonsense of the argument of some fanciful geographers that Islam is intrinsically a religion of the nomads of the desert and the pastoral people of its fringes.[3] The fact is that the four largest Muslim countries in the world today are Indonesia, Pakistan, Bangladesh and India, where the adherents are farmers of rice, wheat, jute and cotton, fishermen and artisans, educated townsmen and illiterate countryfolk; proof that the total, all-enclosing dictates of this faith have a universal appeal that is still very much alive.

1 The totality of Islam

Islam is not a religion and Muhammad is not the founder of Islam. This may seem a statement of extreme Islamic heresy. Yet this is not too far from what two fundamentalist Islamic scholars and reformers have to say about the basic tenets of their faith: 'Islam is not a religion in the common, distorted meaning of the word, confining itself to the private life of man. It is a complete way of life, catering for all the fields of human existence. Islam provides guidance for all walks of life – individual and social, material and moral, economic and political, legal and cultural, national and international.'[1] These words are echoed by every writer, Muslim or non-Muslim, dealing with the most essential characteristic of this faith, a characteristic which it does not share with any of the other 'higher religions'.

Because of this it cannot be repeated too often that Islam is 'not merely a religion'. It is a total and unified way of life, both religious and secular; it is a set of beliefs and a way of worship; it is a vast and integrated system of law; it is a culture and a civilization; it is an economic system and a way of doing business; it is a *polity* and a method of *governance*; it is a special sort of society and a way of running a family; it prescribes for inheritance and divorce, dress and etiquette, food and personal hygiene. It is a spiritual and human totality, *this*-worldly and *other*-worldly.

Consequently, religion and politics are the two sides of a single coin in Islam. However individualistic Colonel Gaddafi may be in his other views or policies, he was being totally orthodox when he said, 'There is no contradiction between religious consciousness and political decisions.'[2] Likewise, however erratic the political *mores* of Zulfikar Bhutto and whatever the truth and sincerity of the statement, he was repeating the best known Islamic political cliché when he announced to an Islamic summit conference: 'the life and teachings of the

Holy Prophet have been the cornerstone of my Government's foreign policy and our land, labour, law, education and other numerous reforms. It has been the governing principle of the Pakistan People's Party.'[3] It has been many centuries since the leader of a political party in the Christian West, however personally devout, would or could have made a similar claim for the interlocking of the spiritual and the secular.

Thus, in any country where the majority of the population is Muslim, politics means Islamic politics: if the politics are secular then the country cannot be called truly Muslim. This is why militant Islam not only has a long history but also has a long future; a future which will last for as long as there are Muslim-majority countries which have not yet approximated their internal and external policies to the teachings of Muhammad in the Koran, and to the other canonical books of Islam.

Because of the subsequent development of Islam it may seem strange that the prophet Muhammad should have stressed frequently that he was not preaching a new faith. As one leading Islamic reformer has expressed it: 'Islam is not the name of some unique faith presented for the first time by Muhammad who should not, for this reason, be called the Founder of Islam.'[4] He was, it is believed, the last of the prophetic line, each reiterating the faith of his predecessor.

Since vast literatures in several languages have been produced on the life and teachings of Muhammad we can refer to these only in outline. Orphaned early, he was until about his fortieth year a moderately successful businessman in the religious and commercial centre of Mecca. The Meccans refused to accept the teachings revealed to him by God, dictated to him by the angel Gabriel, so in 622 AD (the first year of the Muslim calendar) he moved with a small band of followers, in what has been called the *Hijra*, to the oasis town of Medina, on the invitation of the Medinans. There for the next ten years he strengthened and governed the new Muslim community, beat off attacks by his enemies in Mecca, gained supremacy by war and diplomacy over a wide confederation of Arabian tribes, and was finally sufficiently strong to return to Mecca as victor and ruler. At the time of his death he was virtually lord of most of central and western Arabia and was poised for military thrusts northwards into Syria and northeast into Iraq.

Some of the few personal details that are known of Muhammad bear repetition because they tend to be submerged in the teachings of the 'messenger of God'. He was of average height and sturdily built, with a hooked nose and large black eyes with a touch of brown. The hair of his head and beard was thick. His mouth was large and when he laughed, which was seldom though he often smiled, one could see the whole of its inside. In complexion he was fair. He always walked as if rushing downhill, and others had difficulty in keeping up with him. When he turned he did so with his whole body. He never spoke unnecessarily, but rapidly and to the point. He was fond of women and children, and of animals, both dogs and cats; he once mounted a guard over a whelping bitch so that she might produce her pups undisturbed, and he cut a hole in his cloak around a kitten sleeping thereon so as not to awaken it. He liked perfumes and disapproved of the smell of onions and garlic, especially on the breath of worshippers in the mosque. He was always in firm control of his feelings.

Muhammad made a clear distinction between his humanity and his role as Prophet: 'I am a mortal like you. In matters revealed to me by God, you must obey my instructions. But you know more about your own worldly affairs than I do. So my advice in these matters is not binding.' But since Muhammad is the 'Seal of the Prophets' – that is, the last of the line from Abraham through Moses to Christ, and its summation – belief in the prophethood of Muhammad and in his guidance has become one of the three basic articles of Islamic faith; the other two being belief in the unity of God and belief in life after death and the last judgment. Inevitably, the two roles have been merged; the life of Muhammad is accepted as a model and he as the perfect human exemplar. Therefore, for the devout Muslim, Muhammad is above reproach. He may not be criticized. He may not even be portrayed: there have been many riots and protestations in Muslim lands over alleged portraits of the Prophet in Western publications. And in a recent film of his life, sponsored by Islamic governments, he never appeared on the screen although a simulation of his voice was heard.

The Koran is not a 'holy book' written by Muhammad. The word *Koran* means 'recitation', and what Muhammad did was to recite the word of God spoken to him by Gabriel. Fazlur

19

Rahman, one of the most learned and acute of modern Islamic thinkers, speaks of the Koran thus: 'The Koran is purely divine . . . pure Divine Word . . . equally intimately related to the inmost personality of the Prophet Muhammad . . . The Divine Word flowed through the Prophet's heart . . . but Muhammad was not himself divine, wholly or partly.'[5] The Koran, then, far from being a book, however holy, is itself divine, part of the Godhead. Just how firmly and seriously this is believed is shown by the fact that when the revered Egyptian Muslim reformer Abduh wrote, in one of his works, that the Koran was 'created', he thought it advisable to leave this idea out from subsequent editions of the book because the idea of creation might suggest that the Koran was in some way an emanation from God, external to the Divine, which would be a derogation from the sanctity of the 'recitation'. The orientalist W. Cantwell Smith has defined the sacred value of the Koran to Muslims justly in saying that the Koran does not have the same position in Islam as the Bible does in Christianity: the Koran for the Muslim is what Christ himself is for the Christian.

Since the text of the Koran has this sacred quality it is little wonder that proposals to translate it from its own most splendid Arabic into the local tongues of non-Arab believers was strongly forbidden down to this century. Only in the 1930s did Kemal Ataturk dare to try and sponsor an official translation into Turkish – and found no one prepared to undertake the task. Despite continuing protestation, translations in other languages have appeared, but a compromise has been imposed: such translations are acceptable only if the Arabic text is printed alongside. Even misprints in the text have been known to produce violent objection.

Regarded solely as literature the Koran is the supreme glory of the Arabic language. It is divided into 114 *suras*, or chapters, of very unequal length. And, it must be said, of very unequal quality, both spiritual and literary. Since Muhammad was illiterate he himself did not write down his revelations, though there had been some noting down during his lifetime. A definitive collection was begun under his successor and it was completed and revised during the reign of his third successor twelve years after the death of the Prophet. Despite this gap of time the one and only standard text faithfully captures Muhammad's spiritual and secular development. It is generally agreed among non-Muslim students of Islam (and some Muslims as well) that when the suras in the Koran are rearranged in roughly chronological order, which does not obtain in the authorized version, one finds a clear difference between the earlier Meccan suras and the later Medinan ones. The earlier ones are shorter, more powerful, more full of the pulsating spirit of religious revelation, more other-worldly; the later suras are longer, more detailed, more pedestrian and this-worldly. The Meccan revelations are those of a prophet, those of Medina of a ruler. It could hardly be otherwise, for when Muhammad moved from Mecca, with perhaps a group of seventy to a hundred followers, he found himself the head of a community at Medina – the *umma* – which grew in size quite rapidly; eight years after arriving in Medina he was able to field an army of 10,000 men for the march on Mecca; four weeks later the number had risen to 12,000, and ten months later he was able to field 30,000 men for his last expedition. He had to run, control and govern this swiftly growing community, and the legislation he laid down for it is found in the Medinan suras. Thus Muhammad was much more than a prophet. He was a soldier – he took part personally in some of the early raiding battles, was wounded in the face and was known to have killed at least one of his adversaries – then he became a general; he made war and he made peace; he sent out ambassadors and received them; he gathered in booty, divided it and ran a treasury; he laid down laws and administered them. Buddha, though once a ruling prince, did not attempt anything like this, nor did Christ with his twelve disciples. Muhammad was also a family man.

To hold together his community of simple and often rather savage bedouin Muhammad laid down five essential religious duties, the 'five pillars' of Islam. These are: the affirmation of the faith, the *zakat* or obligatory alms tax, the five daily prayers, the month of fasting – Ramadan – and the annual pilgrimage to Mecca known as the *Haj*. The affirmation must be the shortest, simplest credo of any religion in the world: 'There is no god but God and Muhammad is the Prophet of God.' This is all that a convert to Islam has to say to become a Muslim. The zakat not only emphasized the importance of charity, but was also a necessity in the early years at Medina before booty came in as a way to keep the community in funds. Though Islamic law goes into great detail on how much alms tax should be levied it is difficult for us to evaluate its actual incidence because it was taken in kind from a pastoral people. There is however one monetary evaluation: the owner of twenty gold dinars or 200 silver dirhams had to pay five per cent. In recent years zakat has played a large part in plans for a specifically Islamic economic order leading to Islamic socialism. The five daily prayers (there is some evidence that there were originally three) fix the mind of the worshippers on God throughout the twenty-four hours. The prayers also have a practical hygienic value because the worshipper must perform certain ablutions before praying; at a minimum to wash the face, hands and feet. The prayers are said facing towards Mecca. (The original focal point was Jerusalem, indicating how firmly Muhammad believed in his continuation of the Abrahamic tradition.) That five times a day, or even once a day, hundreds of millions of Muslims should face towards the same point on the earth's surface is a singular demonstration of community one-ness.

Fasting, as an act of renunciation, of self-denial, is believed to enhance spiritual virtue in most religions. In Islam it takes the form of abstaining from food, drink, sexual intercourse and, more recently, smoking from first light to sunset for a lunar month. In hot countries, when Ramadan falls in summer, the abstinence from drinking can be a real trial, otherwise it is not too great a strain. Indeed, the meals that are consumed during the hours of darkness, and there are special Ramadan drinks and sweets, usually more than compensate for the missed daytime meals. Perhaps, however, it does teach the rich to learn hunger and so to sympathize with the poor.

The pilgrimage or Haj is so spectacular an event that it will be given extended treatment in the next chapter.

Besides the underpinning of the religious life of the Muslim community provided by these five strong, simple 'pillars of Islam', Muhammad also had to provide for the day-to-day governance of his people which he did in the Medinan suras of the Koran. But there were not enough, for they amount to only about five or six hundred verses out of the six thousand in the Koran. His successors had to find further prophetic backing for Islamic legislation, applicable to the running of the vast

Muslim empire that came into existence within twenty-five years of his death. They found it in the recollections of his chosen companions, his relatives and early followers. These recollections were of two kinds – of what he said, called the *Hadith* or 'Traditions', and of what he did; the two together forming the *Sunnah*, the 'trodden path,' the customary way of life of a devout Muslim, based on what the Prophet is said to have said and done, apart from his words of revelation in the Koran.

The Hadith began to be committed to writing perhaps fifty years after the death of Muhammad. Once their collection began in earnest their fabrication also began, presumably with the very best of intentions: to add a touch here and a touch there that would round out the picture of the Prophet. One ninth-century saying has it: 'In nothing do we see learned men more prone to untruth than in the fabrication of Traditions.' These learned men used the fabrication as a way out of an acute problem facing them: they had to find prophetic sanction for detailed legislation applicable to the governing of an empire. They did so by fathering on Muhammad anecdotes that fitted in with the life and times of mid-ninth-century Baghdad, then the imperial capital, where conditions were very different from those of early-seventh-century Mecca and Medina.

The haphazard recording of Hadith could not be allowed to continue unchecked; six anthologies of them were made by scholars who died between 870 and 915 AD. Two of these collections, by Bukhari and Muslim, are actually known as 'The Two Truthful'. The anecdotes and stories have been categorized as 'true', 'good' and 'weak' depending on whether the original words or action of Muhammad were witnessed to by three or two persons or by a single person; depending also on the reliability of the informant. According to some scholars the Hadith of the highest quality number only 500. What is known is that Bukhari examined some 600,000 'Traditions' and chose only about 7,000 as genuine. Modern scholarship would cut that number down still further. Yet even from that smaller number we gain an incomparably detailed picture of the doings, the personality of Muhammad, such as is not available for Christ or Buddha.

A few examples will give an idea of their quality: 'Be in the world as though you were a stranger or a wayfarer. At evening do not expect to live till morning and at morning do not expect to live till evening. Take from your health for your illness, from your life for your death.' 'None of you truly believes until he wishes for his brother what he wishes for himself.' 'Part of someone's being a good Muslim is his leaving alone that which does not concern him.' 'He who seeks religion through theology becomes a heretic.' 'A prayer in this mosque [Medina] is worth more than thousands performed in others, except that in Mecca, that performed there is worth one hundred thousand more than that performed in others. Worth more than all this is the prayer which someone says in his house, where no one sees him but God and which has no other object than to draw near to God.' 'Do good to your neighbour, you will be a believer, wish for men what you wish for yourself, you will be a Muslim; laugh not overmuch, for much laughter kills the mind.' [6]

But the importance of the Hadith is not in this biographical or historical information. They have come to be regarded as the second most important source for Islamic law after the Koran. Also, because they recount the words and deeds of the Prophet they have acquired his prophetic sanctity, and now are regarded by the devout as holy scripture. 'The Koran and the authentic Hadith' are the words now used to delimit the fundamental scriptural basis of Islam.

We now have to refer briefly to some other basic Islamic concepts, which will recur in later chapters.

Islam is, par excellence, a religion of laws. In addition to the Koran and the totality of the Hadith, or Sunnah, the Islamic judicial system is based on *ijma* and *qiyas*. Qiyas is deductive analogy by which a jurist applies to a new case a ruling already made to fit similar cases. For our study ijma is altogether the more important idea. It is the consensus of the Islamic community or umma. It is through this principle that democracy makes its impact on the conduct of Islamic polity. While it opens up the law to popular opinion it can also be seen as a conservative force, for the consensus has to be that of the whole community, or at least that of a very large proportion of it. Perhaps the most famous case of the exercise of ijma was when the men of religion declared the drinking of coffee forbidden but eventually had to permit it because the consensus of the people as a whole was strongly opposed to the law. Having had to create his own community of believers, starting with his wife Khadijah, Muhammad had an unshakeable faith in its ultimate common-sense and right-mindedness – a faith that events soon after his death did little to justify. One of his most famous sayings is: 'My community will not agree on what is wrong.'

This importance given to the community and its majority opinion arises from the fact that in Islam there is nothing remotely resembling the Church; its corporate functions are taken over by the umma. It follows, then, that there is no priesthood in Islam. Being a legal creed, the men learned in Islamic doctrine are those learned in its legal doctrines – the *ulema*. These religious lawyers can and do become leaders of their communities, and in that capacity can give a lead on what may be purely religious matters. Only in this indirect way, through their legal standing in the first place, do the ulema (more correctly translated as 'men of religion') approximate to clergy or priesthood. The *imam* is simply someone who leads the prayers in the mosque: it could be anyone from the congregation and is not always, or necessarily, an ulema.

Yet another source for legal precedent are the traditions of the Khalifah al Rashidun, the 'right-guided caliphs', the first four rulers to succeed Muhammad. They were Abu Bakr, Omar, Osman and Ali, and their four reigns lasted from 632 to 661 AD. This brief space of twenty-nine years is viewed, nostalgically through the obscuring mists of time, as the 'golden age' of Islam. Why it should be so considered is debatable, for its brevity was because, of the four caliphs, two were assassinated and one was cut down by his enemies, in his home, when reading the Koran. All the divisions that have plagued Islam and the Arab world ever since then were born during that 'golden' age. It was certainly a glorious age, the period when the Muslim Arabs conquered the whole vast area extending from Tripoli-tania in the west to the frontiers of India in the east. So the 'traditions' of what these four glorious but ill-fated rulers said and did were added to the growing corpus of Islamic law.

This corpus, because it was unwieldy, stood in need of codification and this was done by four jurists who died between

767 and 855 AD. These jurists vary in interpretation and in the geographic areas where they are most adhered to. The Hanafite school, which is the least rigid, is found in Turkey, central Asia and India; Shafiism along the coasts of the Persian Gulf and Indian Ocean; Malikism prevails in north Africa; while the Hanbali school, the most orthodox, is found in Saudi Arabia.

Thus by the middle of the ninth century all the components of that total legal entity which is known as the Sharia[7], or Sharia law, were established: the Koran, holy and unchangeable; the six compilations of the Traditions or Hadith in the Sunna, almost as holy and unchangeable; the 'traditions' of the 'four right-guided caliphs', not holy but to be treated with very great respect; and the codification of and commentaries on all these in the four great schools of law. The tendency was towards solidification, and the inevitable happened: somewhere around 900 AD, perhaps a little later, the *ijma*, the consensus of the scholars but not that of the community, determined that enough was enough; or, to use the splendid phrase applied to this fateful decision, 'The gates of ijtihad were closed.' *Ijtihad* means 'independent judgement', so that when the gates were closed on it this meant that from henceforth only past precedent counted. The Sharia became rigidly defined and static, and with it the Muslim community, of which the Sharia was the governing principle.

The trouble – if that is the right word, and Muslims will not think it is – the trouble with Sharia law is that it fully partakes of that inextricable intertwining of sacred and secular that is of the essential nature of Islam (and which is the main root of militant Islam). One sympathetic Western scholar puts it thus: 'Sharia is the revealed law of Islam. Although the term "law" is used, Sharia is not comparable to modern legislation. It is essentially an ideal law. It is indeed an ideal code of conduct with a much wider scope than any modern legislation, since it also includes matters of hygiene, etiquette and the ritual of worship.'[8] This is why the most difficult question facing the Muslim reformer is: should Sharia law be retained or restored or abolished; and in whole or in part?

The closing of the gates of ijtihad and, accordingly, the consecration of the Sharia in its integral totality was something that modern Muslim reformers criticize bitterly, and their aim is to break open the gates closed a thousand years ago by using the battering rams of ijma (popular consensus) and ijtihad (independent judgement). As we shall see, ijma and ijtihad are battlecries in the struggles of militant Islam.

The main result of the bloody ending to the 'golden age' with the killing of the fourth Caliph Ali was that Islam split irremediably into its two major sects, the majority Sunni and the minority Shiah. Political differences on the succession after Ali reflected differences in religious response that were already apparent. The Shiah-type of religious feeling was evident from very early on in the history of Islam, indeed from long before the time when the Shiahs formally became a separate sect. The core of the Shiah faith is that the earthly community should be led by a charismatic, semi-divine leader, the imam, who acts as the mediator between the human and divine, while the Sunni belief is that the individual believer stands directly face to face with God, with no need for an intercessor. Buddhism and Christianity have split in similar schisms along this fault line in the human soul: (Shiah) Mahayana Buddhism and (Sunni) Hinayana Buddhism; (Shiah) Roman Catholicism and (Sunni) Protestantism.[9] Ali became the first of orthodox Shiism's twelve imams, spiritual leaders, although the twelfth is actually the 'hidden' imam who will return as the Mahdi, the man guided by God who will set all things right. Shiism became a separate politico-religious entity when in 1502 it was declared the official religion of the new Persian state being established by Shah Ismail.

The doctrinal differences between Sunni and Shiah Islam are these: the Shiah, of course, do accept Muhammad and the Koran, but while the sources of Sunni law are the Koran, the Hadith of the Prophet, the consensus of the community and 'analogy', the four bases of Shiah law are the Koran, the Hadith of the Prophet and the imams, the consensus of the imams and 'reason'. So the Shiahs have their own collection of Hadith and their own school of law, the Jaafari. The Shiahs perform the pilgrimage to Mecca but their real outpourings of religious passion come at the tombs of the sons of Ali, Hassan and Hussain, at Najaf and Kerbela in Iraq.

Because of these old differences between them the militant Islam of the Shiahs is, as we shall see, different from Sunni militant Islam in content, method and goals.

Since the exponents of militant Islam are more than usually vigorous in extolling the excellence of Islam both as a religion and a polity they are having to face certain accusations against their faith that have been made against Islam for over a thousand years. These are that Islam was spread by the sword, wielded in the *jihad*, or holy war; that the Sharia lays down punishments for some crimes that are cruelly barbaric, especially for the present age; that Islamic economics are unrealistic because they are based on the prohibition of usury or *riba*; and that its provisions on polygamy and divorce impose on women an inferior position in society.

It must be said that all these enactments are indeed sanctioned by the Koran. For the fundamentalist that is the final answer to all non-Muslim objections; and that, quite simply, is the attitude today of the governments of Saudi Arabia and Pakistan.

However, clarification seems called for on the matter of jihad or holy war. The word itself simply means 'effort'. One of the earliest of the extreme sects, the Kharijis, tried to make jihad the sixth pillar of Islam but this was not accepted. Three schools of law, not the Hanbalis, considered jihad an obligation if certain conditions were fulfilled; among them that the unbelievers should begin hostilities and that there should be a reasonable hope of success. In almost all the wars, or rather raids, launched by Muhammad from Medina the pagan tribes attacked were indeed given no other choice but conversion or death, because in those early years Muhammad could not accept submission and an alliance unless it was cemented by, proven by, conversion to his faith. But Jews, Christians and members of other monotheistic religions had the third option of becoming a 'protected community' under the Islamic state, with the payment of an annual tribute in money or kind. Once the Muslim home base of Arabia had been converted from paganism and consolidated, and the Arab armies swept into non-pagan areas, conversion became of minor importance. The armies were too busy advancing and the rulers preferred the cash in hand to the gathering in of non-paying converts.

In any case, this is now merely an academic historical question;

the image of the Muslim armies converting as they advanced has sunk so deeply into the Western mind that no amount of repetition of the truth is likely to dislodge it. What is more to the point is that there is no Muslim army today that could or would undertake jihad. The last time the call to jihad was seriously made was in 1914 when the last of the real pan-Islamic caliphs, the Sultan of Turkey, called on his co-religionists to join the war on the side of Germany, Turkey's ally: it was a total failure. There have been several calls for jihad since then, especially against Israel, none of which have been effective.

The only explanation or apologia that Muslims give for the canonical punishments is that they are hedged around with conditions which are almost impossible to fulfil. Thus there must be four reliable eye-witnesses testifying to adultery before a couple can be found guilty and stoned to death. Likewise, a man can take himself four wives only if he behaves justly to all of them, which is humanly impossible. Also, it is agreed that riba applies to usury and not to normal financial gains on investment. None of these explanations are very convincing, and the reformist Muslim has yet to come to terms with the problem that although certain elements in Koranic legislation may have been suitable for seventh-century Arabia, and may even have represented advances on the customs of the time, they do not conform to the spirit of the times in the last quarter of the twentieth century.

Despite these seeming anachronisms Islam retains its grip on the total life of the members of its community provided they are prepared to think of themselves as Muslims and as members of the umma. This is why in a recent book entitled *The 100: A Ranking of the Most Influential Persons in History*[10] Muhammad is ranked first before Newton, Christ, Buddha, Confucius and St Paul, in that order. Jesus, living 600 years before Muhammad, has probably influenced more people but arguably he has not influenced them as deeply in all aspects of their earthly life.

This is because Christ accepted the separation between God and Caesar and advised to 'render unto Caesar the things that are Caesar's'. Muhammad and Islam have not so much rejected the God–Caesar dichotomy, they have simply never recognized its existence in their universe of discourse and belief.

Islam is so entirely a living faith today precisely because it is a totality, legislating for all of man's earthly activities, not just his spiritual needs. Islam has worn well because it has guided and sustained and strengthened social structures and institutions – the umma, the extended family, the clan, the tribe, and these in turn have sustained and nourished Islam.

2 The vitality of Islam

The coolest spot in which to have a quiet afternoon siesta in
Damascus is leaning, or half-leaning, against the broad pillars of
the Omayyad mosque. That is one reason why Islam is today a
living faith – not that its mosques are cool or quiet but that one
can, without disrespect, have a siesta in them. There are some
minor limitations: it is preferable to be on the farther side of the
tomb of John the Baptist, that is, farther away from the office
of the mosque attendants near the main gate and from the Koran
readers and worshippers who tend to gather, at all hours throughout the day, near the *mihrab*, or pulpit, halfway down the
mosque's great length. It is also a convention that one should
not stretch out at full length, as this is considered too blatant,
and may lead to being awakened by a gentle kick in the ribs
from an attendant. The slowly ticking clocks, none of them
showing the correct time, are a wonderful, irresistible soporific.
It is comforting to observe, before one drops off, that there are
other people in the mosque for non-religious reasons: students
pacing up and down, memorizing their lessons, a group of
friends having a quiet chat, children waiting for their parents
to return from shopping in the surrounding *souk*. From the
steady stream of people crossing back and forth across its
westernmost end it is apparent that that corner of the mosque
is a short cut from the souk of the gold merchants to the main
Souk al Hamidieh; like thousands of mosques in other Muslim
cities, this splendid place of worship is set down smack in the
middle of the busy, congested bazaar area. That is the way it is
with the two most sacred mosques in Islam, in Mecca and
Medina; so it is with the main mosque in Tehran, with al
Azhar in Cairo and the green-tiled mosques of Fez; no longer,
alas, is it the case in Delhi where a tourist-conscious government
has cleared away the 'thieves' bazaar' from the wide flight of
steps leading up to the Jama Masjid; and it is not the case at

Jerusalem, Islam's third most holy spot, where the Mosque of Omar is set on the Temple Mount. In Islam the point is this: casualness and not cleanliness and tidiness is next to real day-to-day 'Godliness'.

The pigeons are another proof of whether a place of worship pertains to a living faith: they are there on the vast courtyard of the Omayyad mosque, one of its walls gleaming golden with the carefully uncovered mosaics of the original Byzantine basilica; they are there in clouds at Mecca and Medina and at al Azhar; they are there too at the base of the gleaming spire of the Buddhist Shwe Dagon pagoda in Rangoon and in the courtyards before St Peter's in Rome and St Mark's in Venice (another place of worship that serves as a short cut). It may be that the birds are there because the worshippers feed them as a pious duty or because the edifices provide convenient roosting places, but across the world and for several religions pigeons seem to indicate a place of active holiness.

Islam has several other, larger and more significant proofs of its vitality. The annual pilgrimage to Mecca, the Haj, is not only a proof of that vitality but has been one of its main causes – likewise of the world-wide unity of the Muslim world. It is ironic that this pillar of Islam should be a relic from Mecca's pagan pre-Islamic past, for Muhammad merely took over a pilgrimage that was already being made to pagan idols in the temple that is now the Kaaba – the black-covered cube that is the very heart and focal point of Muslim worship. His first act on entering Mecca as its new master was to throw the idols out. Some pagan relics remain – the strange black stone embedded in the Kaaba's southeast corner; as part of the Haj pilgrims have to cast seven pebbles at stone pillars – said to represent the devil – in the valley of Mina ten miles from Mecca where the main happenings of the Haj take place.

The Haj is the largest multinational gathering of human beings on the face of the earth today. In the last two years, around a million and a half pilgrims from over seventy countries have flooded into Mecca and the barren valley beyond. More countries are represented at, say, the United Nations General Assembly, but then only in their hundreds; larger numbers of Hindus gather for the Kumbh Mela, the immersion at the sacred confluence of the Ganges and the Jumna rivers, but they are all Indians. The Haj is both multitudinous and diverse. Even fifty years ago 40,000 pilgrims from Indonesia used to make their way in leaky steamships and sailing dhows across the empty expanse of the Indian Ocean. Coming in from the opposite, western, direction thousands of West Africans used to spend a lifetime walking and working their way across the continent. From the north came the pilgrim caravan that gathered at Damascus the pilgrims from Iraq, Turkey and the Levant and which, at Akaba, met the second caravan, bearing with it the new *mahmal*, the embroidered covering of the Kaaba, which Egypt is privileged to provide, accompanied by all the pilgrims from North Africa who had journeyed along the road between the desert and the Mediterranean Sea. And from the northeast came the pilgrims from the sub-continent and Afghanistan who had travelled down the Gulf and across the empty expanse of Arabia. They now come in even greater numbers – 100,000 more each year – but now more than half arrive by air and almost all the others by car or bus; though it is still possible to see a few African pilgrims, their bundles on their heads, trudging up the road from Jedda to Mecca.

The skin colours are every shade of black, brown and pinkish white, but the simple uniform enjoined on the pilgrims makes of them a sea of white, until the main rites are performed. Then, like a butterfly emerging from its chrysalis, national costumes of every sort and colour re-emerge and the unity before God fragments into an international kaleidoscope.

The ceremonies of the Haj take five days in all. It is on the afternoon of the last day but one that the most important act of worship takes place. It is simplicity itself: from noon to just before sunset the pilgrims stand erect facing the small rocky hill of Arafat, that lies at the farther end of the valley of Mina; there they pray, or meditate, or read the Koran, or listen to sermons. But only those who have 'stood before Arafat' can call themselves Hajis.

For the ordinary pilgrim the Haj, in its present vastly expanded form, can be not only an exalting but a terrifying experience. For here one has illiterate Berber villagers from the remote valleys of the High Atlas, Kurds from the equally remote Zagros, pilgrims from the rice fields of Bangladesh, or the coconut groves of Indonesian islets facing the Pacific, people speaking little-known languages, or even less-known dialects or sub-dialects, who have never left their villages before, now thrown into a milling mass, a turbulent sea of nations. No wonder that the professional guides, without whom the Haj would quickly collapse into chaos, often rope their charges together and provide them with distinctive flags and badges.

To the disappointment of the older pilgrims it is now very difficult to die on the Haj (to die while performing it is to ensure Paradise, such is the popular belief). This is so because the Saudi Arabian government has been spending much effort and money to improve communications and health conditions. Quarantine camps, a good water supply and the aerial spraying of disinfectants have made the Haj, once a dreaded centre of epidemics, now disease free. A considerable achievement, for the million and a half pilgrims are concentrated for just one week in a fifty-square-mile area which for the other fifty-one weeks of the year is deserted.

Housing for the pilgrims, however, still remains in short supply, with Meccan landlords demanding scandalously high rents. The poorer pilgrims, in their hundreds, sleep in the spacious arcades of the mosque in Mecca.

The atmosphere of the Haj, which is what really matters, is a combination of religious ardour and friendly joy. Everybody is everybody else's brother or sister, for all are aware that during this time they are especially close to God. The pilgrim chant says it all: 'Labbaik, Allahuma Labbaik – Here I am, O Allah, here I am.' It is noteworthy that even women who normally wear the veil are forbidden to do so during the Haj. To witness the Haj is to see, in real life, that Islam is not just a vital faith, a living religion, it is much more. It is a powerful vibrant force infusing the multitudes with a passionate devotion, and with visible proof that they are members of a vast world-wide brotherhood.

Mecca, the town that rejected Muhammad, sunk deep in a twisting cleft amid steeply sloping hills, has the same hard quality as Jerusalem, the 'city set on a hill', that rejected Christ. Quite different is the open, expansive, green oasis of Medina, which most pilgrims visit either before or after going to Mecca. Guards are mounted around the tomb of the Prophet in Medina to prevent people from praying towards it or from reaching out to touch the enclosing screen; they are lightly tapped on their hands with a cane if they do so. It is mostly the Shiah pilgrims who have to be warned, for this austere remoteness is very different from the scene at Kerbela, where lies buried Hussain the son of Ali. There pilgrims cling to the screen sobbing their hearts out in an agony of grief, and the scene is made all the stranger and more impressive by the rippling disjointed reflections of it in the mosaic of mirrors that lines the inside of the mosque's domed roof.

The down-to-earth, practical aspect of Islam is not absent from the Haj. Businessmen from all over the Muslim world find it very useful for making contacts, and many contracts are signed. It is also, especially for the Saudis, a good time for arranging marriages, particularly since the young women are, perforce, unveiled.

During the Haj a sizable African township springs into existence just outside Jeddah airport, with all the characteristic African colours, sounds and smells: further proof that Islam is a living, growing force, for it is in black sub-Saharan Africa (more in West Africa than in the centre or the east) that Islam's frontier has been advancing. This has been happening steadily for five centuries but the pace has accelerated since the beginning of this century. Paradoxically it was Western Christian colonialism that benefited Islam: it brought peaceful conditions, good communications and, to some extent, the breakdown of the tribal way of life, all of which were to the advantage of the Muslim missionary, who has had far greater success than his Christian counterpart. Islam has long since breached the jungle barrier that some hopeful Western geographers alleged would prevent it from reaching the West African shore. There are now strong Muslim communities all along the coast, and the population of Lagos, the Nigerian capital, is fifty-per-cent Muslim.

This strong Muslim presence in black Africa has had a significant impact on the Black Muslim movement in the United States. African Islam has not only opened the door to Islam for the American black, it has also corrected some of the heterodox excesses of the original Black Muslim movement, which had the most tenuous of links with orthodox Islam.[1]

These are some of the proofs of Islam's closeness to the life of its believers, of its universality and of its growth. Which raises the question of why there should be this continuing assertiveness within Islam which does not exist, in anything like the same strength, in the two other multinational religions, Christianity and Buddhism? (Confucianism never claimed to be a religion and the other 'universal' faiths, Hinduism and Judaism, are uni-national.) Several reasons may be given. The most obvious but least mentioned is *youth*. Islam is just under 1400 years old, Christianity is getting on for 2000, and Buddhism was born 2600 years ago. As living things religions have their own morphology and should not, therefore, be strangers to the waning powers of middle and old age. In the year 1400 AD the Christian Church was incomparably the most powerful and vital force in what had become its European homeland: it was just a century away from the climactic summation of Aquinas, within half a century of the poetic summation of Dante and of the terrors and ecstasies of the Black Death. The new impulse of the Reformation was just beginning to be felt – Wycliffe had just died and the martyrdom of Hus was fifteen years away. Although by 800 AD, the fourteenth-hundred year of its life, Buddhism was showing signs of old age, it was still widely practised through the length and breadth of India (from which it was ultimately expelled) and was the main religion of Afghanistan and central Asia. Islam, then, is now in its vigorous early middle age.

But the devout will say it is wrong, even blasphemous, to talk of religions in temporal terms since they are *sub specie aeternitatis*. Perhaps; let us then say merely that Islam is indubitably the most recent of the major religions. Which fact, by itself, is a source of pride and comfort to some Muslims. In 1976, in answer to a questionnaire, 250 young Turks in Ankara repeatedly made the point that Islam is 'the latest', 'the most recent' of the revealed religions and, therefore, they added, 'the best'.[2]

In addition to placing a value, unreservedly, on new-ness as such, many of the Turkish students and workers went on to say that because Islam is recent in time it has preserved the original purity of its revelations, and that these have not been added to, changed or 'deformed' (a favourite word used) as has been the case with the original teachings of Christ. (This refers to a widespread Muslim belief that the original words of Jesus – whom

36

Muhammad accepted as a prophet and a more powerful one than himself, for he could perform miracles – had been re-written by the Churchmen.) It is true that since Muhammad was scornful of theology (and there is very little theology in Islam) there have likewise been few if any theological accretions to the original message.

This was one advantage that resulted from 'the closing of the gates of ijtihad', in the tenth century. When the body of Islamic law, that is, of Islamic sacred and secular belief and practice, was decreed to have been finally fixed, no scope was given for later addition or emendation. Rigidity meant authen-ticity or approximation to the original – hence the continuing new-ness which is an aspect of youth.

Islam remains vital today because of a crucial synthesis of belief that was achieved in the twelfth century. The earlier splits and schisms within Islam between Sunnis and Shiahs had enabled the First Crusade to invade Palestine and capture Jerusalem. The shock of this defeat produced the strong Muslim reaction that ultimately led to the recapture of Jerusalem by Salah al Din (Saladin) in 1187. But after this military success it was an orthodox Sunni belief that was restored and Shiism was reduced to a minority position in a few widely separated areas of the Arab and Islamic world. Shiism was only in a majority in the frontier state of Persia. Its own success tended to make Sunni Islam increasingly rigid, dogmatic and divorced from the people. There was need to bring into the faith elements of piety, personal prayer, comparison, and even a moderate degree of mysticism, with its direct relationship with God. It has been an enormous boon for Islam that just this synthesis, this healing compromise, was brought about by the great thinker and man of religion, Shuhammad al Ghazali (1058–1111). The foundations of a revived Sunni Islam laid by Ghazali have remained valid down to the present. Thus, through two occurrences in the twelfth century, Islam became solidly Sunni and achieved a stable internal spiritual balance. Because of the first event Islam was spared two evils that afflicted European Christianity because of the even military balance between Roman Catholicism and Protestantism. It escaped the destruction of wars made in the name of religion and it escaped the erosion of spiritual values that is bound to result from such wars. Muhammad told his followers never to harm or make war on a fellow Muslim, and in fact inter-Muslim wars have been surprisingly few, which has helped preserve the material and spiritual strength of Islam.

Other religions have been weakened when their established Churches and priesthoods became targets of criticism because of the inevitable and inescapable gap between lofty preaching and worldly practice. Since Islam has no Church or priesthood it did not attract any such weakening criticism. On the other hand the ulema, the nearest approximation to priests, have done quite well by Islam. They have often been less well educated and spiritually endowed than they might have been, but seldom corrupt. Their main besetting sins have been narrowmindedness and undue subservience to the 'powers that be', but these have not brought Islam greatly into disrepute in the eyes of the community. On the whole the body of ulema through the centuries has done much to maintain the internal cohesion and strength of Islam.

Other points made by the young Turks of Ankara were that Islam is 'simple and easy'. And, since the essentials of Islamic faith and practice are contained in the 'five pillars', simple and easy it certainly is. They also said that it is practical: 'Islam is concerned with practical life and links it with spiritual things – hence its success'; 'Islam gives equal importance to happiness in this world as well as in the next'; 'Islam is very realistic and well adapted to daily life.' Muhammad himself set the tone of down-to-earth practicality, for when asked by a bedouin, 'Shall I let loose my camel and trust in God?' he gave the answer: 'Tie up your camel and trust in God.' Centuries later, Mary Kingsley, a missionary famous for her work in West Africa, admitted that Islam gave 'an easier, clearer line of rectitude to a west African shopkeeper' than did Christianity. And it has a special appeal to the sub-Saharan African because it has no far-fetched abstractions in its beliefs, no complicated rites or rituals. Unlike Christianity it is not obsessed by sex and, in Africa at least, it tolerates polygamy. It makes no great promises and it makes no great demands. From first to last it is commonsensical, and so has endured through the centuries by contenting itself with solutions to life's day-to-day problems.

Adaptability or flexibility of practice is almost the last thing that one would expect from Islam. Because its dogma are few and simple one would expect a rigid insistence on them and on nothing more. But that is not what happened to Islam when it moved from Arab to non-Arab lands. Perhaps it is precisely because its essential framework is rigidly simple that it can afford or dare to permit a rich variety of local variations on the basic theme. Christianity seems to have stopped assimilating local customs after taking on the cult of the Virgin and the festivals of Easter and Christmas. Islam still tolerates local additions so long as the core of belief remains intact.

The most easily observable evidence of this assimilation is in the architecture of mosques. Christian churches in non-European countries are painfully conspicuous because they invariably tend to run towards the style of pointed arch, window and spire of European Gothic (or English Tudor if in former British colonies). Though the Middle Eastern mosque has its set pattern of dome, minaret and courtyard they are not insisted on – consider for example the famous mud-built mosque at Timbucto, reminiscent of Gaudi's cathedral at Barcelona. The mosque at Harrar in Ethiopia with its massive square pillars and low roof resembles nothing so much as an east African trading shed.

Indonesian village mosques are simply huts built of thatch with a quaint little pointed appendage on the roof to indicate their sacred function. When it came to Indonesia, where religious and cultural assimilation is part of the national ethos, Islam itself was prepared to assimilate: 'Muslim teachers advocated and followed a pattern of radical adaptation to Indonesian–Hindu culture. Muslim terminology, teachings and rites were adapted to Indonesian-Hindu thought and practice as far as possible.'[3] This process went so far that it produced a local variety of Islam called *abangan* Islam. Speaking in its defence in the Indonesian constituent assembly in 1957, one of its followers described how 'on holy days our villages are full of the smell of incense and on such occasions our people do not fail to offer specially prepared rice and chicken to our Prophet Mohammed (may God's peace be on him).'[4]

Islam was equally tolerant in the Sudan and Black Africa, and was productive of a fairly distinct Negro-African Islamic subculture.[5] Islam adapted itself to a very gradual penetration of pagan Africa both in the range of its appeal and in the content of its teaching. The first converts would be nomads and traders who were well able to spread the new teaching, and then members of the ruling class would be Islamized. It was not usual for rulers to impose their religion on their subjects, whose conversion would come perhaps several generations later as the ultimate stage.

There were three similar stages during which Islamic doctrine was imparted with an increasingly strong dosage of orthodoxy. In the first stage the prospective convert would not be expected to do anything more than wear Islamic amulets and Muslim-style dress. In the second stage came ritual prayer and the introduction of things prohibited and permitted. This stage has been called 'mixed Islam', and a great many African Muslims have not moved beyond it. In it Islam is in parallel with animist customs and rites, so that right across Africa one has Islamic kinship rites, Islamic demonology with the belief in *djinns*, Islamic divination and magic. In the third stage, which in west Africa came about 1750, Islam moved in to replace the old animistic patterns, almost wholly but never quite completely. For instance, the Sharia has never been fully applied in African Islam. Passing through the three stages of Islamic osmosis has in recent times often taken as little as three generations, but in earlier years the move from stage two to stage three took almost two centuries.[6] This shows how patient and tolerant 'fanatical' Islam could be, but always with the limiting factors that, however 'mixed' the Islam, there was always a dualism, not a synthesis – 'the unyielding nature of the Islamic institutions precluding this'.[7]

This extremely flexible presentation of inflexible doctrines was possible because of the very special nature of the Islamic missionary. These missionaries were almost entirely not the ulema, the established religio-legal scholars; they were instead Islam's holy men, members of the mystical and semi-secret brotherhoods, known as the *tarikas*. And here we come to one of the great paradoxes of Islam and one of its best kept secrets.

Up to about the middle of this century it would have been true to say, if one can quantify such a thing, that the tarikas and all that they produced and stood for, were a good half of everything that Islam had been since its inception. (They should, then, have been mentioned in the preceding chapter where the essentials of Islam were dealt with.) But they were not, because the tarikas are the 'other' Islam. It may seem paradoxical that closed, unorthodox, private groups should have any part, let alone a very important part, in the life of a religion that is so open, simple and fundamentalist as Islam. But that is precisely why Islam did produce the tarikas. If it was to be a truly human, living faith it had to produce them, so as to complement a faith that was a shade too simple, too spare and too austere for the ordinary Muslim believer. The heart of man, and still less the soul (if there be such) is not akin to the mosque, where everything is basic and swept and garnished. Over the centuries the brotherhoods have cared for the personal religious needs of Muslims and given expression to their religious emotions and aspirations. In the mosque, associated with the ulema, the Muslim worshipped God and submitted (*Islam* means 'submission') to His will; but in the meeting place of his brotherhood he *loved* God. This is why Islam, as represented by the brotherhoods, is often called 'popular Islam'. Obviously then the adepts of these brotherhoods or mystic orders, the *takirs* or dervishes, were in competition with the ulema and orthodox Islam. Down to today the attitude of orthodox Islam towards the tarikas varies between rejection and denunciation or, at best, embarrassment covered with silence. That silence has spread to much of the literature about Islam, because most of such books deal with orthodox, established Islam. For every one book written about the tarika half of Islam, there are hundreds if not thousands of works on the orthodox half. It is only in the last thirty-odd years that Islamic scholarship has tentatively dared to give the tarikas their true importance. Before that time bibliographies of books in English on Islam referred the reader interested in the brotherhoods to the same solitary volume, in French, published in 1897.[8] A salute should be given to the pioneering spirit of its co-authors.

The brotherhoods rendered their incalculable, monumental services to Islam in three different ways: they prevented Islam from becoming a cold and formal doctrine, keeping it alive as an intimate, compassionate faith; they were mainly responsible for spreading the faith in east Asia and sub-Saharan Africa; and they were among the foremost leaders in Islam's military and political battles against the encroaching power of the

41

Christian West. We can deal, briefly, with the first two achievements here.

The tarikas responded to an important need. The small brotherly groupings of mystics living in communities appeared as early as the tenth century, though it was in the twelfth century that the first great and powerful brotherhood, the Qadiri, was established. Thereafter orders were founded all over the Muslim countries of the Middle East and spread to every corner of the Muslim world. By 1900, when the movement probably reached its peak, there would have been many tens of millions of Muslims pouring their devotion into the forms provided by the tarikas, themselves numbering around 200.

Let me try to provide a Christian parallel to what happened in Islam from the twelfth to the nineteenth century. Imagine something like 10th-century Christianity in Europe, but without the Church, the Papacy, or any priesthood hierarchy but instead with elders or presbyters attached to churches. Into this unstructured Christianity come the monkish orders, organized and dedicated, the Benedictines, the Franciscans, the Jesuits and the Templars, who then take over and almost monopolize Christian endeavour, civil and military, and nearly become the main channel for popular Christianity. Within the orders something of the secrecy in brotherhood of the Freemasons would have been observed, plus something of the spirit of doing practical good found in the Order of St John or Rotary, plus the missionary spirit of the Society of the Propagation of the Gospel. It would be little wonder if the then Christian establishment, like the later Muslim establishment, resented the take-over and consigned it to silence.

The Muslim holy men were Sufi mystics but their work with the ordinary believer in the tarikas represents the more practical, less exalted, less selfish end of the mystical spectrum. The tarikas and the sort of popular Islam they represent came to have associations with the very widespread and quite non-Islamic cult of saints (the *marabouts* or *pirs*) and the veneration of their tombs. But saint-worship was not a necessary part of the religious life within a tarika.

This life was built around the spiritual power or *baraka* of a mystical leader who gathered his disciples into a monastery (a *zawiya* or *tekke*), and some of these would later move away on missionary journeys to found other monasteries; so that well established orders had networks stretching across the Muslim world. Around the core of full-time practitioners would gather the lay brethren, the average Muslim, and their contributions provided the income of the monastery. Even the founders of a monastery or of an order did not necessarily abandon their worldly occupations, and would carry on trade or a craft. The lay members of course continued with their normal work but attended the meetings of their orders in the zawiya once or several times a week, as a Christian might attend a prayer meeting in the parish hall. At these meetings the brethren were initiated into the disciplines of mystic communion with the Godhead although for most this did not proceed very high up the scale of illumination. There were convents for women illuminati too. The tarikas, in short, provided their members with a powerful combination of spiritual renewal and human companionship. Many monasteries included a school and offered food and lodging to travellers.

Beginning with the Qadiri order, founded in Baghdad in the 12th century, orders were founded in every succeeding century with a burst of tarika activity in the 18th and early 19th. Most orders have resonant names and among the larger and better known are the Nakshabandi, the Bektashi, the Mavlavi, the Shadhili, the Chisti, the Suhrawardi, the Tijani, and so on. Some are world-wide like the Qadiri and Nakshabandi which have been very widespread and influential in Indonesia; others are regional; some orders concentrated on particular trades or professions and controlled their guilds; some are more activist or more reflective than others. They were all things to all men and it was not unusual for a believer to belong to two or three. They were founded in Morocco, Tunisia, Algeria, Libya, Egypt, the Sudan, Syria, Turkey, Iraq, Persia and India. If Libya and the Sudan are national entities today it is almost entirely due to the Sanussi order in Libya and the Ansar or Mahdiyah and Khatmiyah or Mirghaniya orders in the Sudan. Strange as it may seem it was this network of secret mystic brotherhoods with their semi-secret semi-mystic lay followers that sustained popular Islam for eight centuries, and ensured that Islam came through to the twentieth century strong and vital.

The followers of the tarikas did more than this: they were the missionaries very largely responsible for the spread of Islam. And they were successful in spreading Islam precisely because they were not orthodox ulema, because they presented the new faith on a personal not an institutional basis, and with personal fervour. Because of their individual and individualistic approach they could also afford to tolerate variations in local religious practice among their converts.

The story of how vast tracts of Black Africa and the myriad islands of Indonesia [9] were won for Islam by the devotion and force of personality of waves of individual mystics is a story of epic dimensions that has yet to be told – probably by some future historical novelist of genius. This was the finest, truest expression of militant Islam. Time and again in the complicated history of Central and West-Central Africa we come across incidents of Islamization being achieved by Sufi holy men, often through their conversion of a ruling family which then went on jihad; the rulers of this area were altogether too prone to call for jihads, even if they were 'acceptable' jihads, waged against non-believing pagans. But it is significant that two of the greatest empire builders in West-Central Africa, Umar ibn Said in Senegal and Niger, and the more famous Uthman dan Fodio in Hausaland, were both members of tarikas.

The tarikas even proselytized successfully in the Caucasus and in Siberia under the Czars.

It must be said that the Sufi holy men were not the only sort of Muslim missionary that proved acceptable to the black African. Predating them were the Muslim traders who, as a class, seem to have been men of extraordinary spiritual power to judge by the size and number of African areas they were able to Islamize. It was Muslim traders from India who first took Islam to Indonesia and to the coast of East Africa. The traders were particularly successful in winning over the 'top people' in Africa because the latter seem to have decided that it was not only profitable to be associated, through Islam, with the trader but that Islam opened the gateway to a bigger and more interesting world that lay beyond the northern limit of the Sahara.

All these happenings, in far away places and long ago, are distinctly relevant to the issue of militant Islam in our day and age. It was because this sort of missionary brought Islam to

Black Africa and Indonesia that it was accepted freely by the people of those countries. And because of that free acceptance it has remained, not as an alien creed imposed by outsiders, but as something indigenous, rooted in the hearts of the people. That is why Islam's frontier is still moving forward in Black Africa, a fact which the rest of Islam knows, of which it is very proud, and which adds to its militancy. This is why Indonesia is one of the main 'battlefields' of militant Islam today.[10]

Having given various reasons from the past why Islam should be as vital as it is today we might here take note of a possible reason why it should continue to be a popular religion for some time into the future. Fortunately or unfortunately, it is based on one of those hare-brained specious theories about Islam which afflict Western Islamists, even the best of them, from time to time. This one runs: 'Islam is *essentially* (emphasis added) a religion for individuals who have been uprooted from their community, or whose communities have vanished from under their feet.' Such an argument is only on a slightly higher level than those theories that allege that Islam is *essentially* an urban faith and therefore unsuited to and unaccepted by peasants, or that in its outward expansion it could not cross mountain ranges or penetrate bush or jungle belts. All of these, as a matter of fact, are non-factual. But assuming that the 'disaster theory' of Islam is true, it would be a good thing for Islam because individuals are being uprooted from their communities all the time – the millions of French and Portuguese *colons* from North and Southern Africa, the Anglo-Saxon settlers from Southern Africa – so the field of missionary endeavour for Islam remains wide open.

There is an element of good fortune – or perhaps of Allah's blessings – in Islam's vitality, for it seems favoured by a negative factor as well as by its own positive qualities. Islam is in its provenance a Third World religion, a religion of backward areas, that is of non-modernized non-industrialized areas. Hence it has not, unlike Christianity, been attacked in full strength by all the corroding acids of modernity that come with urbanization, industrialization, the mass society, and the affluent society. (Some of the critics of Islam say that it is not just a historical and geographical chance that Islam is a religion of backward countries but rather that it tends to keep people backward. There is, however, a fairly adequate political reply to this particular socio-cultural problem, to be dealt with later.)

It is true that Muslim countries are for the most part still traditional societies and that Islamic traditions are maintained along with the others. But it is also true that urbanization and industrialization do not seem to have so far shaken the grip of Islam on its followers. The lower middle classes – one of the characteristic products of urbanization – are among the most devout, not to say fanatical, elements of Islamic society. The clerks and the small shopkeepers are the most fervent supporters of fundamentalist and reform movements in the partially urbanized societies of Indonesia, Pakistan, Egypt, Iran and Turkey. The area comprising Cairo and its sprawling suburbs is perhaps the largest single industrialized zone in the Islamic world, with a swarming pullulating mass-society, but the industrial labourers in this zone are also devout Muslims. Both in the very heart of fashionable Cairo, and in the industrial estates, roads are blocked as the faithful overflow across them for the Friday noon prayers; the mosques are generally well attended. So far so good, but it remains to be seen what will be the effect of the really massive industrialization under way in Saudi Arabia, the Gulf and, until the Shah's overthrow, in Iran.

In the long run Islam may be weakened by the increasing industrialization of Muslim countries. On the other hand, the strong simplicities of Islam are proving attractive to a small but increasing number of people living in post-industrial Western society who have had too much of the mass affluent society.

Indeed, until now, scientific advances have benefited Islam. Improved communication, especially air transport, has been the main reason for the big recent increase in the number of Hajis, and there are already two powerful radio stations transmitting Islamic programmes world-wide, while the live transmission of the Haj on television a few years ago made a great emotional impact.

In the Islamic world, as elsewhere, one other human product of modern urban society are the cosmopolitan freethinking Westernized liberals, who are heavily represented in the ruling élites. They usually have little time for any sort of religion, including Islam, or they are positively anti-religious. Militant

Islam in Indonesia, Pakistan, Iran, Turkey and Egypt has already identified and stigmatized this class as its enemy and in Pakistan and Iran has actively gone over to the attack to contain or destroy what it considers an antagonistic force.

Once we have seen the proofs of Islam's external vitality and suggested some reasons for it – its closeness to the life of its believers, the multitudes gathering every year for the Haj, Islam's youth, its simplicity and practicality and adaptability, the role of the tarikas as humanizers and missionaries – what is it that keeps this religion alive in the hearts of the faithful, which is where religion truly resides? What are the criteria of life and growth? Attendance figures at mosques or at the Haj? In fact, until the emergence of militant Islam in its present form a few years ago, it was the received wisdom among Islamic scholars that Islam was *not* alive, or at least not very vital. It was thought that from the thirteenth century onwards it had been static, if not in regression, and that Islamic society was almost fossilized and quite incapable of facing the challenges of the modern world.

To counter this accepted doctrine H. A. R. Gibb pointed to the following 'external evidences of vitality' shown by Islam during this 600 year period: 'the establishment of the Ottoman Empire in the Near East and of the Mogul Empire in India, the revival of Shi'ism in Persia, the expansion into Indonesia and the Malay Peninsula, the growth of the Muslim community in China, the expulsion of the Spanish and Portuguese from Morocco, the extension of the Islamic belt in East and West Africa'.[11] Gibb here mistakenly mixes up purely 'external evidences', like the establishment of empires, with the partly internal proofs of missionary expansion. Yet his 'evidences of vitality' are not totally convincing. What is convincing is that we know that throughout these 600 years the ordinary Muslim in Marrakesh or Cairo or Peking lived his daily life in accordance with the precepts of Islam because he knew in his heart that his faith was a living force, as the overwhelming majority of Muslims still do, and as an increasing number of adherents to other world religions no longer do. During those centuries the forms and institutions of Islamic government and society and even of the religious establishment may have been rigid and lifeless, but beneath them the current of faith flowed on, strong and brimming. It still does, not perhaps quite as strongly, but strongly enough. A religion is as old or as young, as moribund or alive as its believers think and feel it is.

Despite all these reasons for and evidences of vitality, Islam could very well have relaxed into torpidity, but it has never been allowed to relax or to become hidebound. From its earliest years Islam has been under challenge – spiritual, political and cultural – from the Christian West, with the pressures at their most intense, and completely inescapable, since the beginning of the sixteenth century.

3 Challenges

How very different the history of Islam would have been, how much more like the infinitely more tranquil history of Buddhism, if its original home had been, say, Indonesia and its main area of belief southeast Asia. But at home at the crossroads of three continents, hard up against an energetic and, eventually, expansionist Europe, Islam has always had to be vigilant in its defence. Islam, the newer faith, took the offensive and provoked the Western Christian challenge by erupting into Europe, not across the nearby straits of the Bosphorus but over the far-distant Straits of Gibraltar. Having been given a very real fright by the Muslim invasion of France (a scare that came to an end with the defeat of the Muslims at the Battle of Poitiers in 732), the Christians came to hate, abuse and attack Islam and the Islamic world for the next twelve centuries.

Why should these two great religions have not been able to coexist peacefully side by side, the Mediterranean Sea their neutral buffer zone? Even to consider such a pacific possibility is to ignore the essential nature of living faiths – that they claim – they *must* claim – to have a monopoly of 'truth'. A 'living God' is a 'jealous God' and cannot tolerate competitors. What particularly set Islam at odds with Christianity was that it was a similar sort of competitor, a monotheistic competitor. The pagans in their outer darkness 'bowed down to wood and stone': they could be patronized. But monotheistic Muslims had to be shown the errors of their ways, even if they were monotheistic ways. The relationship of the two religions could not but be wholly antagonistic in the Age of Faith. Inter-faith tolerance and ecumenical movements are sure indications of a slackening of belief.

Since the confrontation between Christianity and Islam began, as one would expect, on the religious and spiritual plane, it is with the Western missionary challenge to Islam that we shall begin.

It would be both tedious and painful to repeat here any of the unchristianlike abuse that Christian polemicists hurled at Islam and especially at Muhammad himself. The essence of the 'doctrine' was that 'Muhammad was a low-born pagan upstart, who schemed himself into power, who maintained it by pretended revelations, and who spread [his religion] both by violence and by permitting to others the same lascivious practices as he himself indulged in.'[1] These themes, singly or together, remained the burthen of the attacks until the middle of the nineteenth century. Only then, when Islam was clearly no longer a military or political menace to Europe, was a fairer view of the Prophet possible. In more recent times the attitude has become somewhat more rarefied: 'Christianity is essentially a spiritual religion whereas Islam is essentially non-spiritual'; though even this writer says that Muslims are generally lazy, selfish, sensual and dishonest.[2]

It is curious how the conduct of the polemic against Islam today – say, against Arab nationalism or militant Islam – remains the same. Even in the twelfth century a good deal of the truth about Islam was known but was deliberately ignored by the polemicists; they did not want to record the truth; they could not afford to tell the truth because the Islamic enemy was still there and would not go away. Hence the polemical material was very largely addressed to Christians to fortify their spirits against the enemy: 'It corresponded to need: it made it possible to protect the minds of Christians against apostasy and it gave Christendom self-respect in dealing with a civilization in many ways its superior.'[3] Another element that remains true today is that many of the prejudices against the Muslims (or Arabs) were planted by some of the indigenous Christian communities (as is today the case with the Maronites in Lebanon and to a lesser extent the Armenians in Turkey).

Likewise, from that century to this, local Christians in the Islamic world, especially those belonging to the Eastern rite, have been consistently hostile to Western Christian missionary activity. They feared that the brash newcomers would disturb the *modus vivendi* they had worked out with their Muslim rulers.

From the twelfth century onwards one thing was known and acknowledged by the missionaries themselves: that they were not going to make converts from among the Muslims. What the early Christian missionaries seemed to want was to secure their martyrdom by deliberately provocative behaviour in Muslim lands.[4]

The experience of St Francis was typical of subsequent missionary endeavour. After two abortive attempts to reach Muslim territory he finally reached Egypt with the Crusaders in 1219. He preached to the Muslims, who heard him out, refused to indulge in religious controversy, protected the saint and showered gifts upon him. His companions, failing to achieve martyrdom at the hands of the polite Egyptians, pursued it zealously with rude behaviour in Spain and then Morocco where they finally won the martyr's crown.[5,6] One of the principal grievances of the early missionaries was that the Muslims refused to engage in theological debate. This maddening attitude changed only from about 1900 onwards and many of the works of Muslim apologetics that have since resulted make the point that silence is often golden.

The missionaries, especially the Jesuits in the East during the 15th to 19th centuries, had some successes – among non-Muslims at least – because they came as individuals without much backing from the Church and even less from any European imperial power. In fact they operated like the members of the tarikas in Africa. Such were Francis Xavier in Southeast Asia and India, Matteo Ricci in China, and Robert de Nobili, also in India.

But the real missionary campaign against Islam came after the end of the Napoleonic Wars, and during the expansion of overseas imperialism that resulted from general European peace. It was missionary activity closely allied with the extension of imperial power that presented the real challenge to Islam. As we have said, the purely spiritual challenge of Christianity had long since been turned aside in silence even when presented by great souls like St Francis. It was missionary endeavour using and letting itself be used by secular colonial European power that was instantly recognized as an enemy by Islam. How these missionaries from Holland, Britain and France, dedicated and sincere men of God, could have entered into what was basically an unholy alliance with Caesar, is not easy for us to understand. But one has to take into account the evangelical urge, the terrible yearning to pluck the brands from the burning pyre. There is evidence to show that despite the pathetically meagre results in terms of conversions from Islam since the twelfth century, nineteenth-century missionaries, perhaps because of their new and greater evangelical faith, perhaps because of the prevailing self-confidence of Europe, perhaps because of the powerful political backing they were receiving, believed that this time they would be able to make inroads into the faith.

On the ground the confrontation was, necessarily, with Islam. There were six target areas for the missionaries: China and India, where Islam was present (but which are areas that do not concern us here); Southeast Asia; the Middle East; Black Africa; North Africa. In Southeast Asia, the Middle East and North Africa Islam was the prevailing faith, while in Black Africa it was already in control of some areas and was the main contender in others. Thus, throughout the nineteenth century in the Dutch, British and French empires in Asia and Africa, battle was joined between Islam and missionary Christianity.

In Indonesia it is particularly easy to observe the intertwining of missionary and Dutch colonial activity because from the beginning the two were intertwined. It was at first the Dutch East India Company that determined which territories should have missionaries, the languages which should be used in religious services, what salaries should be paid and the assignment of personnel to their posts; after 1798 the Indian government itself took over these clerical responsibilities. Because 'Islam, as usual, offered stubborn resistance to the spread of Christianity', it was chiefly in regions where it had not penetrated, particularly those of animistic cults in the outer islands, that Christianity made the greatest progress.' But it was a superficial Christianity, for in areas like Amboina chiefs were paid 'disciple money' to produce candidates for baptism.[7]

The inter-relationship became even closer after the Dutch government officially took control of the Indies. It was the view of the missionaries themselves that conversion of Indonesians to Christianity 'is favourable for the fatherland since the natives upon embracing the Christian religion will become, heart and soul, loyal subjects'. Hence missionaries were sent into area after area throughout the century and the government helped the opening of schools and hospitals as a means of gaining converts. Another rather different policy pursued throughout the century was a persistent attempt by the Dutch Indies government to reduce the number of Indonesians making the Haj for it was considered that in Mecca they were infected with the 'virus' of militant Islam. This early appearance of the bogey of pan Islam, which became a fixed feature in the Islamic policies of all the European colonial powers, deserves to be noted. In 1825 the pilgrims were ordered to pay 110 florins for a pilgrim permit, when 100 florins was the average overall expense per pilgrim. This order was withdrawn in 1852 but even more stringent restrictions were imposed in 1859: 500 florins in cash was now demanded and on their return the pilgrims had to pass an examination on their knowledge of Mecca and Islam before being granted the title of Haji; also Dutch authorities in Jedde were ordered not to give help to stranded Indonesian pilgrims. The examination test was only withdrawn in 1902 and the money stipulation in 1905. This was done on the advice of the Dutch Islamic scholar Christiaan Snouck Hurgronje, of whom more later. To compensate, as it were, for one relaxation in 1905 the Dutch Indies authorities imposed another in that year by demanding that Muslim religious teachers obtain a special licence for teaching.

Dutch Indies policy swung back and forth between curbing Islam and curbing the missionaries, with the missionaries almost always getting the better of the local authorities, not always pro-missionary, by appealing to Christian sentiment back in Holland. Thus in 1854 missionaries were ordered to get special permits to function in certain strongly Muslim areas in case, as the then colonial minister put it, 'the Muslims, with all their elements of fanaticism and resistance' be unduly disturbed. But in practice the ruling was increasingly ignored. Indeed in 1888 the then colonial minister asked the Churches to increase their missionary activity; and the next year a decree was issued to 'reduce the danger of resistance in heathen areas to the spread of Christianity'. One measure introduced was to forbid Muslim officials from serving in non-Muslim areas, 'neither are Islamic regulations and customs to be introduced.' At the turn of the century official support for the missionaries and discrimination against Islam became even more open. In 1890 the government granted official subsidies to missionary schools, none being given to Muslim schools, and in the succeeding decades subsidies were granted for the building of churches, to schools, hospitals and orphanages, and payment of salaries to priests.

In the 1920s and '30s the Dutch authorities shifted their anti-Muslim policy into the area of Muslim education, which we shall deal with separately below.[8]

Though officially Church and State were separated in 1935 the two remained firmly linked till the Japanese invasion swept the Empire of the Indies away. The 350-year-long tussle between Islam and Christianity in Indonesia was summed up thus by the foremost historian of Christian missions: 'Except through strong political and social pressure, Islam has never yielded many converts to Christianity. Yet in Java in the course of the nineteenth and twentieth centuries converts from Islam to protestant Christianity, though only a few thousands, were more numerous than those made in all the rest of the world during the period. This was partly because the island was under Dutch rule and partly because Islam sat more lightly on the Javanese, who in the course of their history had yielded allegiance to Hinduism and Buddhism before they had become followers of the Prophet, than upon some other Muslim peoples.'[9] By 1935 the living result of the 357 years of missionary work was the presence of well over two million converts to Christianity. What was significant and ominous was that they were solidly concentrated in certain areas, in northern Sumatra, in the Moluccas, Amboina, and other outer islands.

In one of history's ironic acts of belated justice Holland is now having to cope with terrorist acts by young South Moluccan refugees who were led to believe that Holland would ensure their Christian islands' independence from Muslim Indonesia, because of the Dutch Indies policy of consistent favouritism towards converts.

'God has given us Indonesia' was the conviction of Abraham Kuypa, who became prime minister of the Netherlands in 1901. Much earlier on many Frenchmen had reached the same conclusion of Divine generosity towards France with North Africa, but with the task of both Christianizing and civilizing it, for even missionaries if they were Frenchmen had to be missionaries of French civilization as well.

For several centuries the French religious presence in North

Africa was limited to clergy sent there to minister to the needs of French settlers. But when, in 1830, France decided – mainly it would seem for reasons of prestige – to conquer Algeria, it placed its expedition under the sign of the Cross and of humanitarianism. The reasons given were the abolition of slavery and piracy, but the adviser to the French monarch, Charles X, added that the conquest would also be of 'the greatest benefit to Christendom' and the British government also said it would benefit 'all Christendom'. The Holy See made vows on behalf of French arms and on the news of the victory a Te Deum was chanted in Rome. But although the Christian excuse was used not much was done to push the missionary cause till the arrival of Archbishop Lavigérie, who became Archbishop of Algiers in 1867: twenty years later he was named Primate of Africa, surely the largest See ever conferred on any clergyman. He stated quite bluntly what his missionary aims were: 'Algeria is the open port of entry to a barbaric continent with two hundred million inhabitants ... In His providence God now allows France the opportunity to make of Algeria the cradle of a great and Christian nation.' Conversion to Christianity, he said, was the only way the Muslims could be converted from barbarism, and was therefore the only humane policy the French government could follow in Algeria. Under compulsion by Lavigérie some mosques were transformed into churches, extensive financial assistance was given by the state and numerous priests were brought in to carry on the good work. He founded the famous order of White Fathers. These monks were particularly active among the mountain tribes of the Kabyles – just as the Indonesians picked on the animists in the outer islands of Indonesia. But the Kabyles were Muslims too, so that by 1930 after sixty years of work there were not 700 converts among the Kabyles and less than one hundred in the Sahara, further south; among the Arabs of the coast conversions were practically nil, despite a network of missionary schools, hospitals and orphanages (most of the converts were orphans). The traditional anti-clericalism of France gradually asserted itself and in the early 1900s official financial support was withdrawn from the missionaries and religious schools were closed.

Even though Christian missionary activity in Tunisia was mainly directed, not at the Muslims, but at the large Jewish community, the Archbishop of Carthage in 1930 assembled a large eucharistic congress in Carthage, and many of those attending wore costumes recalling the Crusaders. One of the Tunisians whose anti-Christian Muslim nationalist feelings were aroused by this congress was the young Habib Bourguiba.

As in Algeria, the main target of missionary activity in Morocco, where a large number of missionary organizations both Catholic and Protestant took the field, were the Kabyles. But the results there were as disappointing as in Algeria: 'The jealous loyalty of the populace to Islam and the hostility to foreigners proved effective obstacles.'[10]

It must have been, understandably, most galling to Christian Churches, and especially to their missionary wings, that Palestine – the Holy Land and the birthplace of Christendom – should be overwhelmingly a country of Muslims and therefore impervious to the Christian appeal and to conversion. Yet all through the last century and down to the present the attempt was made and continues. Because every grouping wanted to be represented in the Holy Land the result was a complicated mosaic of orders (twenty-odd from the Roman Catholic Church alone) and of 'Churches' (about the same number from the Protestants). If French priests were particularly prominent among the Roman Catholics this was because traditionally French political influence in the Near East sought to buttress itself through the protection of Roman Catholic interests. But the only conversions made were from each other. In fact this inter-Christian raiding into each others' territory is a prime characteristic of Christian activity in the Near East, with the Armenian community and some of the smaller native Churches providing the main hunting grounds.

In the old Syria – which is now Syria and Lebanon – French missionary efforts tended to be educational, culminating in the establishment of the well known University of St Joseph in Beirut. The French consistently supported the local Maronite Church in Lebanon and this special relationship was greatly strengthened when France was awarded the mandate for Syria and Lebanon after World War II. In particular the French so inflated the numerical strength of the pro-French Maronite community that, after Lebanon's independence, it was accepted that the Lebanese president should always be a Maronite. This provision has been one of the prime causes of the Lebanese civil war. So strong has been the link, fostered by the Church, between the Maronites and what they call 'Mother France' that the Maronites have tended not to think of themselves as Arab but rather as part of the Western Christian world: a wholly mistaken belief that could yet bring about the partition of Lebanon.

In Egypt, too, missionary work was very much a game of robbing Peter to pay Paul with the age-old Coptic Christian community providing the converts, especially to the Protestant sects.

The most notorious example of how Christian missionary endeavour could become an integral part of European colonizing policy was provided by the British in the Sudan. It is worth looking in some detail at how the British, with the active assistance of the missionaries, established a Christian anti-Islamic *bantustan* in southern Sudan, because this bantustan was more rigidly controlled and also far larger and more important than any of those being set up in South Africa.

The importance of the southern Sudan lies in the fact that it sprawls across the upper reaches of the Nile where control of its flow could be very damaging to dams or irrigation works lower down the river, especially in Egypt whose life blood is the water of the Nile.

When British administrators took over the administration of what was called the Anglo-Egyptian Sudan, following the defeat by Kitchener of the fifteen-year old Mahdist state which had been set up after the death of the 'Christian' General Gordon at the hands of the 'fanatical' Mahdist mobs, these administrators made it very plain that their main fear was not pro-Egyptian feeling or a survival of pro-Mahdi feeling but of Islamic sentiment that was the basis of the two political loyalties. Since Gordon himself had been very much in favour of missionary work in the Sudan, and because the missionaries had already been active for some decades before the Mahdist uprising, the missionaries assumed that they would be able to resume their work as soon as the British administration returned. But, as in Indonesia, the local administrators were not in favour of missionary activities, especially in the Muslim areas; the same reason applied as in Indonesia – it would surely lead to trouble which they, and not the missionaries would have to deal with. A Dutch Indies administrator had once called missionary efforts to convert Muslims 'silly'; the forthright Cromer was more blunt, saying it would be 'little short of insane'. But, again as in Indonesia, the missionaries counter-attacked by appealing to the metropolitan government, one missionary spokesman pointing out that the Sudan would provide a link in the chain of missions from the Cape to Cairo (thus complementing Rhodes's plan for an all-British highway between those points). The spirit of the Christian hero Gordon was being betrayed. The missionaries had their way, not completely as in Indonesia, but in a compromise by which they were allowed freedom of action in pagan southern Sudan with certain concessions to them in the north. This arrangement, the British government believed, would bring to the southern Sudanese 'elements of common sense, good behaviour and obedience to government authority'. The administrators, now under orders to assist the missionaries in the south, and the missionaries agreed that Islamic influence should be excluded as soon as possible from southern Sudan. To avoid unseemly competition each missionary society was given a separate area for its work. They had the benefit of reduced fares on the railways and steamers.

The main effort of the missionaries was in the field of education, with which we shall deal separately later on. Be it noted that one of the administrators thought that the missionary schools were producing 'softies' and that instead they should try and turn out tough young men 'free from a desire either for hair oil or democratic government'.[11] Indeed education in the south was left entirely in the hands of the missionaries.

The Southern Policy, as it was known, began to be implemented vigorously from about 1917 onwards. Northern Sudanese troops, because they were Muslim, were ordered out of the south and replaced by a locally recruited force. In 1922 the whole of the south, and areas well to the north as well, were declared 'closed districts', for which residence permits were needed. In the same year permits were also introduced for the carrying on of trade. Both orders were meant to keep out Egyptians and northern Sudanese and were so applied. In order that southerners should receive adequate training to replace northerners on the administration special grants-in-aid were made to missionary schools: another similarity with Indonesia.

The missionary schools, of course, instructed only in English; and yet the use of Arabic spread. The governor-general of the Sudan wondered gloomily in 1927 that perhaps 'Arabic after all, in spite of its risks, must be our instrument.' The next year, however, the missionaries and the government, showing greater resolution, decided that the medium of instruction should be one of the six local dialects plus English. Arabic was formally rejected because 'it would open the door for the spread of Islam (and) Arabize the South.'

In 1930 a new memorandum laid down clear policy guidelines for the southern Sudan. Its three points envisaged the building up of 'self-contained tribal or regional units'; the elimination of all northern Sudanese administrators, clerks and technicians and the extended use of English. These provisions were immediately implemented and in addition a new drive to push northern traders out got under way, and if necessary they were deported.

It was considered that all this was not enough to quarantine the south from the north, and so tribes were moved around in order to create a vast no-man's-land between northern and southern tribesmen; it was actually forbidden for tribesmen from one area to be found in the other. Intermarriage between northerners and southerners was stopped; Arabic names were frowned on; and traders were ordered to stop the sale of Arabic dress. Southern Sudanese Muslims were not allowed to practise their religion openly.

The structure of the southern Christian bantustan was complete. But it did not work because isolation meant backwardness, so that there were not even enough competent southerners to run their bantustan.

During and after World War II the Southern Policy was seen to be unworkable and was abandoned in 1949 to the bitter denunciation of the missionaries.[12] By this time the administration, looking ahead towards inevitable independence, was talking about a united Sudan with a single administration and educational system but with safeguards for the south, within a regional or federal structure.

With this degree of separation imposed on the south it was inevitable that independence should bring troubles to the two regions. These culminated in open warfare in 1967, which lasted until 1972, when the north wisely conceded a special position to the south.

The task of missionaries in West Africa, especially along the Atlantic coast, was much simpler than anything they had to undertake in North Africa, Indonesia, the Levant or the Sudan. The entire length of the coast, with a few exceptions, was virgin territory, that is to say pagan, and therefore free from competition with Islam. All that the missionaries had to do was to make settlements along the coast and push inland as rapidly as possible to meet the incoming tide of Islam from the north. However, Islam had already reached the shore of Senegal, Guinea, Gambia and to a lesser extent Sierra Leone.

For between 50 and 75 years a line drawn horizontally about 250 or 300 miles inland from the coast was the frontier between the Christian or pagan area to the south and the Muslim area to the north. There was little direct impact of one on the other, and therefore little competition. In fact, as far as British colonies were concerned, especially Nigeria, administrators, as in Indonesia and northern Sudan, discouraged missionary activity in Muslim areas. The West African Muslims were solid, traditional, law-abiding people (generally quite loyal too) and so were not to be disturbed. So the *cordon sanitaire* drawn around the Christians in the Sudan by the Southern Policy was also drawn around the Muslims in Nigeria and elsewhere in West Africa by a 'northern policy'.

At the end of his massive seven-volume *History of the Expansion of Christianity* Latourette has two summings-up. The first relates to Christianity's long encounter with Islam in the Arab lands on the northern shores of Africa and in the Near East – the cradle of both religions. He makes two points: 'that in proportion to the total population Christians had become fewer than they had been since the second or third century'; and that such conversions and permeation as had taken place 'were predominantly through the missionaries from the Occident and the institutions and churches established by them'.[13] His overall summing-up is a comparison of the record of Christianity with those of other religions. The comparison with Islam is a trifle rueful. He writes: 'For centuries Islam was Christianity's most dangerous and formidable rival . . . It won from Christianity a larger proportion of the latter's territory than did any other competitors. Moreover, it usually held the ground so won. Only in the Iberian Peninsula and Sicily did Christianity regain substantial portions of the populations among whom Islam had once supplanted [Christianity]. In the 19th and 20th centuries . . . in the areas dominated by Islam . . . Christianity lost more numbers than it gained.' Then, to even the balance, Latourette makes these claims: that after the sixteenth century Islam 'made few large gains'; the expansion of both 'was closely associated with the conquests and commerce of their adherents', but the spread of Christianity 'was more often apart from or ahead of these than was that of Islam . . . Eventually Muslim culture became stagnant while the culture of Christianity was continually dynamic. As the presence of Christianity declined in the Muslim world so did its creativity . . . Christianity has done more humanitarian work than Islam.'[14] Some of Latourette's claims concerning the expansion of Islam are factually inaccurate, others he himself contradicts particularly on the dependence of Christianity on secular Christian European power.

Another summing-up of Western Christianity's long campaign against Islam would have to make these points: the spiritual pressure applied by the missionaries on Islam was a Christian initiative; the West was carrying the battle to Islam, which is why the confrontation took place in Muslim, not Christian territory; the main, indeed the sole, object of the campaign was conversion and, as Latourette admits, it failed everywhere. Was it all worth the effort? On the positive side one has to take into account the example set by thousands of brave, sincere, dedicated missionaries; the sick healed; the children educated (but a very mixed blessing this); the reformation or abolition of social evils, like slavery or the killing of twins.

On the negative side is the deep, widespread and long-lasting resentment produced in Islam by the polemical attacks made on it by missionary propagandists, an essential element in any campaign of proselytization. The emotional gulf this has created between the two religions can probably never be bridged. Was it worth creating this antagonism to effect the conversion of a few thousand Muslims?

Clearly the political result of Christian missionary activity in Muslim countries has been malign. It has come about through the creation of separate Christian communities in Muslim countries, whose separateness was deliberately fostered or favoured by treatment given to existing Christian minorities. If the Christian missionaries were unaware that in doing this they were playing the classic colonial game of divide and rule they must have been at best exceedingly naïve. This separateness was perhaps the main cause of the Nigerian civil war in the 1960s. It was certainly the main cause of the fighting between northern and southern Sudanese; of the continuing armed struggle of the Naga tribes against the Indian government and of the Karens against the Burmese government; and of the attempt by the Christian Outer Islands to break away from the Indonesian republic; through encouragement given to Maronite separation it has contributed to the Lebanese civil war.

If these were all the items, positive and negative, on the balance sheet then one would have to say that the Christian missionary campaign against Islam was not justified by the results and should never have been mounted at all. But there has been one other factor that no one reckoned on – the spiritual and religious pressure that the missionaries maintained on Islam did not permit it to relax. It kept Islam militant. And that, probably, has been no bad thing.

2

The well known Islamic scholar H. A. R. Gibb begins the text of a lecture on 'The Reaction in the Middle East Against Western Culture' with a listing of 'the main influences that have impinged on the ancient institutions of Muslim society', divided into 'economic', 'social' and 'political' affairs. Under this third heading he mentions constitutional government, the idea of citizens' rights and duties, equality before the law, and the concept of nationalism. It is true that Gibb is dealing with 'culture' and 'influences' but it is exceedingly strange that he does not mention, however briefly and in passing, that during the 150 years preceding his lecture (delivered in 1951) the entire Islamic world, with the exception of five countries, had been brought under the imperial domination of Britain, France, Holland, Italy, Spain and Russia. When in 1945 Gibb delivered the lectures that became his well known work *Modern Trends in Islam* there were in the whole Islamic world just four Muslim countries that were truly independent – Turkey, Afghanistan, Saudi Arabia and the Yemen (Iran and Egypt were only nominally so). There are now fifty-six Muslim governments that are members of the United Nations.

The continuous, steady and relentless taking over of the lands of the peoples of one religion by the governments of another religion, starting from 1800, was an extraordinary historical phenomenon, which brought crushing political pressure to bear on Islam from Christian Europe. Equally extraordinary was the way in which, responding to this long-drawn-out challenge, the Muslim world rolled Europe back, except in central Asia, in twenty years.

We can only imagine the feelings of educated or semi-educated Muslims in Algiers or Cairo, Delhi or Jakarta during the last century as the news arrived, probably much delayed till 1850 but thereafter with increasing swiftness, of the long series of conquests, annexations and protectorates by which Europe ingested the Muslim world, bite by bite. The process of defeat must have seemed all the more shocking because the Muslim world expanded uninterruptedly from the seventh century onwards. Only the small Crusader Kingdoms established in Palestine for 150 years and the permanent loss of Spain and Sicily had been exceptions to the rule. In the fifteenth century Spain and Portugal had established small coastal enclaves in Morocco, but two centuries later the Portuguese were expelled and Spain retained only Ceuta, Mellila and Tangier. Indeed in the 15th and 16th centuries Islam achieved its widest expansion and even in the 18th the only losses were the delta region of Egypt to Napoleon, and Georgia and the area around the northern end of the Black Sea. There was nothing to warn of the collapse that came from the start of the 19th century.

Listed below are the dates when Muslim territory passed under Western Christian control or conquest was attempted, and of Muslim resistance thereto. It makes no claims to completeness.

1798	Indies under direct Dutch control.
1802–06	Tjirebon War in Java.
1820	Trucial Oman and Qatar under British protectorate.
1821–38	Padri War in Sumatra.

1825–30	Java War.
1830–57	Conquest of Algeria by the French.
1834–59	Subjugation of the Caucasus by Russia.
1837–47	Risings in central Asia against Russians.
1839	Aden annexed by Britain.
1839–42	First war between Afghanistan and British India.
1842	Muslim Amirates of Sind annexed to British India.
1846–9	Balinese War.
1846–64	Conquest of Syr Darya valley by Russia.
1849	Tribal territory of Northwest Frontier Province annexed to British India.
1853–65	First Russian campaign in Khokand and capture of Tashkent.
1856	Muslim state of Oudh annexed to British India.
1857	Final overthrow of Mogul Empire in India by British.
1866–72	Russian conquest of area around Samarkand and Bukhara.
1872–1908	Acheh War in northern Sumatra.
1873–87	Uzbek territory over-run by Russia.
1875–6	Khokand conquered by Russia.
1879	Second Afghan War.
1881–3	Conquest of Tunisia by the French.
1882	Egypt occupied by British.
1883–5	War against the Mahdi in the Sudan.
1885–90	Eritrea conquered by Italy.
1890	Conquest of Senegal by the French.
1891–9	Upper Niger and Ivory Coast conquered by the French.
1891	Muscat and Oman under British protection.
1895	Pamir area annexed by Russia.
1898	Sudan subjugated by Britain.
1899	Muslim Khanates of Baluchistan annexed to British India.
1900–10	Somaliland resists British occupation.
1900	Chad conquered by French.
1903	Battle of Kano, northern Nigeria.
1906	Muslim Sultanates of northern Nigeria become British protectorate.
1912–30	Tripolitania and Cyrenaica conquered by Italy.
1912	Morocco occupied by France and Spain.
1912–15	Moroccan resistance to Spanish rule.
1914–18	Turkey under attack in World War I.
1914	Kuwait under British protection.
1916	Darfur rebellion in Sudan defeated by British.
1919–26	Moroccan resistance to French occupation.
1919–20	Moroccan resistance to Spanish rule.
1919–21	Smyrna and Turkish hinterland occupied by Greece.

1919–21	Antalya area of Turkey occupied by Italy.
1919–21	Cilician area of Turkey occupied by France.
1919	Third Afghan War.
1920	Somali resistance finally broken.
1920	Mesopotamia (Iraq) under British protection. Revolt follows.
1920	Syria and Lebanon under French mandate despite Syrian resistance.
1925–7	Druze uprising against French in Syria.
1926	Campaign to complete occupation of Italian Somaliland.
1941–6	Anglo–Russian occupation of Iran.
1945–9	Indonesian independence struggle against Dutch.
1954–62	Algerian independence war against French.
1956	Anglo–French attack against Egypt at Suez.

Thus we see that during these 150-odd years scarcely a decade, indeed scarcely half a decade, passed without some Muslim area somewhere in Asia or Africa being lost to the Western Christian powers or Muslims fighting against the encroachment of these powers.

If the periods of the wars or uprisings mentioned are added up they come to over 250 years of combat; and this does not take into account the smaller internal armed uprisings, riotings and acts of violence which were endemic, especially after World War I. This being the historical record of militant Islam, it is surprising that Islamic antagonism towards Europe is not far greater than it is.

Once Europe had embarked on the course of empire it was inevitable that the European powers should have to clash with the Muslim world because it lay in a great crescent around the southern and eastern perimeter of the European continent. So we may ask, apart from this compulsion of geography, how far were these endless wars specifically wars of religion between Christianity and Islam? The answer varies with the point of view. For the Muslims, at the receiving end, they were *all* wars of religion waged in defence of hearth and home but also and more so in defence of Islam. The defenders always saw themselves as copying the example of Saladin who expelled the European Crusaders from Palestine. Only some of the European protagonists saw themselves as latter-day Crusaders, fighting the good fight against the 'paynim' hordes; for as the nineteenth century advanced more realistic economic and political reasons prevailed over sentiments based on religious enthusiasm or on prestige or glory. The French were the most likely to hark back to the Crusader spirit, which died hard. As late as 1920 when the French General Gouraud entered Damascus, after the battle of Maissaloun, one of the first things he did was to visit the famous tomb just outside the Omayyad mosque where he knocked on its door and said to its inmate: 'Saladin, listen, we have returned.'

For a variety of reasons the Crusades, the first formal military encounter between the religions of East and West, kept a permanent scar on the souls, or collective unconscious, of both sides. Beneath the scar the wound is still sensitive today and the slightest pressure on it sets it throbbing again. Perhaps this is so because both protagonists were so totally convinced at the time not just that this was a holy war but that it was, particularly for the Christians, a *bellum justissimum*, the *most* just war. The apologists of the just war pointed out that Islam had robbed Christendom, then seen as a unit, of a third of its best provinces. Therefore the Crusaders were fighting to recover what was rightfully Christian property: 'For it had been consecrated by the presence of Christ and conquered by the Roman, later to be Christian Empire.'[15] It was therefore not a war of aggression. Instead it was actually a war of defence because, it was argued, the Muslims had given ample proof simply by their presence in the Holy Land that they were dangerous to Christendom and sought whenever they could to harm Christianity. Thus, having once taken the Holy Land, subsequent Crusades were justified as acts of defence, which is exactly how the Muslim defenders also saw their stance.

Because of the Crusading experience, 'The ideas of conquest and conversion lay side by side in the consciousness of the Christians of the Western world.'[16] And because the Crusades had failed the resultant bitterness produced so much anti-Muslim propaganda in Europe over the centuries that Christians were brought up to expect to be in a relationship of force and violence with the Muslim world.[17]

Among the later Christian conquerors moved by Crusading fervour were, on the French side, Generals Lyautey and Gallieni and, among the British, Laurence, Havelock and Nicholson in

India, Gordon and Kitchener in the Sudan. On the whole these wars threw up larger and more heroic figures from the ranks of the Muslims – such as the impossibly romantic figure of Shamyl[18] in the Caucasus, who after 25 years of fighting Russia died in Mecca; Ababel Qadir, who resisted for 15 years in Algeria; Abdel Krim who fought in Morocco for 5 years; the 20-year epic of the 'mad mullah' Muhammed Abdalla of Somaliland, who wanted to go to Mecca to die but was not allowed to; and the 'Hamlet-prince' Diponegoro in Indonesia.

What were the real motives of the European powers in their assaults on the Muslim world? There was trade – a motive that was notably there even in the Crusades, particularly among the Italians from Genoa and Venice. There were such financial motives as the collection of debts, which played a large part in the events leading up to the British occupation of Egypt and to the French conquests of Tunisia and Morocco. In all three cases Western creditors encouraged feckless rulers to extravagant spending on vain and useless luxuries – like splendid coaches in Morocco where there were no roads for them to be used on. (There is a long tradition behind the Western arms dealers who today press expensive and sophisticated arms on Iranian and Arab rulers whose armed forces do not know how to use them.) There was the route to India, the 'jewel in the imperial crown', which for the British meant that Egypt, Aden, Iraq and the Persian Gulf had to be in 'safe' hands. There was, again, the defence of India against the Russian threat from the northwest, hence the Afghan Wars; and the route to Afghanistan, which had to be controlled, ran through Baluchistan; and the route to Baluchistan ran through Sind, which had to be taken over as well; and for the Russians there was the need for their presence in central Asia, to counter the British threat against their soft underbelly coming through Afghanistan. Least convincing is the claim by the British that the colonies and protectorates all came about 'in a fit of absentmindedness'; or that of the French that they were provoked into an unnecessary campaign in the western Sudan by 'fanatical' Muslim theocrats who insisted on declaring jihad against the French when they merely wanted to tidy up the map of Africa and open their own route to the head-waters of the Nile:[19] 'this animal is wicked, when attacked it defends itself' is after all a French saying. Whatever the reasons of the European powers it was always the Muslims who came under attack; and who, under this long series of hammer blows, were never allowed to relax.

3

Islam as a religion was little affected, as we have seen, by the 350 years of Christian missionary endeavour. As a polity, it was as little affected by the 150 years of colonial conquest and imperial rule. It has been well said that 'It does not matter who rules Muslims so long as he leaves them alone. Even anti-Muslim rulers can make only slow headway against an Islamic community.'[20] But there was one sphere – education – in which colonial rule did have a profound effect on Muslim society: because the foreign rulers, with rare unanimity and unusual purposefulness and pertinacity, sought to give as little education as possible, the wrong sort of education when it had to be given, and also to bring about a schism in the soul of the Muslim community.

What happened was this. The Western powers, the French especially but also the Dutch, British and the Italians, deliberately mounted an onslaught on the minds of the youth of their subject peoples. In most Muslim countries there was a widespread, loosely organized system of education already in existence, traditional, static and not keeping pace with the times, but still providing a foundation on which something more modern yet indigenous could have been built. This local educational system was either destroyed, ignored, or allowed to collapse through 'benign neglect' by the colonial regimes. Since Arabic and Islamic tendencies were looked upon as dangerous and subversive influences they had to be excluded. Therefore the new system that the colonial authorities introduced was wholly Westernized, and used European languages exclusively. Yet the purpose was not to produce thoroughly Westernized young Muslims, for that too would have been dangerous. Education had to serve the strictly limited purposes of the colonial administration by producing clerks and artisans; and in just sufficient numbers to keep the machine going. As far as higher education was concerned the existing universities were also ignored, but nothing was put in their place in the conquered territories. Thus the intellectual élite of Muslim countries was forced to study, during the most formative years, in the universities of the metropolitan countries; which was productive of a thorough if subtle brainwashing, making them aliens in their own countries, of which they became the new rulers.

The French, with their passionate faith in their civilizing mission, were the worst in this regard, but in the end their system did manage to produce a certain number of brown and black Frenchmen with an excellent knowledge of French. The Dutch and British tended to be more slapdash in their methods and less insistent on linguistic excellence or cultural absorption or assimilation.

An American scholar gives this overall view: 'A methodical policy of deracination and deculturization was followed in Algeria in the nineteenth century, was repeated to a lesser extent in Morocco over a shorter period, and carried out most slightly in Tunisia . . . the main effort . . . was to destroy the colonized by a complete denigration of their fundamental values.'[21] And what the French did in Muslim North Africa they also did in the Muslim Black Africa and in the Levant; the British did the same in Egypt and the Sudan; the Dutch likewise in Indonesia. Now for some details on this cultural *Gleichschaltung*.

'*Even according to French official reports* [emphasis added] Algeria was at the time of the conquest thickly covered with the traditional Muslim schools at the primary and higher level, and Arabic and Islamic studies were flourishing.'[22] In Tunisia the condition of education was much the same, with the traditional schools leading up to the Zaitunah mosque school, the Tunisian equivalent of al Azhar. Two schools on modern lines had been established in which technical subjects were taught in foreign languages alongside Islamic and Arabic subjects. So, too, in Morocco the traditional system had the famous Qarawiyin mosque school at its apex and modernization was being injected. Soon after occupying Algeria in 1830 the French set up two systems of education – one imported lock, stock and barrel from France for the colonists, and the other, for Algerian children, called France-Musulman, which however followed the French curricula, used French as the sole medium of instruction and taught Arabic only as a foreign language. Missionary schools were also permitted. The traditional schools, receiving no official support, began to dwindle. Fifty years after the occupation the number of Algerian children in the French–Muslim schools was just over three thousand. In the French-style schools, forty years after the occupation, at the primary level, there were 1500 Algerian Muslims out of 57,000 pupils and at the secondary level 226 out of two thousand. This state of affairs remained much the same till after World War II when some attempt at improvement was made: but when the Algerian Revolt broke out in 1954 only one-tenth of children at primary level were at school. Thus it is clear that the object of the French educational system in Algeria was to deny education to the Algerians.

Algeria set the pattern for Tunisia and Morocco. Even after World War II, when improvements were made in Tunisian education, the reformed traditional schools were brought under official control, given grants in aid but required to teach in French, which was the only medium of instruction. A major concession in 1950, six years before independence, was that arithmetic could be taught in Arabic, but only at the primary level.

In Morocco too French was the sole medium of instruction in the French and French–Musulman system. What was worse was that in an attempt to drive a wedge between the Arabs and Berbers a separate Franco-Berber school system was set up, where there was some use of Berber dialects. The first French president general, a conciliatory administrator, said, 'Arabic is a factor in Islamization because it is acquired with the Koran. It is our interest to make the Berbers develop outside the framework of Islam.'[23]

In 1880 when the British occupied Egypt the country had, besides a small number of schools in the modern sector, over 5000 schools in the traditional system and al Azhar had 8000 students and 300 professors. In 1883 a British official suggested that in the official school system – that is the modern sector – Arabic should be the medium, and in the colloquial not classical style. Far from adopting this revolutionary suggestion the British introduced English as the medium from the elementary level. The large traditional system was ignored for fifteen years when grants-in-aid and some official supervision were introduced. For as long as he could Cromer, the real ruler of Egypt, blocked all attempts to establish a university in Egypt, since he said it would only 'manufacture demagogues'. Cairo University was finally founded in 1907. When in 1922 the British granted 'independence' to Egypt, conditioned and regulated by a treaty with Britain, the country had in its official modern educational sector no more than ten secondary schools with 3,800 pupils (forty-three of whom were girls).

We have already seen how a separate educational system was part of the pattern of isolation that the British imposed on southern Sudan. The whole educational system was handed over to the missionaries, Roman Catholic, Presbyterian and Anglican, each denomination within a specified territory. And despite their differences of nationality and denomination they offered the same type of education: teaching at a lower level through the medium of tribal dialects written in Latin characters (in north Africa the French at least used vulgar Arabic when writing Berber and Kabyle dialects), and at a higher level through the medium of English. The principal object was to supply not much more than four years at a lower elementary school to produce junior clerks and government employees; with the result that in 1920 there were only eleven higher elementary schools in the whole area, and that figure remained stationary for the next twenty years. Sudan's sole institution of higher education, Gordon College at Khartoum, taught in English except in Arabic and Islamic subjects.

Although France acquired the League of Nations mandate for Lebanon and Syria in 1920, exactly ninety years after the conquest of Algeria, it followed exactly the same educational policy in the Levant as in north Africa. In the Lebanon it found an extensive school system, both primary and secondary, run by American, British, and French missionaries. In addition there were a certain number of state primary schools. The French introduced their own primary schools and so favoured them over the state schools that after five years of French rule the number of students in these schools was halved. The medium of instruction in the state and French primary schools was, of course, French. What was even more shocking is that the French did not attempt to bring a state secondary school system into being. At that level the Lebanese either had to go to French schools or private ones. Because there were already French and English colleges in existence no state university was even contemplated. In Syria the French inherited from the Ottoman administration a state educational system with primary, secondary, teacher training and high schools. Their first act was to make French the *première langue vivante* in all state schools from the first year in the primary school upwards. The two teacher training colleges were allowed to die out and also two out of the four secondary schools.

A separate French school system was, as elsewhere, introduced and given favoured treatment over the state system. No institution of higher education was developed except for the schools of law and of medicine which were already there, and French was the medium of instruction in the medical school.

If this was how France moulded the educational system in countries where some sort of system already existed and where there was an already educated class, it can be imagined how totally French was the system introduced and maintained in colonies in Black Africa where it was possible to write on a *tabula rasa*. One of the things written which was recited by the black African students was: *'nos ancestres les Gaulois étaient blonds.'*

The educational record of the Italians in Libya is comparable to that of the French and was based on comparable principles: neglect and Italianization – as an Italian colonial minister put it, 'a progressive and efficient penetration of the native minds by the Italian language and spirit'; but even this cultural 'penetration' was not efficiently prosecuted.

Compared with the other colonizing powers, but only when compared with them, the Dutch in the Indies followed a relatively liberal policy towards the traditional educational system which they found in place when the Dutch government formally took over the country. It was liberal in the sense that they did not try to interfere with the traditional system, knowing full well that it was not going to wither away as it would in Arab countries. That, indeed, was one of the two reasons for Dutch restraint. The traditional system was too well developed in the Indies, too much a part of the people's daily life, ever to fade away. Every village had its school, maintained by the community. These were very elementary schools, for all they did was to try and impart rudimentary religious instruction for four or five years. The religion was Islam: and that was the second reason for Dutch neutrality. They knew Islam to be the very stuff of Indonesian community existence and they had fought too many wars with the Indonesians (some long ones) not to know that the Indonesian, however easy-going, could become very fierce when his religion was encroached on, which it would have been if the Dutch had tried to tamper with the omnipresent Koranic school. So for the whole of the nineteenth century the Dutch and Indonesian educational systems existed side by side. The Dutch system was much like those of the British and French except that, another liberal feature, the Dutch language became the medium not at the primary stage but only at the secondary level. Like the other colonial systems it was severely restricted. There were few secondary state schools and still.fewer high schools and it was not easy for Indonesians to gain admission, with preference being given to children from aristocratic families. In fact the schools were there really to cater for the needs of the Dutch and Eurasian communities. One effective way of keeping Indonesian children out was that they had to pay substantial school fees while Dutch and Eurasian children, whose parents were far better off, could attend free: the per capita expenditure by the government for Dutch and Eurasian children was eighty-seven times that provided for Indonesian children.[24] Thus in 1940 in the higher secondary schools 5700 pupils were Dutch and 1700 Indonesian. The school system, again as in other colonial systems, was meant to produce personnel for the lower and middle range of the administration, and this it did. In 1928 sixty per cent of Indonesian high school graduates went into government service.

From early on in their national struggle the Indonesians realized the importance of building their own educational system – improving the traditional, and introducing nationalized versions of the Western type. The first mass nationalist movements were both mainly educational organizations. In 1925 the Dutch issued what became known as the Guru Ordinance which imposed on secular village teachers, as well as the Muslim missionaries, the obligation to register their intention of giving religious instruction outside their family, together with the texts to be used in such instructions. This was widely and vigorously protested and six years later the missionaries were exempted from the ordinance, while at the same time it was extended to thousands of humble village instructors engaged in teaching the rudiments of Islam. Between 1923 and 1925 similar restrictions were imposed on private schools giving Western-type education. In 1932 it was extended still further to include all types of schools, especially the nationalist variety run by Indonesians. Despite protests the restrictions remained in force until the Japanese invasion but they were honoured in the breach rather than in the observance.[25] However, this meant that at the end of their period in Indonesia the Dutch were trying to watch and restrict indigenous education while making no contribution towards it, and themselves offering only a limited measure of Dutch-based education that was ill suited to the real needs of the Indonesian people.

The cultural offensive mounted by the Western Colonial powers against the societies of their Muslim territories struck at those societies in three different ways. Through the neglect of the traditional educational system it weakened the older set of values, both secular and Islamic. A spiritual and cultural vacuum was created by allowing the traditional roots to wither away unnourished. For the majority of those now without roots the Western rulers did not provide an alternative through their own system of education, for this was restricted to a minority. Even within that minority still fewer were able to go all the way through the Western system to the top levels of higher education where they could perhaps attain a true understanding of the West's cultural and spiritual values. For most young Muslims (and Afro-Asians generally) Western education was a half-baked affair suiting them for nothing more than lower or middle employment in the Western administrative or business structure. And for the 'lucky' few who received the full benefit of Western education, an even worse cultural fate awaited them: complete cultural uprooting. This is why the Westernized ruling élites in Muslim countries are and always have been strongly, even bitterly opposed to militant Islam; and vice versa. A Western scholar of Indonesia puts it starkly: 'The "new" intelligentsia in Afro-Asia is not a product of organic social growth but rather a product of alien education more or less precariously grafted on indigenous non-Western societies.'[26]

How far was this uprooting and replanting in Western cultural soil of the all-important top layer of Muslim and Afro-Asian societies seen by Western colonialists as a result to be deliberately achieved by their educational policies? Not, perhaps, preplanned by the British, even though they welcomed the result once it became apparent. Deliberately planned by the French, but only in the sense that they assumed that anyone with pretensions to culture would want to become a cultured Frenchman: that 'Paris is every cultured man's second capital' is another French saying. But in Indonesia the deracination of the Indonesian élite was a deliberate political decision taken and pushed through to implementation by one of the Western world's most famous Islamic scholars and orientalists.

Under the Ottomans, Libya for some reason had a good school system with numerous traditional schools in towns and villages and seventeen primary schools, one secondary, another for arts and crafts, one training, and one military college. All the state schools and colleges were closed by the Italians, as were many of the traditional schools. Just before World War II there were 102 Arab pupils in the Italian official schools against over 500 in private Libyan schools. When, in 1936, the first high school was set up it was limited to thirty students carefully selected to fill specific posts as junior officials and religious judges. And this was after Libya, like Algeria, had been formally incorporated into the metropolitan motherland.

To the way in which Western Islamic orientalists mounted their special type of offensive against the Muslim world we must now turn.

4

The intellectual life of the Western orientalist must be strange indeed – a life spent immersed in the language, religion, culture, history, social life and ways of thought and feeling of people from a distant and alien continent. The demands on empathy and insight that such studies would normally produce are that much more severe for Western Islamic orientalists for, as we have seen, there has been a constant state of tension between the Western and Islamic worlds extending over the centuries and reaching a peak of antagonism in the last 150 years. Yet until about 1955 ninety-nine per cent or more of the books about Islam were written by Western scholars: they cannot be blamed for this intellectual monopoly, but it must be seen as having been a very strange one.

Analogies are dangerous, for none can be very exact, but let us look at the mirror image of Western Islamic orientalism. Let us suppose that in 1683 the Turks had not been stopped by the

Polish troops of Sobieski at Vienna but that they went on to conquer western Europe; and that they remained the masters of Europe until 1955. Consequently, all books on the Christian religion and culture of their European subjects would have been written by Muslim scholars from Turkey, Egypt, Indonesia and other Muslim countries, with some even by Hindu scholars from India (analagous to works on Islam written by Western Jewish scholars). It would be understandable for Europeans, 'liberated' after 1955, to feel that this monopoly of writings about their faith by non-European non-Christians was unfair and even somewhat ridiculous. But something almost exactly like the reverse of this imagined situation has been the state of affairs in Islamic studies until about 1955, nor has it changed all that much in the past quarter-century.

It surely must be conceded that a local, national religion in countries under foreign rule becomes something very different when those countries are no longer under foreign domination – and the same change would surely be seen in the arts and literature of such countries. What is more, the change from the ambience of subjection to one of freedom would be particularly noticeable in Islam, which more than any other religion is an integral part of the life of its society; and all the more because Islam played a leading role in the long struggle for freedom. Post-liberation Islam is a very different subject of study – more changeable, more dynamic, more authentic – than the distracted and defensive Islam of the pre-liberation period. But, since the passage of time cannot be argued with, it is pre-liberation Islam that has been the subject of study of Western orientalists. Arguably, most of their writing is in need of revision, if not rewriting.

Since the higher education of students from colonized countries was deliberately channelled into the universities of the metropolitan powers, Muslim students of Islam, in the upper reaches of their subject, had to study it under the guidance of Western Islamic scholars at such centres as Oxford, Paris, Leiden, Göttingen and, more recently, Harvard and Princeton. Thus Western-educated Muslim scholars have been looking at their religion through the eyes of their Western teachers. And the vision of those Western teachers has often been askew – almost inescapably so because of the continuous tension between the West and Islam, to which we have referred. Indeed that very learned and judicious Muslim authority on Islam, Syed Hossain Nasr, has gone so far as to write of 'the prejudices and mis-understanding of western orientalists . . . wreaking intellectual havoc among many modernised Muslims'; 'intellectual havoc' are strong words indeed coming from a scholar of such eminence.

Some Western scholars are not unaware of the possibility of prejudice in their writings on Islam. Thus in the preface to his book *Mohammedanism* written in January 1945, Gibb, writing of the first edition of a book by another author, refers to it as reflecting 'the intellectual and emotional limitations of its period' and that it could not escape from 'prejudgement and prejudice'.

It is the 'prejudice' and 'limitations' of two Western scholars of Islam that we will be looking at briefly in this section; for their work was typical of a different variety of pressure, intellectual in this case, that was applied by the West on Islam. The two scholars are Christiaan Snouck Hurgronje, a Dutch Islamist, and Gibb himself, perhaps the most prestigious and influential British Islamist of this century.[27]

Though both men were life-long academics there were two periods in Hurgronje's life in which he was far afield from the groves of academe. The first was when, soon after completing his studies in 1884, he went in disguise to Mecca and lived there as a Muslim for six months. This was an act of great daring, for Mecca was and still is strictly forbidden to non-Muslims (a prohibition for which no sensible reason has been, or can be given). It is important to note that much later on Hurgronje said that if he had not been expelled from Mecca, because of the jealousy of a French consular official, he might never have returned from there. In 1891 he went out to the Dutch East Indies and to the area of Acheh in northern Sumatra, then waging war with the Dutch. His report, based on a seven month sojourn, was not accepted until 1896 when he became civilian adviser to the military commander. Because of the success of the policy he proposed Hurgronje then became adviser on native and Arab affairs to the Government of the Indies, a post he retained till 1906. During this time he propounded and implemented what was called the Ethical Policy of the Dutch and

Indies governments. Though he never returned to the Indies he remained the foremost Dutch authority on the subject and on Islam. He was even offered the Chair of Arabic in the newly founded Cairo University.

Hurgronje believed that no long-term policy could be implemented until the Acheh War was won and he proposed its prosecution with the utmost vigour; he went into the field with troops; and he left Acheh for Batavia because he thought the army was not pressing on with the campaign with sufficient vigour.

When it came to drawing up his long-term policy he based it on a complete misconception of one of the fundamental characteristics of Islam; he believed that a distinction could be made between private Islam, the religion, and public Islam, the polity. In 1925 he wrote: 'Islam from its beginnings has been a political religion.'[28] Perhaps discernment came with time, for that was certainly not what he believed in the 1890s. Towards private Islam he advocated a policy of tolerant but vigilant neutrality. Thus purely vexatious ordinances like restrictions on the Haj or on the teaching of Islam were to be removed. He would have liked to have curbed missionary activity for he realized that 'There is no reasonable hope of the conversion of important numbers of Mohammedans to any Christian denomination . . . it cannot be denied that what they want above all to bring to Mohammedans is just what these most energetically decline to accept.'[29]

So much for toleration. What the government must not 'platonically envisage' is 'all those trends that bear, or tend to bear, a political character'.[30] Against such trends the government must be 'totally intransigent'.[31] Especially, the government must 'decisively reject all demands or pretentions of pan Islamism, which is foreign interference'.[32] He wrote of 'the epidemic of pan Islam'; for him pan Islam and jihad were 'real nightmares'[33] (and as insubstantial as nightmares).

Having tolerated private Islam and contained political Islam, the ethical element in the Ethical Policy was to encourage the fullest participation of the right elements among the Indonesians in the politics and culture of Holland: 'the accession of the natives to a higher civilization'.[34] To achieve the fullest assimilation he was prepared to advise the annexation of the Indies to metropolitan Holland, just as Algeria had already become part of France. 'The right elements' to be given the benefits of Westernization were the traditional chiefs and rulers of the Outer Islands and the aristocratic families of Java: their 'traditional aloofness from Islam made them the logical beneficiaries of Hurgronje's assimilationist schemes'.[35]

There were two reasons why he wanted to wean the 'right sort' of Indonesian away from Islam. The first was 'his basically low esteem for Islam', which the Indonesians knew about and resented.[36] The 'narrow confines of the Islam system' had to be broken out of by Indonesians longing to escape. Since the tenth century Islam had become a closed system and was now in its 'old age'.[37] Consequently 'the treasuries of Islam are excessively full of rubbish that has become entirely useless' but these and other things are not objected to by Muslims: 'Millions of Muslims resign themselves to conditions in which at the present time more Mohammedans live under foreign authority than under their own – facilitated by the historical pessimism of Islam, which makes the mind prepared for every sort of decay . . . The Muslim habit of resignation, not through fatalism but through reverence for Allah's inscrutable will.'[38] It was the bounden duty of the colonial authorities to 'liberate' Indonesians from such a religion, a task to which they should bring 'a missionary zeal of the better sort'.[39]

The other reason why Hurgronje wanted to recruit people away from Islam and into the ranks of Dutch civilization was to split the opposition to Dutch rule. Those Indonesians who were educated into becoming brown Dutchmen would no longer want to be part of the anti-Dutch movement which was dominated by backward and fanatical Islam. 'In the final analysis Western education was the surest means of reducing and ultimately defeating the influence of Islam in Indonesia.'[40] Hurgronje thought he detected signs of Islam's decline in Indonesia early in the century: in 1890 he noted an increase in the number of theological training centres, but twenty years later Western schools were starting to win the case.

This splitting tactic of Hurgronje both succeeded and failed well beyond his expectations. The Westernized Indonesians did split off from the nationalist movement and they did become anti-Muslim. Unfortunately for Hurgronje the gift of Westernized education could not be confined to the scions of aristocratic families. Middle-class youths, like Engineer Sukarno, also partook of it and learnt from the West its ideals of freedom which they then began to demand for their own country. So in the end Hurgronje was hoist with his own petard. His policy did split the ranks of the opposition into Westernized and un-Westernized and it turned the former group, both the aristocrats and the middle-class nationalists, against the Islamic group; and the antagonism between nationalists and Muslims has bedevilled Indonesian politics down to the present. But the process produced those nationalists who brought Dutch rule to an end.

The ultimate political failure of Hurgronje's Ethical Policy is for us of less significance than the fact that it was based on a total misconception of Islam. The division of the religion into private and public Islam was a mistake that no Islamic scholar should ever have been guilty of. Hurgronje preferred to call the Ethical Policy the Realistic Policy, but it was not really realistic because it was based on ignorance, prejudice and fear.

Yet, back at Leiden University, he remained the Dutch government's permanent adviser on Indonesian and Arab affairs. He also taught the young administrators and missionaries going out to the Indies, and the Dutch diplomats dealing with the Arab countries. Thus his ideas were implanted in a whole generation of Dutchmen associated with Indonesia. His ideas being of the sort that we have described, it is little wonder that the Dutch lost their Empire of the Indies and that they fought the loss to the bitter end.

Hurgronje also encouraged Indonesian students to come and study at Leiden where his ideas were planted in the brains of a whole generation of the brightest and best young Indonesian intellectuals – ideas that Islam was an inferior religion and that the West was a superior civilization. By 1926 there were Indonesian protests against Hurgronje's prejudices, but by then the damage had been done and many of the future rulers of free Indonesia had been robbed of national self-assurance and cultural self-respect by Holland's foremost expert on Indonesia and Islam.

Gibb, unlike Hurgronje, was not involved in the foundation or implementation of official policy. He was an academic dealing with history and the movement of ideas; he was almost certainly the more influential of the two because his language is the world language while Hurgronje's work is to a very large extent buried in the unimportant west European patois that is Dutch.

However, as academics they did have one thing in common. They both wrote books on Islam which they termed, or rather mis-termed *Muhammadanism*. This was bad enough when Hurgronje's work appeared as far back as 1916, but it was infinitely worse when Gibb's book appeared thirty-two years later in 1948. The offence is this: for Muslims a reference to their faith, Islam, as 'Muhammadanism' is not merely insulting, it is blasphemous; because it implies that as in Christianity or Buddhism the founder of the faith has become an object of worship. Any such suggestion is anathema to Muslims because it violates the first and most important article of their faith – that there is no God but God and nobody to be worshipped but the One God. (The tendency that has appeared in the last forty years or so to hero-worship Muhammad and to talk of him as the perfect human exemplar, which even fairly orthodox teachers like Mandudi in Pakistan have fallen into is not only exaggerated but is contrary to the true humanistic spirit of Islam.) Hurgronje used the offending word in the title of his book and elsewhere in his works without any embarrassment or apology, which suggests that he was simply unaware of how very offensive it was to Muslim sentiment. The further implication is that, as with his belief that private and public Islam could be kept apart, this great Islamic scholar was ignorant about some of the most important and elementary facts about Islam.

With Gibb, writing a generation later, the case was different. He knew in 1948 that 'Muhammadanism' was an opprobrious misnomer, for he says so in his preface and gives reasons for using it: that the previous work on the subject in the series, the Home University Library, was so entitled and that the publishers wanted to preserve continuity. Interestingly enough the apology was removed from second and subsequent editions of the book, although the title remained the same.

Several Oriental orientialists, just beginning to shake off this inferiority complex towards such people as Hurgronje and Gibb, have come to realize that most Western orientalists do not really seem to like Orientals, that Western Islamists do not like Islam or Muslims and, even more obviously, that Western Arabists do not at all like Arabs.

Even the orientalists themselves have noted this. In his book *Mohammed* Maxime Rodinson, speaking of 'authors bent on systematically running down the Arabs', observes that this is 'paradoxically enough, a fairly popular sport with Arabists'.

Friends and defenders of Gibb point out that he never used the offending appellation after 1948. One hopes that that was so. But it was certainly not the first time he used it. In 1932 he edited a strangely inept work entitled *Whither Islam?*; two of his contributors, Louis Massignon, the greatest French Islamic scholar of the century, and the writer on Indonesian Islam both use the offensive term *Muhammadanism*.[41] Gibb was then the Professor of Arabic in the University of London and he certainly could have edited out the offending word from a book for which he was editorially responsible. We must assume that somewhere between 1932 and 1948 the Professor of Arabic in London and then at Oxford learnt that *Muhammadanism* was insulting; but thereafter did not care.

This is only a matter of a single word, but a word whose use or non-use is most indicative of basic attitudes.

It may seem unfair to quote opinions expressed in a book written in 1932, but a few may be briefly mentioned as examples of the sort of solemn nonsense that great scholars can produce when they leave the past and dive into the turbulent waters of contemporary events. For example, Massignon held the belief that the movement of opinion 'in north Africa was running north–south and not, as before, east–west and that accordingly it is to Paris and not to the East that the great mass of north Africans are turning their eyes.'[42] On the other hand Gibb wrote: 'Nor can it even be said that national consciousness is as yet a fixed and dominant feature in any Muslim country'. One wonders what he thought the numerous wars and uprisings in Muslim countries were all about. In another attempt to detach Arab Islam from its hinterland Gibb wrote: 'In its foundations we have seen that Islam belongs to and is an integral part of the larger Western society . . . Islam stands side by side with Europe in distinction from the true Oriental societies of India and the Far East.'[43] This last idea was also developed by the famous Egyptian writer, Taha Hussain.

It is the underlying bias in Gibb's attitude to which we shall refer briefly, especially as expressed in what is perhaps his best known work, *Modern Trends in Islam*. Since it is supposed to deal with the entirety of Islam one cannot but remark that it was based on a very narrow foundation: there is nothing beyond a single reference to Indonesia, and only second-hand information on India, by which a good half of Islam was excluded. The Muslim Brotherhood is referred to only in a footnote. The fact is that in 1945 the Islamic world was just about to break out into freedom (Pakistan was two years away) and that what Gibb wrote about was its undynamic, distracted, inhibited colonial variety. Seeing how variously independent Islam has blossomed one wonders whether the 'modern' trends of 1945 were even worth writing about.

Gibb commits one of those large generalizations about 'the Arab mind' that have so enraged the contemporary scholar Edward Said; what is noteworthy is Gibb's bias. Talking of the difference between the religious institutions of Christianity and Islam, Gibb writes of 'the absence of a hierarchy and of all that organization of councils, synods and sees which play so large a part in the history of the Christian Church. It may be that this lack of organization is to be related to that atomism of the Arab mind which we have already discussed.' Now why should the absence of clerical *impedimenta* be called a 'lack', an absence of something that should be there? And to say that the 'lack' can be attributed to certain supposed psychological traits rather than to the deliberate prohibitions of the Islamic religion is to indulge in mere fantasy. A recent intellectual fad is called psycho-history. Here Gibb is indulging in psycho-religion. Interestingly enough, after having made clear that Islam has no 'Church' he refers repeatedly to 'the Muslim Church' in his book.

In a way *Modern Trends* is a non-book, because throughout Gibb makes clear that he thinks such trends are not up to much and in some ways even deplorable. He rightly pays tribute to the past achievements of the brotherhoods while acknowledging that they have no future; he also has praise for the ulema and hopes that they have a future, which the modernists, he says, do not. His final summing-up is this: 'The future of Islam rests where it has rested in the past – on the insight of the orthodox leaders and their capacity to resolve the new tensions as they arise by a positive doctrine which will face and master the forces making for disintegration.'

Well, the development of post-independence Islam in the past thirty years has proven Gibb's prognostication completely wrong. The orthodox leaders have not shown any capacity to produce 'a positive doctrine' – not even in Iran, whatever may be the present ambitions of the Ayatollahs. Precisely those modernists about whom Gibb was so dismissive and patronizing ('how difficult it is [for them] to overthrow the age-long domination of atomism and authority') have been trying very hard to achieve the 'positive doctrine'. Gibb's analysis was so wrong because he could not, or would not at that time, come to terms with modern nationalism in the Muslim world. As we have seen he first denied that it was there, and when its presence could no longer be denied he said it was opposed to Islam, which is correct, and that it could never have deep roots in Muslim society, which is totally wrong. Perhaps Gibb's opposition was due to the fact that he realized that this nationalism was going to turn the old Islamic world he knew upside down, and he did not want to have to adjust to a new one. But in fact he did and his later writings, as in the essays in *Studies in the Civilization of Islam* published in 1962, show understanding and sympathy.

Just how the nostalgic backward-looking attitude of Gibb could influence younger scholars is shown by two quotations from another well known Islamist, W. Montgomery Watt. In 1961 in his *Islam and the Integration of Society* he wrote that nationalism, rife in Muslim countries, has been created by the Westernized group, and that it is superficial and has no deep roots. In his *Islamic Political Thought* published in 1968 a somewhat chastened Watt wrote: 'In 1945 Gibb spoke of the dangers of nationalism for Islam and its lack of deep roots in the Muslim soul.' (One cannot but be awed by Gibb's readiness to throw off large generalizations about 'the Muslim mind' and 'the Muslim soul'.) As one reflects on all that has happened since, one is bound to wonder whether Arab nationalism has not in part been transformed. For a time it may have been a useful stick with which to beat the Europeans. In the end, however, it looks as if it has become a partial realization of Islamic solidarity. The sort of Islam that Gibb spoke and wrote about was very different from the one now struggling to be free, far from the quietude of Oxford and Harvard.

In the preface to *Modern Trends* Gibb did something both courageous and honest. In parliamentary parlance 'he declared his interest' of his own free will: something that should be demanded of present-day Islamists. Gibb declared that 'The metaphors in which Christian doctrine is traditionally enshrined satisfy me intellectually as expressing symbolically the highest range of spiritual truth which I can conceive.' 'The highest': Islam then was second (or perhaps, third?) best. How strange a circumstance to spend one's life studying a religion while being convinced that it is an inferior doctrine! However, this open acknowledgement was made.

Other such acknowledgements are necessary today because the object of study of the Western Islamic orientalist, the Muslim world and especially its heartland the Arab world, has been in bitter and often violent conflict with the state of Israel for over thirty years. It would therefore be just to ask of writers on Islam, to say nothing of writers on the modern Arab world, to declare their interest as Gibb did and to say whether they are Arab or pro-Arab, Israeli, pro-Israeli or pro-Zionist. A very large number of present-day writers on Islam and the Middle East patently belong to one of the last three groups mentioned.[43] The Arab writers, of course, stand out because of their names, and their works tend to be taken automatically as being partisan and propagandist. Such is not the case with the Israeli or pro-Israeli writer: their works are accepted as the product of objective scholarship, which in very many cases, they are not.

For example, the British academic Dr Bernard Lewis is a prolific writer on modern Middle Eastern topics. His first books on the Arabs appeared after the establishment of Israel. He is a passionate defender of that country, to the extent that he has testified in its defence to committees of the United States Congress. Should not this political stance affect our opinion of his scholarly objectivity when he writes of countries that are the sworn enemies of Israel (and with the exception of Egypt every single Muslim state is such)?

The time has come, long overdue, for Oriental Islamists to come to the forefront of Oriental Islamic Studies. But since at present Islam remains an embattled faith, because of the Arab–Israeli confrontation, no Oriental Islamist could make claims to objectivity either. Two of the greatest Western Islamists, as we have just seen, were not especially objective, nor very understanding of Islam. The Oriental Islamist would at least have the incomparable advantage of speaking at first hand, while 'intellectual objectivity' is perhaps a mere myth.

One final remark on the Western Islamic scholar: it seems broadly true that when Britain and France were in control of the Islamic countries and were facing Islamic opposition, British and French Islamists tended to be unsympathetic towards those countries, while American scholars were generally sympathetic. But in recent years American scholars have become less sympathetic since Islam has become anti-American and the United States in its turn has become the main pro-Israeli force; European orientalists are now more discerning. This switch in roles seems to have taken place about 1955.

Having seen how in a variety of ways the Christian West has battered away at the Islamic countries, it is now for us to see how the Islamic world responded to those pressures and challenges – the theme of the next chapter.

4 Responses

Much of the response made by the Islamic world to the pressures put on it by the West before independence was achieved in the period 1947–62 and was necessarily negative in character, because during the pre-liberation period there was little that Islam could do except to counterpunch and push back. This was especially so on the political level, where it was a matter of sheer physical eviction of a foreign presence.

I

Before we describe militant Islam's counter-attacks it is right and proper that we should give precedence to the very first organized manifestation of militant Islam in modern times. This was the movement started by Muhammad ibn Abdel-Wahhab (1703–87), because of which the word 'Wahhabism' has become synonymous with militant puritanical Islam. Wahhabism was not in any sense an answer to any foreign challenge, which in the middle of the eighteenth century had not yet really developed and of which Abdel-Wahhab, living in the depths of Arabia, would have been unaware if it had. It was a movement for internal reform and it sent shock waves through the world of Islam because he said for the first time 'there is something rotten in the state of Islam'; the accusation still stirs guilty Islamic consciences today. Abdel-Wahhab advocated a return to Islam of the first generation and opposed everything that had been added since: he was against mysticism and the tarikas; against saint-worship; even against the orthodox schools and the cult of Muhammad as the perfect man. With the support of a petty tribal chief Abdel-Wahhab was able to establish an Islamic state where the Sharia was the law. This state, like the original Islamic state under Muhammad, exploded outwards; but after Abdel-Wahhab's death his Arabian peninsular state lapsed into the obscurity from which his teaching and programme had rescued it. It is ironic that puritanical Wahhabism should be associated with the modern Saudi Arabian state, which Abdel-Wahhab himself would have regarded as a profligate abomination. Decades later we find the moral protest of Wahhabism surfacing in West Africa, the Sudan, India and Indonesia and it is in those later manifestations in other countries that it becomes, through its return to elemental Islam, part of the protest against the corruption of Westernization.

Islam's response to the West on the religious-spiritual plane had to be on two levels – a specific response to the Christian missionary campaign and to the more general challenge of Western civilization or modernization. The answer to missionary endeavour was itself in two parts – one dealing with the material missionary activity, proselytization and conversion carried on very largely through schools and, secondly, the answer to Christian preaching and propaganda against the character of Muhammad and the teachings of Islam. The first answer, to missionary activity, came quickly and easily enough after independence. In many countries the main purpose of the Church was to cater to the needs of the non-indigenous Christian communities, the administrators and the *colons*: and when these withdrew after independence the Church withdrew with them. This was the case in the three North African countries, in Egypt and in Indonesia. In these and other Islamic countries the missionary problem was settled by forbidding them to proselytize in their schools; and in most countries it was decreed that while the preaching of the Christian faith was permitted it was not permissible to criticize other religions or to call for conversion. The humanitarian type of missionary work, hospitals, orphanages and so on, was free to carry on as before. In almost all Muslim countries, these new restrictions were accepted, however reluctantly, by the missionary societies. The exception, where the Church fought a stubborn rearguard action for its privileged missionary position was, as might have been expected, in the Sudan.

The Sudanese government at first adopted a most conciliatory attitude towards the missionary schools, with government subsidies to them actually being increased and religious instruction being provided for Christian children in government schools. But the intention was ultimately to have a unified school system with Arabic as the medium of instruction. This policy was approved by the International Education Commission but it was not acceptable to the missionaries, especially the Roman Catholic ones. These countered with a thirteen-point list of demands which would have virtually restored them to a controlling position over education in the south. The terms were rejected and the Roman Catholic Church and the Sudanese government were on collision course. When the army took over in the Sudan in 1958 it stepped up the spread of Arabic and Islamization as being the only way to achieve national unity. Many centres for the teaching of Islam were opened. Because of vigorous missionary protests, all Christian missionaries in the south were expelled in February 1962. It was only after 1969 when the southern rebellion was called off and the north and south reached an accommodation that the chastened Churches in the south also worked out a *modus vivendi* – no more proselytization with the provision that the mission schools be maintained but as part of the government system.

It was really the *Zeitgeist* that has settled Islam's missionary problem for it. With the decline of the Christian faith in the West, with the loss of the old certitudes of superiority, with talk that 'God is dead', the old qualities of 'missionary zeal' and 'the missionary spirit' have been quietly fading away. The missionaries are no longer putting pressure on Islam because there are far fewer of them in the field and they are not as assertive as before.

While there was still need for a Muslim reaction to Christian missionary effort, this reaction to a large extent came from the Ahmadiya movement which in fact modelled itself closely on the missionary societies. The Ahmadiya started as a reform movement, but its purely spiritual aspect became secondary, or even suspect, when the founder Mirza Ghulam Ahmad started claiming to be not only the Mahdi of Islam and the Messiah of Christianity but also an incarnation of Krishna. Thereafter his movement, founded in the 1890s in the Punjab, became more noted for its missionary activities in East and West Africa, in Indonesia and Western Europe. Despite the efficiency of its organization, including a steady stream of publications and a network of schools, the heterodoxy of its religious ideas has

89

somewhat lessened its impact. One very useful but again some-what heretical innovation of the Ahmadiyas was to sponsor translations of the Koran into English and other tongues at a time when the idea of translating the Koran had not yet been fully accepted. The movement is still very active and remains 'the clearest example of all of the response to the Western and Christian challenge'.[1] It is ironic that this movement which has worked so hard to spread Islam has been declared a non-Muslim sect in its home base of Pakistan.

Perhaps it was because the heterodox Ahmadiyas had the Muslim missionary field very much to themselves in the 1910s and 1920s that the most orthodox of Muslim institutions, al Azhar University, bestirred itself belatedly and started training Muslim missionaries for work, especially in Africa. There was established a training and orientation institute in the missionary section of the university and in 1960 the ministry of religious affairs of the Egyptian government set up a corps of missionaries. As the wave of Christian missionary endeavour swung back, that of Islam rolled forward. Furthermore, the Muslim missionaries, especially those from Egypt, have been just as committed to furthering the political interests of their home countries as were those from Europe. *Plusça change* . . .

The most enduring work from the mass of apologetic literature that was churned out by the defenders of Islam to answer the denigrations of the missionaries has proven to be *The Spirit of Islam* by Sayyid Amir Ali. Though first issued in 1893 it was still being reprinted in the 1930s and 40s. A learned production, elegantly written, it is far too apologetic and defensive, a fact which can perhaps be explained by its appearance at a time when Islam was most heavily under missionary attack. Amir Ali makes too frequent use of that standard tactic of religious polemics – the contrast between the pure theoretical principles of one religion and the debased practice of another religion. Neverthe-less his book had a very great impact on the Muslim community and not only in those areas where English was known. It did much to stiffen backs and resistance when Islamic morale was at low ebb by reminding readers that Islam had had its ups as well as its downs.

It should be said that Islam does not as yet seem to have found an answer to the overall challenge of Western civilization and modernization. Valiant attempts have been and are being made to 'rethink Islam in modern terms', a form of words that has been so bandied about that it has ceased to be a rallying cry or an exhortation, and has simply become a tired cliché. There has been a great deal of talk about the need for rethinking but remarkably little rethinking itself. Reading through the 're-thinking' literature one is reminded of a famous cartoon by Max Beerbohm in which a large bearded figure stands before a bird stand on which perches an eagle staring dyspeptically at the man waving his arms at it: a scene described in the caption as 'Walt Whitman urging the Bird of Freedom to soar'. However much urged to soar, Muslim re-thinking has not yet really taken off, or only in rather short and hesitant hops.

Even the most casual perusal of the rethinking literature reveals three names recurring like an insistent refrain – Afghani, Abduh, Rida. Much, perhaps most, of this literature consists of works by or about them; books about them continue to appear in a steady and apparently unending stream. One is forced to the conclusion that these three men dominate the 'rethinking' scene not just because they were the pioneers but because they have had no followers of equal stature.

It is somewhat difficult to understand why Jamal al Din al-Afghani (1839–97) should have exerted the tremendous influence he undoubtedly did on the scholars and leaders around the Muslim world – not only in his own generation but in the following one as well.[2] He was clearly one of those people whose magnetism comes through the personal touch. For although there is nothing very profound in his scanty writings he was known to have been a fine orator. What was important about Afghani was his general attitude towards the problem for Islam of coming to terms with 'militant Europe', rather than his detailed suggestions for any solution of that problem. A man of mysterious origins (he may not even have been an Afghan), probably a member of one of the brotherhoods, he moved restlessly across the Middle East and Europe – from India to Persia to Egypt to Turkey to Britain to Iran to Russia – teaching, exhorting, plotting (he may have had a hand in the assassination of one nineteenth-century Shah of Persia), advising rulers and then quarrelling with them, speechifying and talking. 'A wild man' he was called: a wild man he was and just what the Muslim world needed at that juncture. Abdel-Wahhab said that Islam had become corrupted and weakened by later additions and dilutions and advised a return to its original simplicities. Afghani faced a much greater problem 158 years later. From his wide travelling he was able to see that Islam as a whole (he seems to have been the first to give general currency to that concept of Islam as a single civilization and historical entity) was under siege by the West. He also saw that it was not making any sort of adequate response because it neither seemed to believe that it could resist nor did it know how to set about doing so. This is where Afghani made his greatest contribution – through his attitude, which was one of a combatant: Islam, he said, having once been great could be great again if it did not allow Europe to trample over it; it must resist because it could resist. The way to resist was to bring about reforms in each Muslim country to make them strong and then to unite them in some sort of loose pan-Islamic federation or confederation. Pan Islam was one of the ideas Afghani popularized and to which he gave a new emotional impetus, but he does not seem to have seen the contradiction between building up strong Muslim national entities and the idea of pan Islam, for the stronger the one the weaker must be the other. The Muslim countries were weak because their societies were corrupt, which could only be remedied by each Muslim truly understanding his religion and following its precepts: this is where Islam entered into Afghani's secular plans. Once Muslims were sure of themselves they would be capable of learning the sciences of the West, to master and not just to imitate them. On the political side Afghani said that Muslim countries did not need Western-style constitutions – the ideal Islamic state was ruled by a just king under the sovereignty of divine law: Afghani spent his life looking for a just king. On the religious side he argued that Islam needed to undergo its Reformation under a Muslim Luther, perhaps with himself in that role; the umma, the Muslim community, could not be rejuvenated and held together simply through personal piety: the ulema had a very important part to play in reforming Islam and in providing Islamic solidarity across national frontiers.

Such ideas are unexceptionable but have not been fruitful of results: what was really important in the Afghani legacy was the underlying attitude of resistance, pride and defiance, coupled with activism. In our times his slogan would have been: don't just sit there, do something about it. For his own age Afghani hammered home a sura from the Koran, 'God changes not what is in a people until they change what is in themselves.'

One person who was moved to activity was Muhammad Abduh (1849–1905), Afghani's greatest disciple but a very different man and a bigger man than his master; it is not surprising that they finally became estranged from each other. As with Afghani, Abduh's contributions to Islam were tangential to his rethinking of it (in his case particularly educational and legal reform). A good Egyptian nationalist, Abduh earned the disfavour of the Egyptian authorities, who exiled him to Lebanon where he was very active in helping the Lebanese set up a fledgling Islamic school system. On his return to Egypt he continued in the same line, but he also tried hard to reform al Azhar. He did not have much success but the reforms and modernization that came in later years were due to his first initiatives. As a Sheikh and later as Mufti, or religious leader, of Egypt he did his best to unify and modernize the system of Islamic law, handing down decisions that were sensible and humane. This was perhaps his most direct contribution to the process of 'up-dating'. On the larger issues Abduh's ideas were always interesting but do not seem to have had much impact on Islamic society. He tried to bridge the gap between modernism and the traditional by showing that there were 'modernist' elements in Islam itself: he too favoured the study of the modern sciences, but without becoming their slavish admirer. Like his master he had hopes of a new and reformed type of ulema and, like him again, he had hopes of an Islamic 'just despot'. In two controversies he actually got down to the specific subject of reconciling Islam with modern thought, but he produced no new or incisive ideas. He was at heart much more a traditionalist than a modernist: he had sympathy for the approach of the Wahhabis; while he favoured ijtihad, independent judgement, he limited it to competent people only and gave no great value to ijma, or consensus. In fact he produced a novel theory of religious education by which religious truths should be adjusted to the mental level of the believer. As an Egyptian he had no great sympathy for Afghani's pan-

Islamic enthusiasms. The two men fell out because of his criticisms of Afghani's over-hasty programmes.

Like Afghani and Abduh before him, Rashid Rida (1865–1935), Abduh's faithful disciple and expositor, was concerned with the question of why Muslim countries were backward in every aspect of civilization. He was probably less fitted than his predecessors to provide the answer, for he was more narrow and rigid in his views. He was, for instance, very approving of the new political importance given to Wahhabism by the military successes of Abdel Aziz ibn Saud (later 'King' ibn Saud). Like Abduh he believed in the positive value of activity and work; he had confidence in the body of the ulema, and in the just despot. Like him he had no great confidence in ijma and would have restricted the expression of ijtihad even more tightly. His one novel idea emerged when he tried to define who should be the real representatives of the umma, of the community, those with the powers 'to bind and to loose'. They could not come from the Muslim nations under foreign rule, nor from the ancient seats of Islamic learning, nor from the Westernizers. Somewhere in between there should be a middle group, an 'Islamic progressive party' who could make changes while preserving the moral basis of the community. But in the last half-century has Islam produced anywhere anything like the Islamic progressive party that Rashid Rida envisaged? It would seem it has not.

These were the first of the rethinkers of Islam and they still remain the foremost. The ideas of Muhammad Iqbal (1876–1938) need not detain us, because although he wrote a book with the challenging title *The Reconstruction of Religious Thought in Islam*, it deals (as far as one can make out through a thicket of philosophic terminology borrowed from Nietzsche and Bergson) with the reconstruction of thought, but in no significant manner with the reconstruction of 'religious' thought *in Islam*. What Iqbal does say, very emphatically and repeatedly, is that 'Islam must be rethought in modern terms', but makes small contribution thereto. Iqbal's best known achievement was, like Afghani's and Abduh's, tangential to his rethinking effort: he was the first to put forward the idea of a separate Muslim state on the Indian sub-continent – which emerged as Pakistan.

Why has Islam's spiritual or philosophic response to the

challenge of modern Western civilization as a whole (not just to the challenge of Christianity, which it has coped with) been so inadequate? A hundred years after the problem was first faced there is still no real rethinking, reshaping or remoulding of Islam such as to give it a living, intimate, organic role in a modernizing Afro-Asian society. Islam as a system of devotion remains very much alive, if less so than twenty-five or fifty years ago. But this system of devotion and of specified religious duties is slowly but surely becoming increasingly 'other', even in the most traditional societies, because even these societies are changing while the bases of Islam have not. And they cannot change so long as they are enclosed in the belief that the Koran is in its totality the very word of God and that Muhammad is the perfect human being. So long as those beliefs remain unchanged (for most Muslims it is blasphemous even to suggest the possibility of change) there is no scope, no 'give', for those modifications that alone can make Islam spiritually contemporaneous with the modern world.

Islam's political counterpunch to the challenge of Western colonial domination has been wholly successful and for Muslims wholly gratifying, for most of the battles in that struggle were fought under the banner of Islam, as we shall now see.

2

'The plain fact is that the longest and bloodiest fighting against the forces of Europe was carried out by Muslims. No European blandishments could charm them into becoming good neighbours. The task was one for firepower, not philanthropy.'[3]

Could there have been an Afro-Asian movement without Islam? This may seem a surprising question because the assumption is that the nationalist movements that rolled up the imperial carpet in Afro-Asia in twenty swift years after 1947 were 'modern' and therefore secular. So they may have been in such leading Afro-Asian countries as Indonesia, India, Egypt and Ghana, but the secular nationalist inheritors came late to the political scene. The foundations as well as much of the new national superstructure were laid down and erected during the preceding 150 years by Muslim forces and Muslim leaders. Without politically militant Islam freedom would have taken decades longer, that is if militant Islam and the freedom struggle had not been one and the same thing earlier on in Indonesia, Afghanistan, the Sudan, Somaliland, Libya, Algeria, Morocco, and West-central Africa – in addition to the very large infusion of Islam in the national movement of Iran and some in that of Egypt.

These being the historical facts, the answer to the question asked above is that without Islam the Afro-Asian movement would probably have aborted. And without the Afro-Asian movement there would have been no 'non-aligned' group of nations, and without that group there would not have been the economic Group of Seventy-Seven, the underdeveloped South in the current North–South dialogue.

Why, in many diverse Muslim countries, should Islam and the freedom movement have been so close together as to be in action one and the same thing? There are three answers. Firstly there is at base the totalist nature of Islam itself: its refusal or inability to make any distinction between religion and politics is necessarily the appropriate and just concern of the faith. Secondly, what other force or organization was there that could guide, inspire and channel the struggle? There was no nationalism, structured or unstructured; that came later and was the product not the cause of the national movements which for many decades were simply movements of revulsion against the Western presence. Not until the 1920s did the secular nationalist political parties appear, and then only in a few Afro-Asian countries. So it was left to Islam with such traditional structures as it had – the Koranic school, the mosque, the Haj – to provide some sort of organized structure for the struggle. Thirdly, Islam, through its ulema, provided the only educated group of leaders available. This was so because in most Afro-Asian countries the usual leadership groups, the princely rulers, aristocrats or landlord class, usually sided with the foreign ruler. But the village sheikh, being that much closer to the people, partook of their nationalist feelings and could not but become the local leader. After all the struggle was against Westerners who were Christians, and Christian missionaries were waging war against Islam. De Lesseps (the builder of the Suez Canal), speaking in an Algerian context, expressed this intertwining very concisely when he said: 'What nonsense has been written about the intractable fanaticism of the Algerian

Arabs ... Fanaticism had not nearly so much to do with the resistance of the Arabs as patriotism. Religion was the only flag around which they could rally.'[4]

If we date the first spiritual counterblow of militant Islam at around 1750, the time of Abdel Wahhab, then we can date the first halting of the ever expanding tide of Western imperialism to the year 1842, the last year of the First Afghan War, when a British column retreating from Kabul was wiped out. That rebuff to a British attempt at domination was the first indication anywhere that the Western powers could be stopped in their tracks or pushed back.

Looking at the long but still perhaps incomplete list of armed struggles between Muslims and Western Christians we see in the early years of the nineteenth century that many of these occurred between the Dutch and the Indonesians. Let us then begin this swift survey of the role of militant Islam in the freedom movements of the Islamic and Afro-Asian worlds by considering what was then the Dutch East Indies.

Islam was as prominent in the military as in the civilian political movements. All the wars listed were announced to be jihads, holy wars. When Prince Diponegoro, the leader in the Java War, called for volunteers, most of them, it is said, were ulema and village religious teachers. This action gave them greater popular prestige and the constant peasant uprisings that occurred regularly through the nineteenth century were 'invariably under the banner of Islam'. The very name of the Padri War shows that this too was a religious war for *padri* was the misnomer (from the original 'padre') applied by the Dutch to the ulema under the mistaken idea that they were priests. The war lasted for sixteen years, and during its course the internal dispute between Indonesian factions of ulema – which gave the Dutch the chance to interfere – was reconciled. Both sides then turned against the Dutch. Members of the tarikas, especially the Qadiriya, provided the organizational framework for the revolutionary protest movement which resulted in the Tjilegon risings of 1888. The Achenese War was ulema-led and organized from start to finish. The last uprising, partly led by ulema, came in 1927 on the west coast of Sumatra.

By that time the main thrust of Indonesian nationalism had moved over into the civilian and political sphere whilst still retaining its strong Islamic coloration. In 1912 the first truly Indonesian political movement, the Sarekat Islam or Islamic League, was founded and rapidly became a mass-movement claiming two million members in 1919. Its programme was an uncomfortable combination of rather conservative Islam and fairly strident anti-colonialism which finally destroyed its inner coherence and popularity. Its ultimately successful rival, Muhammadiyah, was founded in the same year, 1912. It was both more religious and more radical than Sarekat Islam. Muhammadiyah was particularly active in education and in missionary work. Neither of these movements appealed to those among the Westernized élite who still wished to retain their Islamic links, and who formed in 1925 the Jong Islamieten Bond (Young Muslims' League) from which many of the leaders of independent Indonesia emerged. Thus up to 1930 the Indonesian national movement was practically monopolized by Muslim activists. The struggle that developed in the 1930s and '40s between them and the secular nationalists will be discussed later.

Both the great spasms of Algerian nationalism, the first being the struggle under Abdel Qadir from 1832 and the second the war of independence, had strong Islamic content, the first naturally far more than the second. Abdel Qadir's father was a leading member of the Qadiriya Order, a *marabout* or holy man, and his son's one ambition had been to become a marabout like his father. When war was declared on France in May 1832 it was after prayers, and as a jihad. Because Abdel Qadir regarded it as such he pressed the point that any Muslims co-operating with non-Muslims engaged in war with a Muslim prince after the declaration of jihad were no longer Muslims, and when defeated could be treated as infidels. The sustained support of the Qadiriya Order for him through the fifteen-year war was one of Abdel Qadir's main sources of strength. During the hundred-odd years between the defeat of Abdel Qadir and the beginning of the war of independence it was left to the orthodox ulema to maintain Algeria's identity, because many of the tarikas supported the French. This was why in 1871 the French tried to form a cadre of loyal ulema who would be paid servants of the administration; the scheme failed because there were no takers.

In the 1930s the ulema tried to revive the Islamic spirit of the people by a campaign of opening Koranic schools. For the first few years after independence the Algerians were embarrassed to admit that during the testing years of war their Islamic faith had not only given them inward moral support but that prayers and attendance at the mosque had become assertions of Algeria's identity. Unlike Abdel Qadir, the leaders of the independence war were not men of religion, and in fact the national movement frowned on the cult of marabouts; many of them were, however religious men, notably Colonel Boumedienne, so it was not surprising that the constitution of free Algeria describes it as an Islamic state.[5]

The religious motive in that fateful First Afghan War was acknowledged by the defeated British themselves. An official despatch talks of 'the universal hostility of the whole people of Afghanistan, united against us at the present moment in a war which has assumed a religious, as well as a national, character'.[6]

Across the Afghan frontier to the north where Russia was pressing forward in a series of wars of conquest against the Muslim states of Central Asia these wars assumed a religious as well as a national character. The twenty-five-year war of Shamyl in the Caucasus was one such. Shamyl was styled as 'the Imam', had been a pupil of Afghani, was both the spiritual and secular leader of his tribes, and had declared his struggle a jihad. The first Russian through the gate of Tashkent when it was stormed in 1865 was a Russian Orthodox priest holding his cross high before him. Yet the Russians rarely saw their advance into Muslim areas as being a Christian crusade: they were more intent on trying to extract commercial advantage. Indeed Catherine the Great encouraged the conversion to Islam of the Kazakhs, believing that this would give them a more stable social structure. And the Russian Orthodox Church carried out no missionary activity anywhere in the Muslim world, not even in the Holy Land. Yet from the perspective of the Central Asian Muslim the oncoming Russians were always *kafirs* – infidels. One Muslim grievance against the Russians, which went back to the sixteenth century, was that Russia hindered the transit of Muslim pilgrims to Mecca: even as late as 1842 the Russians were still refusing to grant free transit. From 1885 a series of sporadic revolts broke out; they had but one pattern:

they ended up as movements of a religious nature, sometimes as jihads, led by religious leaders frequently of the Sufi orders. After the failure of these successive jihads to stop the Russian advance, and despite the Russian policy of non-interference in local and Islamic affairs, resentment of the very presence of the infidels built up during the century and exploded in a carefully prepared jihad launched at Andijan in 1895 by a Naqshibandi sheikh. Despite considerable popular support the rising was fairly easily crushed and the Russians, just like their fellow colonialists, blamed it all on Muslim 'fanaticism'.[7]

India is not strictly speaking within the purview of this study because it is not a Muslim country. But since the British Indian Empire was advancing, in northern India, against the Muslim Mogul Empire, or what little was left of it, a specifically Muslim reaction was forthcoming from time to time. Thus during the Indian Mutiny we read of the mutineers in several places being led into battle by mullahs under the green banner and behind the uplifted Koran, and of other bands of mutineers calling themselves Wahhabis. While stating that before 1860 there was a strong sentiment of anti-British hostility among the ulema in India, one Muslim scholar argues that after that date the strength of anti-British sentiment among them has been exaggerated, and that only one ambivalent *fatwa*, religious decree, was issued against the British.[8] If the Indian Muslim ulema were quiet after 1860 it was because of the British belief that it was the Indian Muslim community, especially the upper class, that was mainly responsible for the mutiny, thus 'attempting to rehabilitate their Mughal Empire'. For twenty years the Muslims were sternly repressed and excluded from government employment because they were followers of a 'disloyal religion'. In addition the fundamentalist sect of Wahhabis was active and 'disloyal' and 'In the various uprisings against the British in the north and in Bengal, they proclaimed a holy war against the infidel.' In 1912 there was a surge of pan-Islamic sentiment among Indian Muslims aroused by the defeat of Turkey in the Balkan wars and the loss of Libya: there was some talk of jihad but no action.[9] What is quite clear is that later on most ulema were opposed to the idea of Pakistan, a logical consequence of their opposition to the Muslim League, which was accused of consistent loyalty to the British in the 1920s and '30s.

In Egypt the class of ulema did not play a more outstanding role in opposing the encroachment of British power than any other sector of the populace, nor did it shirk its share. At least one from among their ranks, Muhammad Abdu, did try to organize popular resistance following the uprising of Colonel Orabi against the Khedive and the British in 1881–2. The Egyptian ulema, centred on al Azhar, has been, and still is, noted for its docility.

The case was utterly different in the Sudan where the uprising of the Mahdi, his defeat of the Egyptian Army under Gordon, the establishment of the Mahdist state and the ultimate overthrow of that state by the British – all this between 1881 and 1898 – was from beginning to end a strongly Muslim reaction and nothing else. This is so evident a historical fact that there is no need for any detailed explication of its Islamic nature.[10] The entire Sudanese setting was so strongly religious that the victorious Kitchener was referred to as the Dajjal, the Muslim equivalent of the Anti-Christ, whose forces of Evil had temporarily overthrown those of the Good. But this was not the end of the Mahdist experience in the Sudan. There were twenty other Mahdist-type uprisings in later years: there was the Katifiyya rising in 1908, a protest against economic and social sufferings which prodded the British into starting the Jezira Scheme, one of the outstanding achievements of their period of rule. Then there was the Nyala rising, launched both for religious and economic reasons, and the Darful rebellion in 1927, a religious movement led by a Sufi dervish. The spirit of resistance among the neo-Mahdists was kept alive in the following decades by their belief that one day the true Mahdi Isa would manifest himself and drive out the British.[11]

Similarly Islamic were the wars in West and West-central Africa in which the French got themselves entangled in the 1880s and '90s – similarly Islamic because they were waged against theocratic Sultanates who invariably insisted on declaring jihad.

As completely Mahdist and Islamic as the upheaval in the Sudan was the long-drawn-out jihad of Muhammad Abdallah in

Somaliland. A Koranic scholar, he was a member of the militant and puritan Salihiya order and a great many of his followers were styled Hajis or Sheikhs. The 'state' he founded was based strictly on Islamic law, of the Shafi school.

When the Italians blundered into what is now called Libya in 1911 they could hardly have foreseen that because of the Sanusi Sufi order they would complete the task of conquest only in 1932. For sizable periods of time during those twenty-one years and over varying areas of territory the Sanusi were *de facto* rulers. On more than one occasion a Sanusi 'state' was proclaimed in the interior of the country.[12] It was inevitable that following this long struggle under the Sanusi aegis an independent Libya should emerge after World War II as a state under Sanusi rule: probably the only state the world has ever seen to be created by a mystical brotherhood. It still survives but under a rather different sort of mystical Muslim brotherhood – the Revolutionary Command Council of Colonel Gaddafi.

The uprising in Iraq following the imposition of the British Mandate – some Iraqis still refer to it as the 'national war of liberation' – had its full share of Islamic inspiration and guidance. Among the leaders were the Shiah holy men from the shrine cities of Najaf and Karbala, who issued a fatwa enjoining on Muslims the religious duty of jihad. (A British historian of Iraq refers to their actions as 'self-interest Mujtahid promptings'!) It was a 'damn near-run thing' for the British, and a British participant later wrote that if only there had been bold leaders 'to direct and organize the well armed forces of disorder and to arouse their latent fanaticism, Iraq might have been overwhelmed for a time by a band of zealots not less formidable than the Wahhabis of central Arabia.'[13]

A review of the close living connection between Islam and Afro-Asian nationalism highlights one strange and important factor. So many of the nationalists, the men who became the historic symbols of their country's freedom, were not merely Muslim men of religion, but members of the mystical Sufi brotherhoods, the tarikas. Beginning with the forerunner, Afghani, we have Prince Diponegoro; several tarika leaders including Shamyl in central Asia; the Mahdi and Muhammad Abdallah, Abdel Qadir and Abdel Krim; and the Sanusi –

clear proof of how important these partially underground groupings have been in 'popular' day-to-day Islam.

The green-and-white flag of independent Algeria was the flag designed and used by Abdel Qadir. By adopting it the Algerians asserted the continuity between their struggle and that of its politico-religious progenitor – a reminder of the umbilical link between militant Islam and the freedom struggle. Islam did not have to choose the difficult path of allying itself with and leading these struggles against imperialist rulers, which at the time must have seemed hopeless. And in some Muslim countries the ulema in fact did not join the struggle. But that was the exception. As a rule the struggle against the West was for Islam and by Islam. By being prepared to pay the price and joining in with the movement of the people, Islam for 150 years received successive blood-transfusions from the struggle to push Europe out of Asia and Africa and back into Europe. That struggle is politically complete, but the blood still courses through the veins of Islam.

The Muslim and nationalist resistance to the Spanish and the French in their respective zones of Morocco was of shorter duration than it was in Libya or Somaliland but its after-effects were perhaps more enduring. A tribal leader of the Rif mountaineers, Abdel Krim, opened hostilities in 1921 and the next year he declared the foundation of an Islamic republic, with himself as president. He expressed his political aspirations in religious terms; improbably claiming descent from the Prophet and declaring his war to be one of religious liberation. After his defeat and surrender in 1926 his personal myth survived long years of exile in Cairo and gave a nationalist colouring to the freedom movement in Morocco.[14]

In Iran the Shiah ulema, whose position within that country has always been very much stronger than that of the ulema in any Sunni country, have always emerged as leaders during the country's crises. They, with the bazaar merchants, led a successful protest against the Shah's grant of the tobacco monopoly to a foreigner in 1891; with the merchants and the new Westernized liberals they wrung a constitution from the Shah in 1906; the mullahs were responsible for advising Reza Shah to set up a monarchy rather than a republic in 1924; they also opposed the drawing up of a civil code under Reza Shah; Ayatollah Kashani gave strong support to Mosaddeq during the oil crisis of 1951; they were responsible for the agitation and violence against the Bahai sect in 1955, and for the 1963 outbreaks against the Shah's reforms, especially the land reform. They led the movement that overthrew the Shah in 1979. It is a very mixed record of good and bad: but it proves beyond doubt that in Iran militant Shiah Islam is very much alive and militant and that consequently its leaders are, and always have been, very powerful.

There were some Muslim countries where Islam played little or no part in the national movement, the most startling of these exceptions being Palestine, the central political cause in the Muslim world today. We must ask why.

3

The reasons why Islam was not militant in a few Muslim countries are these – either the docility or timidity of the ulema, or the multiplicity of sects in these countries. It was either one or other reason: in no Muslim country did both apply. Neither reason applied to Palestine; but Palestine is a case by itself, in this as in many other ways.

Tunisia is the clearest, and only, example of the ulema's docility inhibiting militant action, even though the Tunisians of the interior resisted the French for two years after the invasion of 1881. But the ulema were not the only docile ones in Tunisia; the Bey, who was kept on his throne by the French, was on his best behaviour and so too were the aristocratic families and the landlords. The Tunisians to this day are genuinely pleasant people, surprisingly different from either of their neighbours, the Algerians and Libyans.

Docility kept the Egyptian ulema from playing a leading role in the struggle against the British, though they did take part. As in Tunisia, the tone of docility was set by a pliant ruler, the Khedive.

In Syria, Lebanon and Iraq, religion – Islam or any other – had to be kept out of the freedom movement if that movement was to receive support from members of the different religious communities in these countries. Inter-religious and interdenominational unity was particularly urgently required in Syria in 1920 when the French took over as Mandatory power. The policy of 'divide and rule' was immediately applied. The mainly Christian areas on the coast of geographical Syria were split off to form Lebanon, with some adjacent Muslim areas added to it. The rest of Syria was split into four separate autonomous areas, two of which were based on separate, heterodox, vaguely Muslim sects – one for the Druze sect in the south and the other for the Alawites in the northwest. The Syrians did not then, and still do not, accept the separateness of a 'Christian Lebanon'. Therefore if in 1920 or at any time thereafter they had stressed the Muslim character of the freedom struggle, even though Syria is three quarters a Muslim country, they would have pushed the Lebanese Christians farther away from the larger Syrian motherland, and deeper into their already existent minority psychosis (which is presently in full bloom). Likewise if the Sunni majority aspect of the movement had been emphasized the nominally Muslim Druzes and Alawites would have taken fright. As far as these two communities were concerned the restraint worked, and faced with a pan-Syrian protest movement the French were compelled to scrap their autonomous areas. This necessity for communal restraint has been an element in Syrian politics ever since, and was the determining force once again when the Syrians rose against the French in 1945.

The Lebanese were also protesting against the French at the same time in a brief and sometimes farcical national struggle. Since there is no majority community in Lebanon but only a mosaic of minorities, neither Islam nor Christianity could be stressed.

The ulema in Iraq, as we have seen, did play the usual leading role in the 1920 uprising, but that was possible because beforehand the religious leaders of the Sunnis and Shiahs had formally decided to cooperate to face a national emergency. It is because these two communities are evenly balanced in Iraq (only officially so, the Shiahs have long claimed to be in the majority and almost certainly are) that the Iraqi national movement never again had recourse to Islamic support: the delicate equilibrium might not have been achieved again, one or other community would have been forced into opposition.

Thus in Lebanon Islam had to be detached from the national movement because there was no majority community; in Syria because the Sunnis were in too large a majority; and in Iraq because the Muslims were evenly divided between Sunnis and Shiahs.

These were the negative reasons. The positive reason was that in these three countries, as well as in Egypt and in Palestine, secular national political parties had emerged which deliberately cut across religious divisions. Nowhere was this more striking than in Palestine.

Several years before the official beginning of the still continuing struggle between the Palestinian people and the Zionist incomers, in November 1918 the Christian minority in Palestine had joined in the anti-Zionist effort alongside the Muslims. Their motivation at that time remains the same today: Christian and Muslim Palestinians have to stand together against a common enemy. By 1910[15] the standard bearers of the opposition to Zionism were the newspapers *Karmil* and *Falastin*, both owned and edited by Greek Orthodox journalists. The Palestinian Christian community has always numbered around nine or ten per cent of the total, about half being Greek Orthodox.

In November 1918 in response to the Balfour Declaration and the British mandatory power's commitment to the creation of a 'Jewish National Home' in Palestine, a Muslim-Christian Association was founded, and by the following year it had become the main organization of the Palestinian national movement and remained so until just before World War II; it had a network of branches throughout the country.[16] When a somewhat more militant Palestine Arab Party was started in 1935, the vice-president and the secretary were both Christians. A guerrilla organization had already been started in 1931, called al Jihad al Muqaddas, and it was energized in 1933 by Emil Ghawri, a Christian activist. It was directed by a committee composed of fourteen Muslims and three Christians, becoming sufficiently important for the leader of the Palestinian community, Haj Amil al Hussaini, to assume its command. There was some tension between the Muslim and Christian communities in 1932–3 but it was coloured by the energetic intervention of leaders such as Haj Amin who emphazised the overriding importance of a united front. This united front was maintained through the stresses of 1936–9 when the Palestinians launched, first a country-wide general strike that lasted for six months, and then an armed rebellion that went on for over two years. The leadership for this phase of the struggle was in the hands of the Higher Arab Committee, and of its ten office bearers two were Christian. What brought the Christians and Muslims even more closely together was the proposal to partition Palestine. This was as strongly opposed by the Christians as by the Muslims, perhaps even more strongly by the former, because under the plan the predominantly Christian area of Galilee was awarded to the Jewish state.

This communal unity was a remarkable achievement for a movement led by a Muslim man of religion. On their own the Palestinian ulema and village preachers played a leading role, and large numbers were arrested by the British.

The unity of the Palestinian communities has continued to the present day and the leaders of two of the Palestinian guerrilla groups, George Habush and Nayef Hawatmeh, are Christians. The unity now is not based only on the need to face a common enemy but on a common devotion to the cause of Palestinian nationhood in a secular democratic state. Many of the Palestinian leaders, like Yasser Arafat, are personally devout Muslims but the Palestinian movement, as its members would put it, went beyond the stage of militant Islam from its very beginning.

4

For militant Islam today the real field of battle is the school-room. Having regained their land from foreign soldiers and administrators the Muslim peoples are now trying to reclaim their brains and souls from the continuing influence of foreign teachers. In essence the problem is one of switching the medium of instruction to the mother tongue, and of Islamization. The seemingly humdrum matters of teacher training, curricula and school textbooks are actually of far greater and more long-lasting importance than heroism in ancient battles or present-day squabbles over constitutions or legal systems.

Gibb has well defined the general principles and objectives of this vital if peaceful battle: 'The real significance for Islam is the inward reaction towards the (Western) cultural values which are seeking to find their place within Muslim society under cover of these borrowings. Everything depends on the capacity of Muslim society to defend and protect its values and cultural traditions against the western invasion. If it fails in this task it is lost as a Muslim society, it will inevitably become a more or less faithful copy of western society with secondary characteristics peculiar to the different countries and languages.'[17]

The tactics of 'the Western invasion' were to destroy existing indigenous educational systems, either by dismantling or neglect, to provide as little Western education as possible, and that in a European language, and to create a schism in the soul of the society by educating the élites into a state of alienation from their own cultural background.

The educational challenges to the new governments were, then, to revive and reform the traditional system, to integrate it with the modern system, to expand both, to increase the use of the mother tongue, and to narrow or close the cultural schism. In studying the Islamic response to these challenges, we make, in this section, an abrupt movement forward in time, to the years roughly between 1955 and 1978, the period when changes in Islamic nations' educational systems began to develop under newly independent governments. The nationalist movements achieved their task of expelling outsiders from their territories between 1945 and 1965.

The French were the most ruthless of the cultural invaders but their victims, especially in North Africa, have made the most effective counter-attack, while the victims of the Dutch have unexpectedly done least well in their campaign of cultural reclamation.

'Unexpectedly' because from as early as 1902 the Indonesians had seen the importance of a national system of education, and by the 1920s no less than three independent school systems were operating: the Kartini, the Budi Utomo and the Tamam Siswa.[18] The two main national mass-movements, Sarekat Islam and Muhammadiya, had both concentrated on building schools, especially the latter. Also, as we have seen, the Dutch tried (but failed) to bring the traditional village schools under their control. So there was no problem over the structure of a national educational system or the use of the mother tongue. The main problem was the integration of the traditional Islamic system and the now national but Westernized system which the

Indonesians had inherited from the Dutch. What has happened is that both systems have been maintained, both have expanded, especially the Westernized system, but both remain apart from each other, and as they expand it becomes less and less likely that they will ever come together. This means that the schism in the soul of Indonesian society will split not merely the élite level but fissure (as it has already begun to) that society right down to the primary school level. This cannot but greatly aggravate the tension which already exists between Islamists and nationalists. If the picture is not hopeless it is because of the existence of a third type of educational system – the continuing Muhammadiya schools which have always tried to blend modernist education with instruction in Islamic values. This system has schools at all levels throughout Indonesia and even several universities. Through them we have Indonesia's real cultural-Islamic response; but no thanks to the Indonesian government or to the orthodox ulema.

Egypt's education counter-attack only came in 1953, a year after Colonel Nasser took power. It was decreed that a national primary school system would replace the existing one, offering free and compulsory education for boys and girls from age six to twelve. The curriculum included the Koran and religious instruction (with alternative instruction for non-Muslim pupils), Arabic, 'patriotic education' and the full range of other subjects. Special stress was laid on religious and patriotic education and Arabic. The teaching of a foreign language was abolished because it could not be made universal. From then on the school system was vastly expanded, inevitably at the cost of quality. The high-level split between Islamic and Western University systems was closed when in 1961 al Azhar, Islam's leading theological establishment, was brought under government control and was obliged to teach modern subjects – to female students as well as males. These two reforms wiped out the disabilities imposed by the British system; but the solution of Egypt's basic educational problem is another matter.

The Sudanese, because of the long-established missionary school system, found it much more difficult to rid themselves of the British legacy. For lack of Arabic textbooks and teachers English remained the language of instruction in secondary schools till the early 1970s. It is still the medium in Khartoum

University except in the Arabic and Islamic departments. A concession made to the southern region was that in the first two school years, local dialects written in Arabic not Latin characters were to be the medium; pupils are taught religion but none but their own. In the north there are intermediate and secondary religious schools leading to higher religious education at the Islamic University in Omdurman.

The Moroccans learned the hard way how difficult it was to 'Arabize' the system left behind by the French. Arabization in fact became an internally divisive issue, with the leftist leader Mehdi Ben Barka arguing for the retention of French as a compulsory subject, 'to open windows on to Western culture'. Plunging headlong into expansion plus Arabization in 1956 the school system was soon in chaos; there was a sharp pulling back and then a period of moderate change, which however has been at a very slow pace. In the late 1960s secondary education was still mostly in French, but at the elementary and secondary levels the pupils are given a good grounding in Islam, its history and culture.

The educational picture is much the same in Tunisia: Arabization proceeding rather slowly including 'religious and civic instruction' and Islamic teaching. As in Morocco the traditional Koranic schools have been integrated with the general school system.

As might have been expected the Algerians have pushed their counter-offensive far harder than either their eastern or western neighbours. In the 1976–7 school year the three systems of schooling were integrated: foreign, mostly run by the Roman Catholic Church; national Westernized; and Islamic, run by the ministry of religious affairs. They all now became part of a nine-year system. The Islamic traditionalists disliked the integration of their schools as little as did the missionaries; but the former were compensated by the introduction of religious education in all schools. Algeria faced the same problems of Arabization as Morocco and Tunisia but has pushed it more vigorously, being less reluctant to receive teachers from eastern Arab countries, especially Egypt, than the other two states. In all three a large quantitive expansion has meant a qualitative drop.[19]

Perhaps because it started out as a self-proclaimed Islamic

state Pakistan faced special problems in asserting its Islamic cultural identity, particularly because the ruling élite and the higher levels of the bureaucracy were thoroughly Westernized and alienated. While there was a vast expansion in the number of schools, with the inevitable drop in quality, and although Urdu replaced English as the medium of instruction up to and including the universities, the Islamic element in Pakistani education was almost entirely limited to the traditional *madrassahs*, as is still the case in Indonesia. However, unlike Indonesia there has been no mixed system of Westernized-religious schools such as the Muhammadiya. It was only in 1972 that the Bhutto government introduced drastic educational reforms. The large number of private schools and colleges with over 3000 students were nationalized, as well as the 350 madrassahs. That was the original intention; but when the traditionalists, as in Algeria, objected to the loss of control over their schools the Pakistan government caved in and decided that 'the status quo shall be maintained', 'doubtless with a political end in view' – to quote the words of a distinguished Pakistan academic.[20] The details of the educational reforms need not detain us except for one – the introduction of Islamiat (study of Islam) and Deeniat (theology) as compulsory subjects up to the last two school years when there are separate studies for Sunni and Shiah students on the rituals of their two sects.

In Syria, private foreign, mostly missionary, schools were partially integrated into the national educational system but the religious schools were not; Arabic became the medium of instruction. Although the multiplicity of Syria's religious sects obliged religion to be kept out of politics it was brought back into the schools as a compulsory subject – each sect studying its own faith.

Thus all the nations that constitutionally regard themselves as Islamic states have brought the teaching of Islam into the curricula of their public educational systems. This process of putting Islam back into the education system of countries where it was not before has been going on during the past twenty-five years, while in the Christian West the last remnants of religion have been being pushed out of public education; proof, if there was need for it, of bold militant assertiveness on one hand and of defensive apologetic withdrawal on the other. But of course merely including so many hours of instruction in Islamic subjects per week in a school curriculum is not going to make millions of young Pakistanis or Sudanese or Moroccans into good Muslims – although Tunisia especially has produced a well thought out programme of religious instruction that makes Islam a relevant part of the nation's life. Religious instruction cannot be just a programme of a Muslim state; to be effective it has to become part of the way of life of an Islamic society.

What the Islamic nations have accomplished – however partially so far – in redeeming, controlling and changing their educational systems in a specifically Islamic direction, amounts to the greatest single achievement of militant Islam to date. A massive achievement it is, of long-lasting import. If it has not been recognized as an aspect of militant Islam this is only because it has been going on in separate countries over a space of years in inconspicuous school rooms and ministries of education. But this Islamization of the minds (and perhaps the hearts) of hundreds of millions of young Muslims is more truly militant and Islamic than the chopping off of hands.

While the Muslims were reclaiming their education and system of values there have been two cases of Muslim educationalists going the other way, seeking to identify the culture of their country with the West and with Western forms. This was a comparatively small matter compared to Turkey's total identification with the West under Kemal Atatürk.

The first of the two educationalists, Sir Sayyid Ahmad Khan (1817–98), was in himself something of an oddity. He knew very little English but was passionately loyal to the British Indian Raj and spent his life trying to convince his community that it must be loyal too and, above all, should not join with the Hindus in the Indian National Congress Party; he had no use for parliamentary democracy. To produce loyal young Muslims he started the Muhammadan Anglo-Oriental College at Aligarh, modelled strictly on Oxbridge lines with a mostly British staff teaching in English. This became the premier Indian Muslim educational institution. The Muslim community, which never accepted Sir Sayyid's British loyalty, insisted that English should not be used in the teaching of Islam in his college; it also ignored his ventures into Koranic commentary. One wonders why Western Islamists should give any attention at all to this aberrant figure, yet they do.

Another aberrant figure was the famous Egyptian educationalist and *littérateur* Taha Hussain, a very different sort from Sir Sayyid. Born in 1889 and blind from childhood, Taha Hussain was a writer of great distinction; he was a cabinet minister in the period after the second world war and became Egyptian minister of education where he strove mightily and partially sucessfully to modernize the Egyptian educational system. What concerns us here are his ideas on where Egypt lies on the map of civilization. It was his belief that Egypt and Europe have a single intellectual heritage and that, accordingly, Egypt is not a part of the Orient, to which countries like India and China belong. Egypt must therefore stop looking eastward for inspiration and start looking across the Mediterranean to Europe. Taha Hussain asked whether the ready acceptance of Islam made Egypt an Eastern nation: no more, he replied, than did the acceptance of East-born Christianity 'Easternize' the European mind. There simply did not exist any intellectual or cultural cleavage between the two groups of people that face each other across the Mediterranean. It was his belief that political and economic circumstances set them against one another, and that Egypt was a part of Europe. His countrymen have largely ignored Taha Hussain's flawed advice. And if anything was needed to convince them of the folly of cutting oneself off from one's racial and cultural roots, it would be the sad example of Turkey under the reforms of Atatürk.

When Ahmad Khan, Taha Hussain and Atatürk advocated that their community or nation should accept the West and even 'join' it they were expressing a response (even if they would have denied it) to Western pressures, but a response that was more of a reaction than an effective answer to an inescapable problem. For the religious, political and cultural pressures of the Christian West on Islamic countries would not cease because one or other Islamic country joined up with the West. These pressures by their very nature could not cease until one or other side gave up being Christian or Muslim. That is what Atatürk did: going far beyond Ahmad Khan and Taha Hussain, who remained good Muslims; Atatürk abandoned Islam and actively suppressed it.

5

The sad fact about Kemal Atatürk is not merely that he was a very shallow reformer, but that he has been proven an unsuccessful reformer. The main reason for his failure is that he did not know his people. He refused to acknowledge that the Turks always have been and for the foreseeable future will remain very devout Muslims.

Just how far he was from understanding what his people really wanted is illustrated by this incident. Quite a few years ago, during one of my periodic visits to Turkey, I was driving in a taxi from the lovely town of Bursa to the ski resort high on the snowy slopes of Uludag (one of the three Mount Olympus's) that towers over the former Seljuk capital. To pass the time the taxi driver switched on his car radio, and to my delight the music that flowed out was the great chaconne from the second unaccompanied partita for violin by Bach. The pure lofty clarity of the music exactly matched those qualities in the chaconne, surely the most powerfully abstract composition in the entire Western classical repertoire. This was to *my* delight, but not to that of the taxi driver. Muttering angrily he switched to another local station – more chaconne – and then to another – still more chaconne. A Sunday morning nationwide hook-up for Turkish listeners to hear Bach: how very civilized; and how very *Western*! The driver snapped off the radio, but since I was paying the piper I called the tune and got him to switch it back to the offensive Bach. I owed that moment of delight directly to Atatürk who, I recalled, had decreed that Turkish radio should only play Western music, because Turkish music to his ears sounded like the yowlings of a cat with a stomach ache. I did not then know that, through Atatürk, I also owed that moment to a obscure Turkish sociologist called Ziya Gokalp, who came from the remote southeast corner of Turkey and who probably was not even a Turk – of whom more presently. The point is that the ban on Turkish music on Turkish radio has long since been lifted. Just one example of how Atatürk's 'reforms' have been abandoned by his ungrateful people.

Leader of a country that had been defeated by the Western Powers in World War I and left shorn of all its Ottoman territories, Atatürk decided that the only way Turkey could stand up to the West was to become as Westernized as possible.

Accordingly in the 1920s and '30s he ruthlessly jettisoned huge chunks of Turkey's Ottoman and Islamic past: not just the music, but Islam itself. I set out here a listing of his very comprehensive Islamic 'reforms': in 1924 the Caliphate, the supreme politico-spiritual authority in Islam vested for centuries in the Sultan of Turkey, was abolished; so were the Sharia courts (an attempt to produce a modified version of the Sharia had been debated during 1923–4 in the national assembly, but there was a sharp division of opinion and Atatürk personally decided to do away with the lot); in 1925 came the forcible dissolution of the Muslim religious orders, the tarikas, and the closure of their meeting places, the *tekkes*, and of the religious schools, the madrassahs; the tombs and shrines of saints were also closed (the tarikas were very strong and widely popular in Turkey where some of them, like the Bektashis, had originated); in 1926 a new civil code, adapted from the Swiss code, was passed in replacement of the Sharia; in 1928 the constitution was amended to delete the clause, 'the religion of the Turkish state is Islam', and the Latin alphabet replaced the Arabic script; in 1933 the call to prayer was decreed to be made in Turkish not Arabic; in 1937 the constitution was amended to include 'laicism', secularism, as one of the six cardinal principles of the state; in 1938 a law prohibited the formation of societies based on religion, sect or tarika, and political parties were prohibited from using religion for political purposes; and as late as 1949 the penal code was revised to provide punishment for acts contrary to the constitutional principle of laicism: this was simply a strengthening of an important amendment of the penal code in 1926 which forbade propaganda against secularism.

The opponents of this dismantling of the Islamic structure argued that what was happening was not secularism, which meant the separation of politics and religion and the neutrality of the state, but the persecution of Islam and the erection of secularism into a sacred and untouchable principle. Thus clerical robes and clerical titles were banned in public; so was the teaching of the Arabic script (shades of the anti-Arabic language policy of the French in north Africa) and parents had to get permission from the ministry of education if they wanted to arrange for the private religious instruction of their children by anyone other than a family member. To go on the Haj was made impossibly difficult and only one or two hundred were allowed to make it each year. Even a staunch defender of the Kemalist revolution has had to concede that these reforms were not really secularist: 'These measures were not meant to separate religion from secular institutions or to reform the former: they merely removed institutions that were incompatible with the basic principles of a secular state . . . to put it in a nutshell Kemalist secularism was nothing but rejection of the ideology of an Islamic polity.' [21]

The vast mass of the Turks, the peasants of the bare uplands of Anatolia and the icy mountains of the east, simply turned their backs on Atatürk's anti-Islamic reforms and took their religion underground into the mysticism of *tasawwuf*, and into what was left of the closed brotherhood of the tarikas: and, when they could get away with it, they smashed busts of Atatürk. The Tijani brought its opposition to Kemalism out into the open in 1949. Islam will out: that, quite simply, was the final result of all Atatürk's anti-Islamic reforms.

Was Atatürk's rejection of Turkey's Ottoman heritage, of which the repudiation of Islam was the most important part, based more on a disgust with that part or more on a positive admiration for Europe? Probably more the former than the latter. If one wishes to venture into the dangerous, though shallow waters of psycho-history, then attention should be paid to Atatürk's first personal experience of the West, the years he spend in Sofia, 1914 and 1915, as a military attaché. Society even in that petty Balkan capital judged him an uncouth Turk. He had tried to impress Europeans and had failed: a very proud man, he was going to try again.

If a larger, theoretical explanation has to be given for his rejection of Islam then it can be found in the work of Ziya Gokalp, part sociologist, part philosopher and the intellectual father of the Kemalist 'revolution'. He came from Diyarbekir, a strongly Kurdish area, hence the suspicions that he could have been partly of Kurdish origin; just as the wholly Turkish origins of Atatürk, coming from the opposite end of the empire, from Thessalonika, are also sometimes questioned. Whether or not Atatürk read much of Gokalp's sometimes obscure writings is doubtful, but his ideas were in the air. Thus it was Gokalp who first said that Turkish music was really Byzantine in origin and 'morbid'. It must be said at the outset that Gokalp was not anti-Islamic. Ironically, he had Sufi inclinations and knew about mystical practices, yet the tarikas were among the first of Atatürk's targets. What he wanted was a Turkified Islam: no Caliph and no Sharia but back to the Koran and the Hadith, with the Koran in the Turkish language. Islam was compatible with a modern state. It need not hinder Turkey's 'complete' adaptation to Western civilization; for Western civilization is no more Christian than Eastern civilization is Islamic. (Gokalp had his own personal and idiosyncratic definition of civilization.) Indeed the beliefs and practices of the Christian Church were, Gokalp believed, a hindrance to Western civilization. When the reasonable beliefs of Islam penetrated Europe Christianity reformed itself and produced Protestantism. It was then that Europe became strong, thanks to the strong simple beliefs on which a Turkish Islam should be based. (Along with this went a second racialist theory that Islam, being essentially an Arab religion, was fundamentally incompatible with the genius of Turkism: one aspect of Gokalp's thought was pan-Turkish or pan-Turanian.)

Atatürk rejected all this Islamic argumentation of Gokalp, retaining only some of his 'Turkism' ideas. The man in power crushed Islam for no better reason than that he saw in it the only real threat to his power.

One final irony about Gokalp's work is that most of it is unknown to the modern Turk because it was written in Ottoman Turkish in the Arabic script, and so was a victim of Atatürk's linguistic reform![22]

Even in Atatürk's time it was recognized that there had to be some religious structures, and so in 1924 there were established within the government a department of the affairs of piety (through which Atatürk kept strict personal control on everything concerning Islam) and a department of Evkaf (religious endowments); a faculty of divinity was founded at the University of Istanbul. But suppression could not go on forever, because it was just too contrary to the strongest sentiments of the ordinary Turk. Islamic instruction in schools was reintroduced in 1948, as were theological schools to train religious functionaries (imams) under state auspices. A faculty of theology was added to Ankara University.

Nothing shows the strength of Islam in Turkey more clearly than the number of pilgrims making the Haj. It was permitted from 1947. In 1934 there were one hundred pilgrims, in 1952 over ten thousand and in 1970 just under fifty thousand, and this was with continuing restrictions on foreign currency. From 1947 onwards the relaxations followed quickly on one another: numerous religious periodicals appeared; religious programmes reappeared on the state radio, and it was once more permitted to visit the tombs of saints. In the 1950 general election the Democrat Party quite openly breached the Kemalist prohibition against the political exploitation of religion and as a result captured more than three quarters of the seats. One of the new government's first acts was to permit the call to prayer to be made in Arabic once more. Then came a great increase in the number of mosques being built and renewed activity by the tarikas.

The Bektashis, Nakshabandis, Qadiris and Mevlevis had all maintained limited activity underground despite police harassment. The partial relaxation of the early 1950s allowed two new Turkish brotherhoods to appear. The first, the Risala i Nur of Said Nursi now operates openly and is said to have a following of half a million members: it even has its own daily newspaper. The other grouping is the Suleymanciler or Sulemanis, named for its founder Suleyman Hilmi Tunaha, which is still clandestine but is said to have many members among Turkish workers in Germany. The president of the government department of religious affairs claimed that in the 1972 Turkish Parliament five deputies of different parties belonged to this mysterious group.[23] Both groups are militantly fundamentalist in their programmes and are far more politically activist than the tarikas proper.

Although the military coup in 1960 was made in the name of Kemalism, which the Democrat Party was said to be undermining, even the soldiers did not undo the religious permissiveness that the Democrats had made an important part of their policy. The exploitation of Islam by Turkish politicians when the Justice Party took office in 1965 will be considered below.

If one re-reads the lyrically optimistic chapter on Turkey in W. Cantwell Smith's *Islam in Modern History* one sees that all his worst fears for Turkish Islam have come true, even though he strongly discounted this pessimistic possibility. For what has happened is that the Turks of the ruling class, the people who really mattered according to Cantwell Smith, did remain strongly Muslim; they wanted a reformation, but their ideas on it were too vague and so they returned to 'the traditional forms and institutions'; writing in 1957 Cantwell Smith said, 'The dominant and emphatic conviction of this class itself is that such will not be the case.' But it has happened, and the present state of Turkish Islam is worse than that before Atatürk, for now it is being deliberately used by cynics and fanatics to achieve political power. This situation is the direct result of the short-sighted reforms of Kemal Atatürk, who believed that Islam could be totally excluded from the public life of a country composed of devout Muslims. The angry response to that Westernizing challenge is still driving forward in Turkey and with increasing energy. The Kemalist Lilliputians tried and failed to tie down the Islamic giant.

It is not for us here to evaluate the failure of the Kemalist revolution in other spheres of Turkish life, but one verdict on the economic situation may be given. In *Turkey: an Economic Appraisal*, written in 1949, an American economist and planner said, 'Why does a popular revolution, after nearly a quarter century of glamorous successes, leave most of the people – perhaps 18 out of the 20 million – almost where they were before? Nothing in Atatürk's declaration of principles prepares us for the concept that 'the state is superior to the individual', or for the spectacle of a glorious streamlined Turkish state resting on the bowed necks of the Turkish peasantry.'[24] The economic condition of Turkey in 1949 was positively paradisal compared to what it is like now.

Thornburg's book is a rarity in the modern literature on Turkey: it is critical. In spite of the evident failure since the beginning of the Kemalist revolution Western writers on Turkey remained obstinately cheerful and the biographies of Atatürk are still hagiographies. The reason for this Western favouritism is not far to seek. Atatürk gave to the West that sincerest form of flattery – imitation. But for wholesale imitation to succeed, the imitators have to be very clever and hardworking, which the Japanese are and the Turks are not.

Atatürk was also held in high regard by Afro-Asian leaders, even by so discerning a student of history as Jawaharlal Nehru. Atatürk's economic ideas of *étatisme* and five year planning (borrowed from Russia) had a very great impact on the new states of Asia, where they had the same uniformly deleterious effects as they had on Turkey itself. It could be that his military success against the Western Powers at Gallipoli bedazzled these anti-Western Asian leaders into admiring his religious, cultural and economic reforms which are still bedazzling, but only in the horrendous consequences of their failure (which is still unfolding in his hapless country).

Looking back over the responses made by Islam to the various challenges and pressures of the West one may draw the conclusion that the responses were somewhat more than adequate. The spiritual challenge had been partly met; and the political and cultural wholly. But for the Arab countries the political pressure has remained as a result of their conflict with Israel, which they see as a continuation of the former confrontation because Israel is seen by them, by itself and by the West, as an outpost and bastion of Western civilization holding out in the very centre of the Islamic world.

The failure to produce a real 'rethinking of Islam in modern terms' remains a hole in the heart of Islam, for only the zealots do not think it necessary. The spiritual state of the Muslim world in the period soon after independence came to all Muslim nations, say at around 1965, was one of animation – but suspended animation. Looking for a Luther was the motto of the day, as the Muslim states began to try and bring new order into Dar al Islam, the House of Islam of which, at long last, they were now the free masters.

5 Militant Islam today: the contemporary response

I

By 1975 the owners of Dar al Islam must have felt that the roof of the brand new House of Islam had fallen in on their devoted heads. In the preceding decade the Muslim world had received two major hammerblows and several minor ones. The Arab heartland of Islam suffered a crushing military defeat in the 1967 war with Israel, a humiliation that was felt personally not only in Egypt, Jordan and Syria, the actual combatants, but by all the other Arab states and indeed the non-Arab Islamic nations as well. The defeat was so complete that it revealed the weakness not just of the Arab military machine but of the whole of Arab society, which is an Islamic society. Then in 1972 came the split in what was then the largest Muslim state, Pakistan, a split brought about through hatred and bitterness, mass suffering and war. The link of Islam had not proven strong enough to hold an Islamic state together against the pulls of regionalism.

These two events were by themselves bad enough to shake the foundations of Dar al Islam; but there was also fighting between Algeria, Morocco and Mauritania, tension between Iraq and Iran, an increasingly unstable situation in Turkey; the Keeper of the Two Sanctuaries, King Feisal of Saudi Arabia, was felled by an assassin's bullet. Furthermore, the ground was bestrewn with many a fallen idol – Sukarno, Ben Bella, Nasser and, most recently, Bhutto. From the mid-1950s on, by when the larger Muslim countries had become independent, came other and more basic political reasons for self-doubt and disillusionment. None of the various political systems the Muslim states had adopted seemed to work satisfactorily: parliamentary democracy had been tried and failed; army regimes had been no more successful; likewise the system of single-party left-wing socialism. Could Muslim countries ever find a way of governing themselves aright?

In this grim situation the Muslims have reacted as did Marshal Foch in the bad days for Allied arms in the spring of 1918, when he said: 'My flanks are in retreat, my centre is not holding: I shall attack.' Precisely because of their setbacks the Muslim peoples turned more than ever to Islam and Islam became more militant. It is this defiant spirit of militancy in Islam, surfacing in several Muslim countries simultaneously, that caught the attention and the headlines of the rest of the world: a wave that is still moving towards its crest today. But while defiant militancy was the public reaction, the private turning towards Islam was done 'in fear and trembling', to find something enduring that would give strength and comfort. One reaction fed the other. As more people prayed at home, went to prayers in the mosques, the Islamic leaders, some sincerely, some with opportunistic cynicism, decided that with this renewed popular Islamic resurgence the time had come for them to enunciate or implement more militantly Islamic policies, at home and abroad.

Another smaller and not so reputable reason for the present surge in militant Islam is the effect of Saudi Arabian influence and finance, both of which increased greatly when the oil revenues of the world's largest oil producer quadrupled as a consequence of the 1973 Arab–Israeli war. With their Wahhabi background the Saudis would naturally wish to see orthodox Islamic regimes established in as many Muslim countries as possible. Their impulsion towards this goal could be discerned in Pakistan, North Yemen, the Sudan and Egypt. A similar impulsion towards the same goal and using the same methods came from the Libya of Colonel Gaddafi directed towards Indonesia, Turkey and Egypt.

The two wider and more general reasons given above apply to almost all Islamic nations and certainly to all Arab nations but in not all of these countries, not even the Arab ones, has militant Islam appeared. As far as the Arab States are concerned, in three of them – Iraq, Syria and Algeria – politically militant Islam would not be permitted by the regimes which claim the monopoly of political power, even though Algeria may have a ministry of religious affairs and Islamic teaching. So if militant Islam has manifested itself in other Islamic countries it is because either the governments were themselves encouraging its appearance, which was mostly the case, or because they were not able to prohibit it. Very often inability to control came first and then, in the second stage, came official support.

Hence governmental reactions to militant Islam have had varied and very mixed motivation. In Indonesia a reluctant government has been trying to pre-empt and outbid the Islamic groundswell. In Pakistan militant Islam was at least partially a diversion from internal and external difficulties, in addition to being an expression of the continuing demand for an Islamic state, that was Pakistan's very *raison d'être*. Much the same combination of pressures applied to Egypt, the Sudan, Morocco, Saudi Arabia and Turkey. In Libya the striving for an Islamic polity seemed genuine enough, at least as far as Colonel Gaddafi himself was concerned, but it partook of his erratic nature. Algeria too wanted a genuine but strictly limited degree of militant Islam, which was well within the ambit of governmental policy; and it has emerged in Iran because the religious structure of the Shiah community was able to provide leadership for a revolution against the regime of the Shah. It is to be noted that all the countries named above are anti-communist and they are all, with the exceptions of Algeria, Libya and the new Iran, pro-West. The West's suspicions and fears of militant Islam do not appear to be well grounded in rational calculation. Old atavistic fears of Islam as such have little to do with reason.

2

After 150 years of struggle, having defeated the religious, spiritual, political, military and cultural pressures that the West applied from outside, Islam has had to try and find a response to a new Western cultural challenge during the last twenty-five years; a challenge that is all the more dangerous because this time the enemy is not wholly foreign but is partly a native fifth column within the gates. We are not referring to the over-arching civilizational challenge of 'the West' as a whole, that complex of forces denoted by such concepts as 'urbanization', 'the mass-man', 'technological advance' and 'the affluent consumer society'. That challenge will continue for generations to come. This new challenge is more penetrating, for it is made on a narrower sector called the 'youth culture', which poses tremendous problems to Islamic society in this post-Beatles age of ours. From the vantage point of this outside observer it truly seems that the four young men who constituted The Beatles pop group must be accounted among the true revolutionaries of our time.[1] They started something much bigger than just a new musical style.

Ayatollah Khomeini has identified this new enemy, for in his scathing denunciations of Western civilization, root-and-branch, he often makes mention of 'music', a seemingly strange reference – he is obviously not referring to Bach or even to Stockhausen (though the last named provides ample provocation). The Ayatollah is referring to pop music which has literally become a universal phenomenon thanks to the Western-cum-Japanese technological product, the cheap transistor radio.

Why are the songs of pop music so dangerous as to arouse the wrathful denunciation of one very powerful militant Muslim? They are innocent enough stuff – but not at all innocent in the context of the youth culture. For what the lyrics usually say is that two young people should choose each other, if necessary defying the family (because of the 'generation gap'), if necessary defying society. The underlying moral is that two atomistic individuals choose their own path in life, not two families, as it has been from time immemorial in Islamic and Eastern societies. Such goings-on, if accepted in an Islamic country, would mean the end of the family structure and the end of a traditional society based on interlocking families. This, some may say, is making heavy weather of something the youngsters listen to on the radio. But it is not unreasonable to assume that impressionable young people cannot listen with passionate attention to something year after year, without it affecting their opinions on social behaviour, even if they are not just yet rushing out to do what the pop song lyrics tell them to do.

The songs are only one part of a whole pop culture that is world wide. Along with admiration for the pop groups goes the attraction of their lifestyle, including such possibilities as drugs, 'doing one's own thing', dropping out (of school, college or family), long hair and casual colourful clothes especially that omnipresent symbol of youth culture – blue jeans. Girlie magazines and pornography are only, perhaps, a step away. Anyone noting the addresses of the young people sending in requests for pop music to, let us say, the World Service of the

BBC becomes aware that this youth culture is both world-wide and vigorously alive. It hits Islamic society hardest because Islam is the most demanding, the most solidly constituted, the most resistant society of those produced by the three main indigenous Afro-Asian faiths. One doubts very much whether middle-class Hindu parents in India or Buddhist parents in Southeast Asia would mind very much whether their children hero-worship the Rolling Stones; Muslim parents in Pakistan or Syria or Algeria would. Just let us say that Muslim society, even urban society, tends to be that much more traditional and old-fashioned.

The onslaught of this youth culture can be unnerving to young people with a traditional background, who feel swept off their feet. This is the case even with many educated young women in the Arab countries or in Iran when they are confronted with the ideas of Women's Liberation. In recent months, in newspaper interviews, girls draped in the black *chador* on the campus of Tehran University and in the long white robe and wimple on the campus of Jordan University near Amman have said that they have taken to wearing the traditional garb (often to the dismay of their mothers and grandmothers who fought to get out of it) not for religious reasons but simply because it gave them a feeling of identity. Thus dressed, they knew who they were: in blue jeans they were something that was neither this nor that. Only a non-Westerner can really understand this cultural timidity and bewilderment – alas! for inter-cultural understanding.

When Islamic leaders like Ayatollah Khomeini (or like the sermonizing Shah before him) denounce the West as a source of decadence and muddled values, they are launching themselves into battle against the world-wide culture of pop and jeans. The wearing of jeans can be forbidden, so can the showing of films; but how can TV programmes be banned when they are beamed directly from satellites, and even the cheapest transistor radio can pick up programmes from powerful foreign medium-wave stations. As more than one dictator has found to his cost, the transistor revolution is both irreversible and inescapable.

Yet with historical irony the wheel has come full circle: the Christian (or post-Christian) West, which for centuries derided Islam as a religion peculiarly productive of voluptuous sensuality and sexual licence, is now being derided by Muslim Savonarolas and Calvins for infecting the Muslim world with those very same evils. And under their stern reproachful gaze the only answer the West has given so far is to shift uneasily and guiltily on its feet: which does not make these critics any the more likeable to the West.

Ayatollah Khomeini, at least, seems to know that militant Islam faces a new challenge from the West that he identifies with its 'music', and which is now presented from within each country by its Westernized younger generation. The challenge is all the stronger because by now millions of young Indonesians, Iranians, Turks, Algerians and Saudi Arabians have studied abroad and have, as it were, drunk from the original spring of Western youth culture. A return to the original simplicities of the Koran may be the best and easiest way of solving the problem of how to 'up-date' Islam as a religion; but something more sophisticated than a return to simplicities will have to be the answer to the problem of a younger Muslim generation that has been Westernized: a whole new dimension has been added to the claim that 'youth will have its day' and 'its say'.

3

Before considering how militant Islam meets this and many other challenges of the modern world we must first define it by saying what it is not, who its protagonists are, and how they set about dealing with each other, as well as with the problems facing Islam.

There are two things which militant Islam most emphatically is not: it is not 'Muslim nationalism' and it is not pan Islam. By Muslim nationalism is meant both the feeling within countries inhabited by Muslim peoples that such countries constitute separate nations and the inevitably concomitant nationalist feeling that each such nation is in some way not merely different from but superior to other countries, especially its neighbours. For the militant, or even the non-militant but devout Muslim such nationalist feelings are condemned not merely because they are narrowminded or chauvinistic but because they are irreligious, un-Islamic.

The Muslim critics of nationalism feel so strongly on this matter that they do not mince their words. Thus: 'The concepts of secularism, humanism, nationalism, materialism and rationalism which are all based on partial truths, became deities in their own right; one-eyed superbeings. They are responsible for the present Euro-American spiritual crisis. The partial truths in all these powerful ideas can all be satisfied by Islam.' That was a former prime minister of the Sudan.[2] A Pakistani critic writes of 'the forces of nepotism, tribalism, ethnocentrism and nationalism' as things equally and obviously undesirable.[3] Iqbal, the spiritual father of Pakistan, was fiercely critical of nationalism and everything pertaining to it. In putting down his simple, soldierly ideas for a new constitution for Pakistan, the former president Field Marshal Ayub Khan gave this listing of basic principles: '(a) Singleness of God . . . (b) All human beings are equal before God . . . (c) True that in such a society national territorialism has no place, yet those living in an area are responsible for its defence and security and development.'[4] When the new constitution of free Indonesia was being drawn up the Muslim reformers fought President Sukarno for years to keep out the inclusion of nationalism as one of the five principles or Pantja Sila of the new State.

This very strong Islamic opposition to nationalism may seem strange because Muslim religious groupings took such a leading part in the long drawn out nationalist struggle, as we have seen. But for militant Islam there is nationalism and nationalism and, in a further paradox, while negative nationalism is deemed both necessary and admirable, positive nationalism is almost an evil.

It was negative nationalism, it is argued, that inspired the struggle against the imperialist Christian West – better defined as love of country or patriotism. Such a struggle *against* an aggressive foreign force is truly a jihad and is an obligation on the true believer, because only in a free country can there be 'religious self-respect'.[5] This is the basic responsibility for the 'defence, security and development' of an area by the people living in it to which President Ayub referred. But these struggles, though only *against* something and therefore negative, were laudable for they set no other god before God. The fighters went into battle not under the colour of some new territorial entity but under the green banner of the Prophet; the only symbol carried before them was the Koran; the battle cry was not the equivalent of 'God for England' but the simple chant that Turkish soldiers used when they went in with the bayonet against the Koreans: 'Din, din, din – the Faith, the Faith, the Faith.' The actual battlefields may have been in Morocco or Somaliland or Sumatra but for the martyrs it was in and for Dar al Islam (in the 1950s a Muslim rebel group in Sumatra called itself Dar al Islam).

The new doctrine of positive nationalism is hateful to Muslim reformers for several reasons. To divide mankind into smaller, mutually antagonistic units is to deny that oneness and universality of mankind that the Koran speaks of.[6] God is One and so are his children. If Islam does not accept the natural, God-created differences of race, colour and language – a fact demonstrated so effectively in the amalgam of the Haj – who is man that he should set up artificial barriers even between people of the same race, colour and language?

Secondly, nationalism is wrong because it not only divides mankind but it splits up the umma, the world-wide community of the faithful, and by doing so has weakened it. 'This new emotion has established "modern states" but it has destroyed the unity of the Muslim world and left it a prey to Christian and Zionist imperialism. While the whole world moves towards internationalism, Muslims with a tradition of internationalism are regressing to regional and provincial loyalties.'[7] Instead of the Dar al Islam being the large, single home of the whole umma some of the family members are trying to lock themselves into single rooms. Keeping in mind the historical age of Christendom we may compare this disapproval of nationalist divisiveness to the regret felt by the last of the Latin-speaking Europeans, who in the fifteenth and sixteenth centuries saw the unity of Christendom being fragmented into the new nation states of Europe.

Thirdly, and 'worse, this narrow nationalism, which is a Western product, has established "a new object of worship", the materialist nation, destructive and incompatible with the "nationalism of divine principles" decreed by God in Islam. The modern nation has become "a partner with God"; the secular nationalist is guilty of shirk'[8] – or blasphemy. The Muslim reformers were right to sense in nationalism a dangerous competitor to their ideal of exclusive loyalty to Islam, for if there is any force that could counter militant Islam it is Muslim nationalism – just as it is the only force that has countered the powerful current of communism in Afro-Asia.

Lastly, it is the 'Western' character of the nation state that is objectionable. It is a Western creation and importation; and the machinery of the nation state can only be worked by members of the Westernized élite who are not only trained and experienced administrators and technicians but who are also, because of their Western background, secular or even anti-Islamic in their thinking. This is why Ayatollah Khomeini rails against the fact that even though there has been a revolution nothing seems to have changed because the work of government is still being carried on in large ministry buildings in Tehran. A Pakistani critic is equally vehement: 'Politically the concepts which enthrall us are the concepts of nationalism and sovereignty. Once a nation state is established, whether it is the result of distribution of plunder among the victors, or a grudging dispensation granted by a receding imperial power, it acquires a universally acknowledged right to defend its solidarity and sovereignty. Within the nation states our effort is to preserve the legacy of imperialism: corrupt systems of elections, alien modes of education, and outlandish procedures of administration . . . We imitate all the secular skills in public affairs . . . We talk in cabinet rooms of hard realities, pragmatic moves, and contemporary compulsion, and then when we emerge from there we proclaim the glory of Islam.'[9] Thus in its originating concept, its provenance and its *modus operandi* the Islamic re-reformers found the nation state repugnant.

The nationalist Muslims naturally made reply, which should be recorded here. President Sukarno arguing for the inclusion of nationalism in the Pantja Sila said that nationalism is not anti-Islamic or anti any ideology: 'It is above all the feeling of desire, the desire to go back to one's identity, the desire for freedom, the desire to smash the chains binding one's hands, the desire to be in control of one's own affairs, the desire to shape one's own cultural identity . . . this is nationalism . . . The paradox is that in Europe people want to abolish national borders. Here people want to establish national borders. In my opinion Islam does not prohibit us from founding a national state. People always think erroneously that being a nationalist means worshipping your country. No! in loving my country do not worship it.'[10] For all his eloquence Sukarno was not really answering the Islamic objection to the nation state because the nationalism he describes is of the pre-independence variety of which Islam approves. He was on much surer ground when he argued that in an Islamic state the Christians would become a conspicuous minority. The Christians, many of whom had taken an active part in the national struggle, should not, he said, be reduced to minority status. 'The Christians will say "we have not fought and died to become a minority".' Sukarno here hit on one of the major weaknesses of the Islamic state.

In the pages of his *Political Biography* we see Ayub Khan wrestling with engaging honesty with the fundamental incompatibility between an assertive universalist religion and equally assertive particularist nationalism: 'The ulema thought in terms of a glorious though nebulous past and a vast but undefined future of Muslim brotherhood. And this more than anything else damaged the growth of Muslim nationalism and retarded the progress of Muslims in the sub-continent . . . Those who thought that a national outlook was incompatible with the concept of universal brotherhood were really suggesting that the Muslims of the sub-continent should not try to establish a homeland of their own because there were homelands enough of Muslims in other parts of the world. Why have a home of your own when there are so many Muslim homes in the Middle East?'[11] Yet another president of Pakistan, Zulfikar Bhutto, raised this problem of incompatibility: 'There has been a certain ambivalence in our Muslim minds about the role of nationalism in Islam, and its compatibility with the establishment of an Islam community. Nationalism as the motive force of a people's liberation . . . is a motive force which we will do nothing to weaken. Patriotism and loyalty to Islam can be fixed into a transcendent harmony. As Muslims we can rise higher than our nationalism without damaging or destroying it.'[12] An adroit politician, he raised a very real problem only to evade it with fine words. The debate on this question, still being carried on in Pakistan, is a 'dialogue of the deaf' between the nationalists and the Islamists.

The field marshal's references to Pakistani feelings about 'Muslim homes' and 'Muslim homelands' elsewhere points to one of the major characteristics of the Islamic umma – its strong feeling of one-ness and solidarity. In 1912 the Indonesians were greatly exercised by Turkey's losses in the Balkan Wars and the Italian invasion of Libya. That solidarity of sentiment still remains and is still quite lively; but it has always been on the level of sentiment. When one Muslim country faces troubles the people and governments of other countries do feel genuinely concerned, they express concern, and if it is a natural calamity they may send money or relief supplies or medical teams. But there has never yet been any more concrete expression given to this sentiment of solidarity. During the various Arab–Israeli Wars volunteers have enrolled in Pakistan and Malaysia but none have ever yet turned up on the field of battle. Islamic solidarity received a severe shock and subsequent debunking soon after World War I when Muslims everywhere, particularly vociferously in India and Indonesia, opposed Atatürk's abolition of the Caliphate. It was only after several years of agitation that they realized that they could not force a Caliphate on a totally non-cooperative Turkey.

All attempts to give a formal, organized structure to this sentiment of solidarity have either failed or produced only minimal results. In the first flush of Islamic enthusiasm Pakistan, soon after its creation, launched a variety of international Islamic organizations to deal with economic, educational, health and communication problems and so on. They all faded away, and now Saudi Arabia is trying its hand through an Islamic secretariat based in Jedda, where there is also an Islamic News Agency. They have not heeded a pointed statement by President Nasser made at Karachi in 1960: 'Our country does not favour the creation of an Islamic federation.'

Nor do the Muslim reformers favour this sort of pan Islam because these organizations are not truly supranational but simply international: to produce cooperation and coordination between existing nation states. When the national bricks of which these international structures are composed are declared faulty the final structure will be considered more faulty still. Since it operates only on the secular level political pan Islam will always be defeated by the separate national interests of the Muslim states: witness the creation of Bangladesh, the wars in the Yemen, on the Egyptian–Libyan border and in the western Sahara. Thus subsequent history has shown that the reformer Afghani's campaign to liberate Muslim countries so that they could then join together in a pan-Islamic federation or confederation was basically unrealistic; even if at the time his message enthused and energized a demoralized Muslim world.

What the Muslim reformers, or at least the Muslim Brotherhood, would like to see is something they call *Islamism*. In this scheme the 'bricks' of a new order for the Muslim world would be Islamic states not national states, which would move through regional cooperation to overall Islamic unification. But even this nebulous plan is something that is said to be for the distant future.

If so-called pan Islam is something that is objectionable in theory to militant Islam and if in practice it has produced the most negligible results, why is it that pan Islam has always sent shudders of fear running down the spines of Western governments? Why is the present resurgence of militant Islam deliberately and repeatedly coupled with pan Islam in the Western media? The answers that suggest themselves are: obvious ignorance, a wish to be deliciously scared like children safely tucked up in bed asking for ghost stories, and a thoroughly guilty political conscience.

A prime example of a Western attitude to pan Islam, combining the first two motivations, was contained in a recent article in a London weekly magazine, in which the author said, 'When Jan Morris wrote in 1954 "the idea of pan Islam is all but dead," Allah must have chuckled, knowing that so long as he had oil up his sleeve, and the rapidly failing West as his only competitor, Islam would not only live, but rapidly become more powerful than ever.'[13] What pan Islam today has to do with oil which emerges from Allah's sleeve is somewhat unclear, but what the author believes in ignorance is that pan Islam is alive today, and is a threat to the West. Western confusion about pan Islam goes back a long way. In 1881 the British agent in Cairo expressed his 'alarm' at the pan-Islamic spirit which 'appears to be endeavouring to spread in the country'. Many years later he explained, 'I used the expression *pan-Islamic* because, at that time, the word *National* had not come into fashion' – a significant confusing of religion with politics.[14] Writing in 1915, the British intelligence chief in Cairo, Clayton, wrote: 'We are dealing with political suspects of all kinds and pan-Islamic propaganda.'[15] This was the same blurred picture as of 'Islam

132

the menace, "pan Islam", "fanaticism" which resisted the civilizing missions, Islam in alliance with national feeling'.[16] Yet the death blow had been dealt to political pan Islam a number of years before Clayton wrote, when the Turkish Sultan, as Caliph, called on all Muslims to join Turkey and rise against the Allied Powers. In the succeeding years of World War I pan Islam was shot and speared to death by Muslim Indian infantry and cavalrymen fighting the Muslim Turks in Mesopotamia and Palestine. When the new 'King of All Arabia' called the first pan-Islamic conference in Mecca in 1923 it caused a great stir throughout the Muslim world, but the conference actually never met. The then James Morris was wrong about pan Islam in 1954 only in being forty years behind the times. Indeed none of the 'pan-' movements have ever amounted to anything much – pan Slav, pan Teutonic, pan Turanian, pan Greek (the Megali idea), or pan American. For better or worse nationalism has always had the last word.

For connoisseurs of the absurd, the full romantic Western myth of pan Islam is laid out in the novel *Greenmantle* by John Buchan: 'There is a dry wind blowing through the East, and the parched grasses await the spark. And the wind is blowing towards the Indian border. Whence comes that wind, think you?' and so on. Indeed, the emotive root of the pan Islam concept, of the wrathful Muslim world rising as one in some vast jihad against the Christian West, was just a bogey, an inverted revival of the Crusader complex created by guilty colonialists like Marshal Lyautey in Morocco, the Arab Bureau (including Clayton and Gertrude Bell) in Cairo in World War I and, before them, Snouck Hurgronje in Indonesia. Such people knew better than most that the West had been pressuring and challenging the entire Muslim world in every sort of way since 1800. They could not believe that given the chance, as in World War I, the Muslim world would not unite and rise in revenge. They almost seemed to have hoped that it would. Now once again, after a further half-century of Western pressures, the Muslim world through the 'oil weapon' seems given the chance to revenge old wrongs: and the West cannot believe that it will not take revenge. So the old pan Islamic ghosts ride again, and the skeletons rattle in the West's dusty cupboards.

For serious militant Islam these Western horror stories are sour jokes. But nationalism remains a continuing and very serious problem for any future Islamic state or Islamic order.

We now have to see what sort of Islamic leaders have been trying to make the contemporary political Islamic response. Manifesting itself across the varied range of Muslim countries, which differ so greatly in geography, history and political system, it was inevitable that militant Islam should be exemplified by very differing sorts of Muslim leaders: at least three types may be distinguished. Firstly, there is the professional politician, essentially secular, Westernized and non-Islamic, who simply harnesses the still-living force of Islam to achieve his political goals. These we may call the 'exploiters'. The second type consists of men of religion, and may itself be subdivided into two groups; there are the 'established' men of religion – the ulemas, sheikhs, ayatollahs, who are active in politics; and there is the more passive sort, the members of the tarikas who, for all their mysticism, still have popular influence and therefore political power in some Muslim countries. The first section of this group are the 'reiterators' because for them it is sufficient to go 'back to the Koran' by a strict reiteration and literal implementation of its teachings. The third and most serious type of Islamic militant are those men, not professional politicians and not professional men of religion, who are religious men and have gone into politics in order to try to implement their Islamic ideals in public life. These are the 'rethinkers' for they are trying to achieve that most difficult objective 'to rethink Islam in modern terms'.

Militant Islam, represented by these three types, is to be found in countries that are one-man dictatorships, or one-party dictatorships; in monarchies and multi-party republics; in Muslim countries that are very rich from oil revenues and in others that are very poor; in countries that encourage militant Islam, or merely tolerate it, or suppress it and drive it underground. In short militant Islam has been a generalized Muslim phenomenon since World War II and particularly dynamic and conspicuous in the past decade.

'Exploiters' is a harsh term to apply to anyone, but it usually can be applied with justice to those politicians who make promises in the name of religion which are not kept or who, with fanfares, demand the observance of the purely outward practices of a religion, and who do so at a time when this would be politically expedient and popular. The Muslim exploiter par excellence was, of course, Muhammad Ali Jinnah, the founder of Pakistan who brilliantly manipulated the hopes and mostly the fears of Indian Muslims to bring that state to birth. From the start his leadership of the Indian Muslim movement was wildly incongruous; here was a man completely Westernized from his fingertips to the polished toecaps of the black-and-white correspondent shoes for which he had such an unfortunate predilection. He was a member of one of the smallest and most heterodox Shiah Muslim sects, the Khojas, and was observably not a practising Muslim – if indeed he had any religious faith at all. The incongruity lies in the passionate loyalty given to him by his Muslim following rather than in his assumption of the leadership of their cause, for he never promised them an independent Islamic state. All Jinnah wanted was to carve out of India a Muslim state, that is a state in which the Muslim would constitute a majority and of which he would be the undisputed lord and master. He cannot but have known that this was not what the Muslim masses wanted. The slogan of their movement was 'Islam in danger'; if it was to be rendered safe in a new state it could only be in an Islamic state. If Jinnah did not understand this most obvious aspiration of his people, and if they did not know that he was unaware of it, then Pakistan was brought into existence not in a fit of absentmindedness but as a result of the most colossal misunderstanding in recent history.

In any event, only three months after the establishment of Pakistan the ulema in the new state began a full-fledged campaign so as to have its constitution based on the Sharia. This reaction came so swiftly because it was quite clear by that time that Pakistan was going to be a secular, non-Islamic state. It was Jinnah himself who put the matter beyond doubt in his inaugural address to the constituent assembly, when he said, *inter alia*: 'You may belong to any religion or creed or caste – that has nothing to do with the business of the state . . . you will find that in course of time Hindus would cease to be Hindus and Muslims cease to be Muslims, not in the religious sense because that is the personal faith of each individual, but in a

135

political sense as citizens of the state.'[17] *Muslims cease to be Muslims?* That is not what the Muslim masses had toiled and died for. In what way did this fine liberal doctrine differ from the liberal sentiments being expressed at the same time by Gandhi and Nehru in secular India across the borders? Jinnah went further; he is quoted as saying, 'Pakistan is not going to be a theocratic state ruled by priests with a divine mission,' and he then went on to make the same point to be made a few years later by Sukarno, that a religious state would reduce people not of that faith to the status of second-class minorities. His right-hand man and successor, Liaquat Ali Khan, repeated the argument: 'The investment of power in the people eliminated any danger of the establishment of a theocracy ... any persons who still use the word "theocracy" in the same breath as the polity of Pakistan are either labouring under a grave misapprehension or indulging in mischievous propaganda.' Since then Pakistanis have been among the most fervent critics of any linking of a Muslim or Islamic state with 'theocracy' but it was begun by their first two leaders.

This wide gap between what the leaders of Pakistan wanted and what the Muslim masses of Pakistan wanted has been the main cause of all the travail that Pakistan has gone through ever since, and is still going through. One of the first results of this misunderstanding or exploitation was that it was only in March 1949, a year and a half after the founding of the state, that the constituent assembly was able to agree on the most important, Islamic, clause in its 'objectives resolution', which was to lay down the Islamic *raison d'être* of Pakistan. This said that Pakistan was to be a state 'wherein the Muslims shall be enabled to order their lives in the individual and collective spheres in accord with the teachings and requirements of Islam as set out in the Holy Koran and the Sunnah'. Which left the door wide open for every sort of personal or collective interpretation or misinterpretation of those 'teachings and requirements'. Agreement on this vague formula was reached only after prolonged debate, and it continued so that it was only in 1956 that Pakistan's first constitution was adopted, where the Islamic mountain in labour produced a barely Islamic mouse: the Islamic clause of the objectives resolution was repeated with the addition of just two Islamic provisions – that the Head of State must be a

Muslim and that Pakistan was 'an Islamic republic'. Two other Islamic provisions which were to take effect in the future were included: an organization for Islamic research and instruction was established; and a commission was appointed to report in *five* years on how the laws could be made to conform with the fundamental teachings of Islam and 'to draw up in a suitable form such injunctions of Islam as *can* be given legislative effect'; after these were accepted by parliament no law repugnant to these injunctions could be passed.

For the next fifteen years the politicians of Pakistan including Field Marshal Ayub Khan continued to fiddle with the Islamic elements of the country's constitution. There was a second one in 1962: Pakistan ceased to be an 'Islamic Republic' but became one again, on amendment, a year later. The word 'Sunnah' was dropped from the preamble, leaving the Koran as the sole guide, but that was also reinstated. An advisory council of Islamic ideology was added to the existing Islamic research centre, all meant to ensure that laws conformed to Islamic principles. This huffing and puffing was just so much more political exploitation of Islam.

Then in 1972 another major exploiter of Islam took charge in Pakistan – Zulfikar Ali Bhutto. After the *débâcle* of Bangladesh he had been swept into power at the head of his new-style Pakistan People's Party. He was another leader in Jinnah's Westernized mould, but even more worldly and sophisticated. He was a new man to face a new situation and with large promises of a new deal, including the vote-winning slogan of 'Islamic socialism'. As a student in Los Angeles he had confessed: 'I do not say my prayers regularly. I do not observe all of the fast. I have not yet performed the Haj. Therefore, religiously speaking, I am a poor Muslim. However, my interest is soaked in the political, economic and cultural heritage of Islam.' How did he set about solving the intractable problem of giving the Muslims of Pakistan the Islamic polity for which they had split off from India? One of his first acts was to lift restrictions, imposed because of a shortage of foreign exchange, on pilgrims going on the Haj (which Turkish politicians had found a popular gambit some years before). There was also a new constitution, in 1973. There was no mention in it of Islamic socialism nor even in his five year plan. The reference to the Koran and Sunnah were retained, as was the 'repugnancy' clause. Like its predecessors a reference to the Islamic obligation of zakat or alms was mentioned in an isolated clause far down in the constitution and the hope was expressed that it would be possible to eliminate riba, usury, 'as early as possible'. But it was laid down in this constitution that the teaching of Arabic would be encouraged; Islamiyat (religious instruction) became a compulsory subject for students and 'error-free printing of the holy Koran would be ensured.' This repetition of tired old Islamic clichés, with the addition of a certain amount of window dressing from a politician who had come in with a strong mandate for change, sincerity and integrity amounts to nothing more than the exploitation of Islam. In Bhutto's case it was the more heinous because unnecessary, and because he was aware of what had been going on before him in this regard: 'It has been my struggle in Pakistan not to exploit the name of Islam,' he once said. 'Islam is against exploitation; and hypocrisy is the greatest sin in Islam. But some of us have been super-hypocrites.'[18] He provided a good example of super-hypocrisy when in 1974 his government declared that the Ahmadiyas were not a Muslim sect. In 1953 the ulema, frustrated at not being able to make Pakistan more Islamic, diverted popular discontent against this small sect. Ahmadiya beliefs are indeed heretical and non-Islamic (so are many of the beliefs of the Khojas, Jinnah's community) but Ahmadiya missionaries had served Islam well. Nevertheless in the subsequent rioting there were killings and destruction of Ahmadiya property. To their credit, the then rulers of Pakistan were thoroughly ashamed of the whole affair and tried to make amends. The ulema merely bided their time, and having pushed Bhutto into a quasi-Islamic constitution (they feared that with his Westernized background he might go for secularism) they kept up the pressure on the Ahmadiya question. Finally in the name of the purity of Islam Bhutto declared the Ahmadiyas to be non-Muslim. In doing so he was guilty not merely of exploiting Islam but of moral cowardice towards a harmless and defenceless group of Pakistanis. As internal conditions in Pakistan became more difficult for Bhutto, he played with increasing hypocrisy to the Islamic gallery. In May 1977, two months before he was overthrown by General Zia al Haq, prohibition was introduced, gambling was prohibited and Friday was declared the weekly holiday instead of Sunday. But this additional window dressing coming four years after Bhutto took office was too late.

If we have described at some length Pakistan's unhappy struggles to achieve an Islamic constitution it is because it took place in a country brought into existence solely on the basis of Islam, and because constitution-making has been the main preoccupation in Pakistan's internal politics for the last thirty years.

When General Zia al Haq ousted Bhutto in July 1977, he too seemed to be courting cheap Islamic popularity, for soon afterwards he decreed amputation the punishment for theft and public whipping for other offences. But the changes he introduced in February 1979 are of a different order. The timing of these Islamic reforms makes them totally suspect, for in that month General Zia was under great pressure from abroad and some pressure from inside to stay the execution of Bhutto. The reforms therefore can be interpreted as exploiting Islam in a diversionary tactic. That being said we note that this time the general has not 'fiddled about' with the Koranic prescriptions; the complete range of canonical punishments has been introduced – for theft, adultery, drinking and bearing false witness. In addition the supremacy of the Sharia has been established over the legal system by the fact that citizens have been given the right to challenge the Islamic validity of any law before special Sharia benches: a stop-gap measure until such time as the entire body of the law is revised in accordance with the Sharia. The first specific measures have been taken, through the national investment trust and the Investment Corporation of Pakistan, to eliminate riba, usury. A very detailed and comprehensive plan has been introduced for the levying of zakat, alms tax, and for the utilization of the funds thus collected. The Pakistan government has made a large contribution to the newly established zakat fund and 'large sums of money' have been made available by King Khaled and Prince Fahd of Saudi Arabia as well as by the president of the United Arab Emirates. This is the second suspicious element in this reform move because the contributions could suggest that the Zia regime has been bribed by these orthodox rulers to bring Pakistan into line with their brand of Islamic traditionalism. Because of the seriousness, detailed nature and wide scope of these reforms it cannot be said with certainty that they are another example of the exploitation of Islam but, with the record of the previous rulers of Pakistan in mind, the suspicion remains.

The next example of the exploitation of Islam is of a less serious nature, for it comes after all from 'laughter-loving' Egypt. In May 1971 President Sadat announced that Egypt should have a new permanent constitution in the framing of which allowance would be made for Egypt's ancient traditions and 'above all else and before all else, our mission of faith'. Those words were interpreted as meaning that an Islamic element was to be introduced into the new constitution and there was a lively discussion throughout Egypt, especially in the columns of *Al Ahram* newspaper, on just how Islamized the constitution was to be.[19] In September 1971 the people of Egypt in a referendum gave 99·9 per-cent approval to a document which had two 'Islamic' clauses: 'Islam is the religion of the state; Arabic is its official language; and the principles of the Islamic Sharia are *a* [emphasis added] principal source of legislation ... The state shall be responsible for maintaining the balance between woman's duties towards the family and her activity in society, as well as her equality with man in the fields of political, social, cultural and economic life, without detriment to the laws of Islamic sharia.' As before, and as would occur later in Pakistan, the Islamic mountain was put to labour to produce a mouse.

In January 1977 severe food riots occurred in several places in Egypt. The first public appearance thereafter of a badly shaken Sadat was for prayers at al Azhar mosque, with maximum publicity coverage. In February 1977 after a meeting with Muslim and Coptic religious leaders, Sadat said that 'religion must be a basic and compulsory subject in our schools' and that 'appropriate steps' would be taken in that direction for the coming school year. Egypt had already had religious instruction in its schools but admittedly for only two hours per week. Egypt being Egypt, no steps of any sort have yet been taken but the declaration of intent went down very well with the men of religion. Later in 1977 draft laws were presented on prohibition (which nearly went through before the tourism lobby stopped it) and on amputation for theft: nothing came of this last move and nothing is ever likely to under Sadat who is too sensitive about his image in the West as a Westernized moderate.

Having derived what advantage he could from talking about Islamic revivalism President Sadat, after making peace with Israel, has swung to the other extreme; he could hardly do otherwise after his peace initiative was denounced by the overwhelming majority of Islamic governments and Islamic popular movements. Sounding like a recording of Atatürk, Sadat said in mid-April 1979: 'No politics in religion, no religion in politics,' a totally untenable position for the sort of devout Muslim that the Egyptian leader claims to be.

Two other political exploiters of Islam are Turkish politicians: Necmettin Erbakan, the leader of the National Salvation Party, and former colonel Alparslan Turkes, leading the National Action Party. The real political interest of both these leaders lies elsewhere than in Islam – Erbakan's in a vast and rapid industrialization of Turkey and Turkes' in pan Turanianism – but both use Islam to gain grass roots support. The door to political respectability was opened for them by the Justice Party of Suleyman Demirel in the 1965 general elections; this party had already been exploiting Islam, for which he was later ousted by the army. In the 1973 elections Erbakan's party did surprisingly well and Turkes' appeared officially on the scene. Both were given places in the coalition government formed by the left-of-centre leader Bulent Ecevit – a cynical alliance if ever there was one. Erbakan demanded the usual top-dressing reforms: to prohibit usury, drinking and gambling, plus sport stadiums, plays on non-Islamic themes, the mini skirt and foreign tourists (who would bring their corrupt foreign ways with them). The coalition pact he forced on Ecevit provided for government assistance in the building of mosques, 'moral' instruction in primary and secondary schools and the accelerated training of imams. The result in the educational field is that while Turkey has 89 teacher training schools, in 1977 it had 244 schools for imams with 50 more to be opened. Turkes' exploitation of Islam takes the form of emphasizing the division between the Sunni majority and the large Shia, or *evlevi*, minority in eastern Turkey whom his propaganda accuses of practising and approving of adultery. It is because of the activities of these two parties, particularly the 'Grey Wolf' gangs of Turkes' group, that the campuses of Turkish universities have become battlefields.

Two half-states have also indulged in the same sort of

Islamic gesturing – when the Emirates introduced public flogging in 1977 and Kuwait banned the sale of pork, forbidden food in Islam, and considered banning co-education. The hard pressed regime of President Numeiry in 1974 took the same path towards introducing amputation and floggings with a committee to Islamize the constitution.

Even Muslim monarchs have not been above playing the Islamic card. In the last days of his reign King Farouk produced a wholly spurious genealogy tracing his descent from the Prophet. King Hassan II of Morocco makes the same claim, and despite a jet-set lifestyle now and again tries to invest himself with religious charisma. While even the recently deposed Shah, that most Westernized of monarchs, claimed in his autobiography to have seen religious signs and visions. None of these royal claims were or are very credible but the important thing is that they were made.

It is this class of political exploiters of Islam who give Islam a bad name and give militant Islam an even worse name. For what the rest of the world sees is a secular leader in a Muslim country who suddenly and for obvious reasons of political convenience 'gets religion'. They are educated, sophisticated men – professional politicians, professional men or generals, men of the world. But not knowing the deeper truths of their religion all that they have recourse to are the easily available appurtenances of Islam – its system of punishments. So it is entirely natural for the rest of the world to believe that if men of this calibre, experience and education embody their Islamic policies in amputations and whippings, there cannot be anything else to Islam except a very harsh penal code. But of course there is a lot more to Islam than the canonical punishments, and one should not in any case evaluate any religion, society or culture (Islam claims to be all of those) simply on the basis of its penal code. For men of religion – of any religion – to be backward looking is in this day and age almost taken for granted; but for secular Islamic leaders to take the soft option and to reach for the sword and the whip whenever they are in trouble is inexcusable. Perhaps Islam should count itself lucky that there have been so few exploiters of Islam among its secular leaders.

4

It would be positively un-Islamic for the professional men of religion in Islam not to take an interest and an active part in politics, for that would mean that they are indifferent to the fate of the umma, which they are not. One reason why the ulema are given a place in political life is because by and large they are a respected body of men in every Muslim country except Turkey and possibly Afghanistan and South Yemen. They are known to be conservative and traditionalist but that indeed has been one of their achievements – the preservation of the traditions of Islam in living, not mummified, form. Before looking at the 'politicking' of the ulema this tribute to their historic role seems in order: 'Traditional Islam has been held together through the tradition and organization of the ulema. These people, the learned men of Islam, have managed to this day to preserve their status as the proprietors of the symbols of Islam. Their exclusive right to interpret Islam has only recently come into dispute. They have also managed to preserve the medieval statement of Islam in all its essentials. This has been a great achievement for an institution as formless as this one.'[20] (In this section we will be dealing exclusively with the ulema in Sunni countries because the Shiah men of religion have their own special characteristics which merit separate treatment.)

As individuals ulema can be found active in the politics of every Muslim country, even if underground. In some countries they have organized themselves into recognized political groupings. Such are the Nahdatul Ulama in Indonesia; two groups in Pakistan, the Jamiat al Ulema i Islam and the Jamiat al Ulema i Pakistan; the sheikhs of al Azhar in Cairo and the Rabitah Ulama al Maghreb in Morocco; lastly the entire body of sheikhs in countries like Saudi Arabia which claim to be, already, Islamic states.

The Nahdatul Ulama was founded in 1926 in East Java which still remains its stronghold. It was originally started as a protest movement against Turkey's abolition of the Caliphate but it soon stated its local objectives which were to strengthen unity among the ulema, the spread of Islam, assistance to mosques and care for orphans and the poor. There were no political objectives in its programme and throughout the NU (to use the Indonesian acronym) has been rather quietist in the political field. In fact one of the first things it did was to go into business using funds from the religious endowments or *wakf*. It has always retained its links with the merchant class, and in class terms has spoken for the religious-minded bourgeoisie. It did not seek to confront the Dutch Indies administration and was given official recognition; by 1942 and the Japanese invasion it had 120 branches all over Indonesia. It trod warily under Japanese occupation and was recognized by them, though at the end of the Japanese period it did rise in arms against them. In the elections to the Indonesian constituent assembly the NU won eighteen per cent of the votes, and that has remained quite steadily the measure of its strength in Indonesia. During the debates on the place of Islam in the constitution, the NU propounded the integral Muslim line – that Indonesia should be an Islamic state based on the Koran and the Sharia, and this it has continued to assert, if quietly: this has been part of the NU's talent for survival. When the other Islamic party, Masjumi, was banned in 1960 the NU survived even in the radical atmosphere of Sukarno's final years, which is why it participated in almost every cabinet till the military take-over. Thus also it has been accused of opportunism and of not having a distinctive programme or ideology of its own. It has not needed to, for by endlessly re-stating its traditional and scholastic goals it is left free to man-oeuvre politically to ensure its survival. In 1971 General Suharto forced all the religious parties to join in what was called the United Development Party. And this party, to the surprise and chagrin of the military, won nearly thirty per cent of the votes in the election of 1977 and defeated the army's party in Jakarta. This figure indicates that the political strength of Islam remains intact in Indonesia despite implicit, and often explicit, army dis-approval. The dynamic element is represented by what survives of the modernist and reformist Masjumi Party, but the NU remains, quietly, the orthodox representative of one fifth of the Indonesian electorate.

The two ulema groupings in Pakistan follow more or less the same policy as that of the Nahdatul Ulama: a rigidly orthodox position on goals, not presented with any great vehemence, and tactical flexibility in methods. The most striking difference is that in Pakistan the ulema, though organized, did not form a political party as such but were content to remain a pressure group. They began with an initial disadvantage in Pakistan because many, perhaps most, of them had been opposed on Islamic grounds to the formation of the separate Muslim nation state of Pakistan. They soon made amends by becoming decently patriotic, by such acts as approving the Pakistani invasion of Kashmir. In the following years they took a very active part in debates on the constitution pressing for a full Islamic state based on the Sharia – but, as we have seen, to no effect. Such was their badgering of Ayub Khan whom they never forgave for removing the 'Islamic' appelation for the Republic of Pakistan in his 1962 constitution, that he devotes almost ten pages of his *Political Autobiography* to berating them.[21] His main charges against them are two: that they do not know the modern world; and that they want an Islamic state not as a matter of religious conviction but because it is only in such a state that with their limited outlook they will be able to gain power. Referring to their previous opposition to the formation of Pakistan he comments bitterly: 'If they had not been able to save the Muslims from Pakistan they must now save Pakistan from the Muslims.' After the downfall of Ayub Khan, in which the two associations of ulema, true to form, joined at a late stage and in no great strength, the ulema achieved a victory against the secular Muslim reformists. In the 1956 constitution an advisory council on Islamic ideology had been established to study the feasibility of an Islamic constitution; to this body had been added, in Ayub Khan's 1962 constitution, an Islamic research institute. The ulema considered the mere existence of the two bodies an insult to themselves and persistently suggested that the institute should be under the control of the ulema – an audacious request considering that the two bodies had been set up precisely in order to produce the sort of modernized Islamic thinking that the ulema were incapable of producing. What they achieved was to hamstring the two bodies and to force the institute to part with its director Fazlur Rahman, one of the clearest and wisest Islamic thinkers in the world today.

Under General Zia al Haq retribution has overtaken the Pakistani ulema: he has stolen almost all of their clothes, at least the main outer garments. They can, and almost certainly will, say that Pakistan still does not have an Islamic constitution and is not an Islamic state; but their most pressing demands have been met by the general, and as far as one can see not because of pressure from the ulema. The Pakistani ulema like their Indonesian counterparts could afford to rest their case on the Koran and Sunnah because, as in Indonesia, there was a reformist Islamic group to make the running. In Indonesia it was the Masjumi, in Pakistan it is the Jamaat i Islami of Pakistan.

The ulema which were grouped around the theological head-quarters of the Islamic world – the University of al Azhar at Cairo – need not detain us long. They quite simply have done and said what they have been told to do and say by the Egyptian government. The most charitable interpretation is that they have never recovered from the thorough shaking up they were sub-jected to under President Nasser. He in effect changed al Azhar out of all recognition; not being able to recognize itself, the oracle of al Azhar has been dumb ever since – a sad fate brought down on this ancient Islamic institution by its own traditional, but now overdone, docility. Al Azhar did express an opinion in the debate on the possible Islamization of the Egyptian consti-tution, which was the usual ulema claim for an Islamic state based on the Sharia.

The existence of an ulema organization in Morocco, the Rabitah Ulama al Maghreb, has been registered but it must be even more quietistic than the al Azhar group, for apart from the fact of its existence little is known of it.

The brotherhoods or tarikas, that very important and certainly most dynamic element in Islam over the centuries, have not played a significant part in militant Islam. Most of them are not activist and those that are are on the wane, even in areas like North Africa, where they were formerly omnipresent and strong. But they are there as a popular force and as a possible Islamic alternative. For instance, when Ayub Khan was facing opposi-tion from the ulema he turned for religious support to the *pirs*, the holy men outside Pakistan's religious establishment. The two new brotherhoods in Turkey, Risala i Nur and the Sule-manis, already have some political importance – particularly the former which played a role in the foundation of Erbakan's National Salvation Party and is also giving open support to the Justice Party. In the Sudan the Mahdiya brotherhood is the base of the Ansar movement which in turn is the foundation of the Umma Party, so much so that the brotherhood is, and has been, involved in everything the Ansar and Umma do politically – including the abortive coup against Numeiry in July 1977. The Ansar/Umma group under Sadek al Mahdi were for a time reconciled with Numeiry but have split away again because they oppose his approval of Sadat's peace with Israel. The Mahdiya brotherhood are likely to continue to play an active and perhaps violent part in Sudanese politics.

Overall we can see that the Muslim men of religion, even those in organized groups or political parties, have not played a very activist or dynamic role in militant Islam. But they are of great importance as a strong, silent pressure group waiting and watching in the wings. Much of the action taken by the militants in several Muslim countries was to counter or anticipate possible criticism from the religious establishment. This has been especially so in Pakistan. The ulema, conscious of their age-old traditional role of reiterating Islam's truth, can afford to bide their time. The rulers of the day can bully this or that group of ulema in such and such a country. But nobody can bully Islam, and the ulema say that collectively they are Islam.

5

We now come to the most serious, dynamic and, for the future, important element in militant Islam today. It is also the least known, not only in the West but in the Muslim countries as well. Names like Jinnah, Bhutto or Sadat are household words, and the collective 'ulema' or 'ayatollah', are also well known. Almost unknown are the groups that are trying the very difficult task of 'rethinking Islam in modern terms'. These are: the Muslim Brotherhood in Egypt; the Party for the Liberation of Islam in Jordan; the Jamaat i Islami of Pakistan led by Maulana Abul al Maududi; the Masjumi Party in Indonesia led by Mohammed Natsir; the group around Allal al Fassi in Morocco; the Iran Liberation Movement of Mehdi Bazargan, the present prime minister of Iran; the Mujahidin al Khalk in Iran whose spiritual father was Dr Ali Shariati; and, with reservations, the Libya of Colonel Gaddafi.

These men and groups, though Westernized, are not Westernizers but modernizers; though Islamic believers, they are not fundamentalists but reformers. There are wide variations of approach and even of objective between them: while some want an Islamic society within an Islamic state, *based* on the Koran and the Sunnah, others want an Islamic society within an Islamic order, *derived* from the Koran and the Sunnah; some accept violence as a means, others do not. What unifies them is an attempt to make Islam, which is indubitably alive today, relevant to the special needs of today.

Writing over fifty years ago, Rashid Rida, who was one of their number, hoped for the emergence of what he called an 'Islamic progressive party', somewhere between the ulema and the Westernizers, which could make changes while preserving the moral basis of the Islamic community. Such groups have emerged and have presented their programmes of change but have not so far made much impact; they are not well known, even in the Muslim world.

The best known of them is the Majallat al Ikhwan al Muslimin, the Society of the Muslim Brothers, because its use of violence has brought it notoriety and because it has always operated, and still does, in many Arab countries outside Egypt. The society[22] was founded in 1925 by Hasan al Banna who was then twenty-two years old; it was his sole creation and still bears the stamp of his powerful and truly charismatic personality. In his teens he became a member of the tarika of the Hasafiya Brothers and remained a member for twenty years: just one more Islamic leader to be influenced by Sufism. He became a member of several societies for the purification of Islamic life and the combating of missionary influence, and when a student in Cairo he reproached the al Azhar authorities for being ineffective in the face of missionary and atheistic currents. It was during his nineteen years as a government primary school teacher that he started the brotherhood in Ismailia with six members who accepted his authority as 'soldiers for Islam'. After four years of hard work the brotherhood had branches all over the Suez Canal Zone and had started its consistent programme of building mosques, schools, clubs or small home industries. Soon after his transfer to Cairo he started the formation of 'scout' battalions and the publication of magazines; recruiting went on so successfully that by 1939 the brotherhood was a force that had already attracted the attention of Egyptian politicians; so much so that in 1941 Banna was arrested for his forceful denunciations of the

British. About a year later Banna founded what came to be called the 'secret apparatus' of armed men. Publicly the Muslim Brothers started still more schools and technical institutes, for students and adults, some small industries, and welfare and medical services in their own hospitals, clinics and dispensaries. Sporadic contact was also maintained with Nasser's Free Officer movement through Anwar Sadat. In the middle 1940s the brotherhood, because of its size, discipline and anti-communist stance, received favours from various Egyptian governments including permission to start a daily newspaper in 1946. Inevitably the brotherhood moved into competitive antagonism with the main secular nationalist party, the Wafd, and violent clashes between them occurred all over the country, especially at the universities. These were temporarily set aside when in 1947 Palestine was partitioned and the first Arab–Israeli war began. Armed and trained volunteers of the brotherhood preceded the Egyptian army into Sinai and took an active though small-scale part in the fighting. In Cairo, meanwhile, throughout 1948 the brotherhood engineered a whole series of violent acts, including its first assassination, so that when the government accidentally unearthed evidence of the 'secret apparatus' it dissolved the brotherhood altogether in the December of that year. Ten days after the dissolution a brotherhood gunman assassinated the prime minister, Nokrashi Pasha. Six weeks later Banna himself was gunned down by members of the government's political police.

It was three years before the ban on their existence was lifted and the Muslim Brothers could resume activity under a new leader, Hudaibi, a judge of twenty-five years standing and a very different sort of man to Hassan al Banna. Following Egypt's abrogation of its treaty with Britain armed clashes took place within the British-controlled Canal Zone in which brotherhood volunteers took part. These clashes in turn culminated in the burning of central Cairo on Black Sunday, 25th January 1952, in which the brotherhood participated prominently. This in turn led to the army coup in July of that year, led by Nasser. Because of their numerous past contacts with the army the brotherhood greeted the coup with joy; most likely it was asked to join the first military cabinet but decided not to. The Muslim Brothers were exempted from the dissolution that was imposed on all other parties, but the *entente* was not to endure because the brotherhood was too powerful and independent a group for any government to tolerate. Its dissolution was once again ordered in January 1954, but the order was not strictly enforced. There could not ever be real cooperation between the army regime and the brotherhood, and on the 26th October 1954 the brotherhood attempted the public assassination of Nasser in Alexandria. Six culprits were hanged including Hudaibi and the movement was efficiently crushed.

It remained so for twenty years. Then, under the regime of their first contact with Nasser's group of Free Officers, the brotherhood has slowly begun to come to life again publicly, or rather semi-publicly, because it is still officially banned. Given official tolerance, its tight organization, and the devotion of its membership it has become incontestably the single most powerful organization in Egypt outside the army. In impressive displays of the power of its semi-clandestine organization, it has without any public announcement arranged large prayer meetings in the centre of Cairo with members attending from all over Egypt: dress rehearsals, perhaps, for a more turbulent occasion. In fact an army-cum-brotherhood regime is the only likely or possible successor to that of Sadat. The brotherhood strongly condemned Sadat's visit to Jerusalem and has bitterly denounced the Camp David peace treaty.

Apart from its violent and bloody history the Society of Muslim Brothers was most notable for the superb organization imposed on it by Banna. In its tightly structured headquarters the most interesting of the six committees in the secretariat was that dealing with the Muslim world subdivided into six subsections, indicating the importance given by the brotherhood to its foreign relations. Others of these committees dealt with 'labour and peasants', 'students' and 'the professions'. There were four ascending degrees of membership and the basic unit was called a 'family' rather than a 'cell', and usually consisted of five and sometimes ten members. Membership figures for the brotherhood can only be guesses. One such guess is that it had somewhere between half a million and a million members and active supporters at its peak. Its large-scale humanitarian and small-scale industrial enterprises, and its 'Society for Islamic Social Insurance' were one beneficent aspect of the brotherhood's activities. But with its battalions of 'rovers', in effect a private army which claimed to number 40,000 at one moment, and the 'secret apparatus' which even Banna did not fully control and which practised the 'art of death' (to use a phrase of Banna's), the brotherhood appears as an overly-militant and positively menacing organization. So it was; and so, in secret, it probably still is. But it also had a third aspect: it attempts to lay down, through innumerable pamphlets, the Islamic answers to political, social and economic problems, with which we shall deal in the next chapter. The brotherhood, it is claimed, had branches in many Arab countries; the Sudan, Iraq, Jordan, Yemen, Saudi Arabia and North Africa have been mentioned. Its members are said to have played a leading part in the student demonstrations in Morocco against the presence of the ex-Shah of Iran in that country. Its strong presence in the Sudan is confirmed by the fact that when in 1978 Numeiry tried to Islamize the Sudanese constitution he released from jail Hassan al Turabi, the local leader of the brotherhood, former dean of the law school of Khartoum University where the brotherhood has a strong base, to join the committee on Islamization. The brotherhood is also said to be very strong both on the campus and in the faculties of the University of Jordan in Amman.[23]

These Jordanian brothers may in fact really be members of a Palestinian counterpart of the brotherhood. This is the Hizb al Tahrir al Islam, or Party for the Liberation of Islam, founded sometime in the 1950s by Sheikh Takieddin Nabhani who was a judge in the Sharia Court of Haifa in pre-partition Palestine and subsequently settled in Nablus. He died in 1978. The party has been banned almost from its inception so facts about it are hard to come by, particularly concerning its membership and organization, though some of its ideas will be referred to later. Its members are said to be found not only in Jordan but all over the Levant, and for a time it had its own newspapers in Beirut. Its presence in Libya has been officially confirmed by Gaddafi. The Party for the Liberation of Islam differs from the brotherhood mainly in that while the latter did not wish to be thought of as a particular party, rather as a *jamia* or 'society', this group is a *hizb*, a political party as such, and so more akin to the Jamaat i Islami in Pakistan.

One final comment on the brotherhood deserves quotation

since it comes from an Israeli commentator. After mentioning the brotherhood's programmatic linked slogans: 'Allah is our God. The Prophet is our Leader. The Koran is our constitution. Jihad is our way. Death for Allah's sake is our supreme desire,' the Israeli writer says: 'There is little doubt that its essence, its message and its teachings will live as long as Islam itself.'[24] Well, for the next fifty years – two more generations – anyway.

Though the Muslim Brothers and the Jamaat i Islami are very similar in their objectives and in their organization, the ways in which these organizations set about trying to achieve their objectives are very different indeed. Not for the Jamaat the conspirational secrecy, the military apparatus and the ruthless violence of the brotherhood. At its peak the brotherhood was a mass movement; the Jamaat, not necessarily by choice, has been an élitist movement.

There exists one considerable similarity at the time of writing. If the brotherhood is the single most powerful factor in Egyptian political life after the army, in Pakistan the Jamaat is the dominating civilian element in the government because of the army, or at least because of the support of the army's leader, General Zia al Haq.

Like the brotherhood the Jamaat is the creation of one man – Maulana Abul al Maududi who was born in 1903 in south-central India of a not especially prosperous family. Many of his ancestors were leading members of Sufi orders but he himself does not seem to have Sufi connections. For the most part self-educated, Maududi began life as a journalist and remained one until he founded the Jamaat in 1941. Because of doctrinal objections to nationalism he was very strongly opposed to the creation of the Muslim nation of Pakistan: 'What is selfishness in individual life is nationalism in social life. A nationalist is naturally narrow-minded and niggardly.' His writings, mostly on Islamic subjects, attracted the attention of Iqbal who invited him in 1937 to carry on his literary work on the premises of a *waqf*, or charitable foundation, at Pathankot in the Punjab. In 1947 this area was allotted to India under partition and Maududi moved across the new nearby frontier to Pakistan. Failing to come to terms with the new state of whose existence he disapproved, he continued to voice that disapproval and was jailed by the Pakistani authorities from 1948 to 1950. Thereafter he became reconciled to the new Muslim state and for the past forty years has devoted his very considerable mental energy and that of his disciplined and well organized party to the task of converting this Muslim state into a full-fledged Islamic state. As the lukewarm wording of the Islamic clauses of Pakistan's three constitutions indicate, neither the Jamaat nor the two organizations of ulema met with much success – until the advent of General Zia.

Despite an equivocal statement of support for Pakistan's invasion of Kashmir (because the Pakistan government had admitted aggression) he was imprisoned. In local elections in 1957 in the Punjab the Jamaat fielded fifty-three candidates; even though it gained 200,000 votes it was able to elect only one candidate. It has had the same humiliating record of electoral failure ever since. One of the Jamaat's less creditable actions was its vigorous support of the agitation against the Ahmadiya community in 1953 which resulted in violence and fatalities. For his part in the movement Maududi was arrested and sentenced to death. He refused to appeal for mercy and the sentence was eventually commuted to fourteen years' imprisonment. He remained in jail for two years, up to April 1955. In 1956 the Jamaat declared itself satisfied with the rather meagre Islamic clauses of the 1956 Pakistan constitution which was however swept aside by the military coup of 1958. Military rule of any sort was declared un-Islamic by the Jamaat and it was officially banned along with all other political parties. It came to life again only after Ayub Khan permitted party political activity in 1962. It was again banned in 1964 and Maududi was jailed again for six months. Though its opposition to Ayub Khan continued, the Jamaat was among the first to declare that the Indo-Pakistan war of 1965 was a true jihad, though it was very unhappy with the way it was ended in the Tashkent Declaration under Russian auspices. The party took a prominent part in the popular movement that brought about the downfall of Ayub Khan in 1969 and campaigned vigorously in the 1970 general and provincial elections. It put forward 488 candidates of which only eight were elected. The Jamaat consoled itself with the fact that two and a half million votes had been cast in its favour even though it had a full-time membership of only 2,500. In 1971 it supported Pakistan in the military action in east Pakistan that ended with independence for Bangladesh. Under the Bhutto regime the

Jamaat joined in the renewed agitation against the Ahmadiya which forced Bhutto to agree to declaring it a non-Muslim minority. Only after General Zia al Haq took power in July 1977 did a spectacular change in the Jamaat's fortunes take place, because of the general's support for the movement. It became an important constituent of the Pakistan National Alliance which provides civilian backing for the Zia regime.

Thus the Jamaat has had a rather inglorious and unsuccessful record, riddled with inconsistencies and self-contradictions of policy. But, as with the Muslim Brothers, it has simultaneously done a lot of serious rethinking of Islam which may be its more enduring legacy.

The Jamaat is tightly organized but with all real power vested in the leader or Amir, Maududi himself. Its small membership is due to a high measure of selectivity – granted only after long probation. But it is an effective membership because one in every fifteen members is a full-time paid worker; the part-time sympathizers are said to number several hundred thousand. Like the brotherhood the Jamaat gives great importance to publicity and propaganda and produces it in quantity: Maududi himself has written over one hundred and twenty books and pamphlets, and has made over a thousand speeches. It has an active public welfare department: as far back as 1952 the party was running 50 fixed and 11 mobile dispensaries. It later established several hospitals. Special sections work among peasants, workers, students and ulema.

The Jamaat Party has always had a peculiar position in Pakistani public opinion. People do not vote for it but they respect it, equally because of the intelligence and integrity of Maududi himself, because of the singleminded devotion of its followers, and because of the consistency with which it has maintained its ultimate aim. It has had very changeable relations with the two ulema organizations, usually opposing them, yet they almost fear it, and in times of crisis they willingly have allowed Maududi to be their spokesman. Though not a man of religion, he is recognized as having by far the most comprehensive grasp of the theory and practice of Islamic polity of anyone in Pakistan. Hence these two comments by outside observers: 'To many Muslims in Pakistan Maududi is just another commentator; to others he is a commentator turned politician. To all, however, he does reflect and represent the value of Islam, the spiritual importance of a faith that will not be abandoned; however differently individuals might interpret it. In this lies his strength.'[25] And: 'I am almost inclined to think that only Sayyid Abul al Maududi and his Jamaat i Islami have a well defined objective and work for it with singlemindedness of purpose and determination, making use of means copied from totalitarian political philosophies and movements.'[26]

At its birth in November 1945 the Masjumi Party of Indonesia was a political illegitimate. At first it was not even a separate party but, as its full title denotes, simply a coordinating body – Masjumi is one of Indonesia's inescapable acronyms for Madjlis Sjuro Muslimin Indonesia, or Consultative Council of Indonesia Muslims – and its membership and leadership had to be drawn from existing bodies, namely Nahdatul Ulema and Muhammadiya. It was not long before Masjumi developed into an independent organization. It was wholly a creation of the Japanese occupation regime and its earlier policy statements overflow with fulsome protestations of loyalty to Japan's 'greater east Asia co-prosperity sphere' – in other words, the Japanese Empire. If quite quickly Masjumi acquired respectability it was because it was joined and led by people like Muhammad Natsir. Even though he had all his education in Dutch schools in Java (and had turned down the offer of a scholarship to study in Holland – shades of Snouck Hurgronje!) he very early on showed his interest in reformist Islam, and joined a party advocating such policies. In the early 1930s Natsir induced his party to launch an 'Islamic education' project which led to the establishment of a number of schools, and also a teacher's training school. He therefore had a record of public service behind him when he became one of Masjumi's leading figures in 1945. As had been the case with Muhammadiya and Sarekat Islam before it, Masjumi rapidly ballooned into a huge unorganized mass party. From the start its leadership was split between the older, traditional leaders and the younger group called the 'religious socialists', who took their ideas from Abduh, and of whom Natsir was one. After the Japanese exit Masjumi played its part in the final struggle against the Dutch, was one of the constituents in the first independent government, and Natsir was one of the several Masjumi cabinet ministers in coalition cabinets. In 1950 Natsir became prime minister of Indonesia because by then Masjumi was the largest party in parliament, holding 50 of its 237 seats – and that level of around twenty per cent has remained Masjumi's popular strength ever since (much the same as that of Nahdatul Ulema, so that these two Islamic parties between them control forty per cent of the Indonesian electorate). However, the fervour of independence did not long endure and three years later Masjumi left the government never to return. It had already tried and failed to have Indonesia declared an Islamic state. By 1956 Masjumi moved into vocal opposition to Sukarno's slide towards 'guided democracy' and one-man rule. But Sukarno seemed to be riding the crest of a popular wave and Masjumi's opposition was brushed aside. In frustration the party backed a coup in 1958 based in Sumatra where a rival government was established. It was a hurried, badly planned move and was quickly snuffed out. Natsir and other leaders were imprisoned and Masjumi was banned in 1960 and has stayed banned ever since. After the army ousting of Sukarno the ban has been eased to the extent that the party's existence was accepted but under a new label – Parmusi – to act as a counterpart to its old rival Nahdatul Ulema. But in 1971 all the religious parties were obliged to coalesce into the United Development Party, which took thirty per cent of the votes in the 1977 elections – ten per cent less than it should have, because of heavy army pressure.

Because it has always functioned as a party, and not as a 'society' like the brotherhood and, partially, the Jamaat, the Masjumi has not had a tight or secretive organization. It functioned in the open, giving much emphasis to propaganda and to social welfare, especially education. In the same way in Egypt the Islamic UDP is accepted as the most credible successor to the present army regime.[27]

Born in 1910 in Fes, from which his famous clan took its name, Allal al Fassi was barely out of his teens when he became interested in the problem of rejuvenating and modernizing Islam. Attracted to the teachings of Afghani and Abduh he soon saw that the activism of the former was less valuable than the thoughtful reformism of the latter. But because Morocco was in the throes of a nationalist movement al Fassi's work for militant Islam had to await the liberation of his country. He was one of the two leading figures of the Istiqlal Party in that struggle and was exiled by the French for nine years, 1937 to 1946, in Gabon. Though set free he was not allowed to return to Morocco and in the years to follow led the fight for freedom on the world stage, especially at the UN. Only in 1956, after an absence of nineteen years, could he return to his country. When he became minister of state for Islamic affairs in 1961 al Fassi was able to gather around him a group of like-minded reformers. This never became a formalized body but it was through these disciples that he made his active contribution to militant Islam rather than through his own Istiqlal Party, which remained a purely political organization. In fact al Fassi's real work for modernist Islam came through his writings, particularly his spiritual autobiography *Self-criticism*, published in 1952. He had his ministry publish a series of books on Islam for, as he said, 'It is rather paradoxical that so far the books on Islam have been written by Western scholars.' The time had come 'to give the word to those who really live Islam'.

After Hassan II became king, al Fassi found it increasingly difficult to remain in the government; he quit it in January 1963 and has remained in opposition ever since. This act of protest was directed against the king's refusal to move towards the economic liberation of Morocco, to complement its political independence. Since then al Fassi has written much, and worked in the Istiqlal as much as was permitted to him after a serious road accident that left him partially paralysed; since 1970 he has been in active and open opposition to the regime of Hassan II. Al Fassi has thus, perforce, had much time to develop his thoughts on Islamic renovation, to be discussed below.[28]

It is singularly unfortunate that not much is known,[29] or has been published in English or French, on the secular militant Islamic group that, in tandem with the Ayatollah Khomeini, is now in charge of Iran. This is the Iran Liberation Movement of Dr Mehdi Bazargan, the present prime minister. Until about 1963 it was a part of the middle-of-the-road, liberal National Front coalition of parties, but it differs from the other parties in that alliance by being specifically an Islamic party. Parallel to, but unconnected with the ILP was the activity of Dr Ali Shariati, whose pictures now adorn the streets and buildings of Tehran alongside those of Ayatollah Khomeini and Dr Mossadeqh. An academic, he acquired a doctorate in sociology from the Sorbonne, and after his return to Iran he taught that subject at the universities of Meshed and Tehran. He produced a volume of his lectures, *Islamshenasi* – 'Islamology' – and many pamphlets. His object was to reconstruct Shiah Islamic thought in the light of Marxism, existentialism and phenomenology. Camus was one of his mentors, and his style in polemic is akin to that of Sartre – punchy and, in Persian, very effective. His politics were radical and he called for a revolutionary overthrow of the secular state and the regime of the Shah, and also of what he called Safavid Islam, the religious and political views of the established ulema and ayatollahs. Against this he set Alavid Islam – Islam, but always Shiah Islam, it must be noted, in its state of original purity. He was very Persian in his idealization of Ali and Hussain. In the middle 1960s he lectured publicly on his ideas of religious reform in the Hussainieh Ershad – the centre for Hussaini studies in Tehran which drew large and enthusiastic audiences of young people, especially from the university. His views took the younger educated class with a shock of surprise, for the educated young assumed that Islam was a 'backward' 'Arab' religion. Yet here was a Westernized intellectual using the latest intellectual terminology, telling them that while Marxism and existentialism had failed to solve the problem of morality for Modern Man, Islam had the answers. His achievement was to make Shiah Islam seem relevant, respectable and revolutionary to his young listeners. He was obviously a person, like Afghani, the full impress of whose personality depended on face-to-face contact; in writing, in *Islamshenasi* for instance, his ideas seem thin and arid; his attempts to reduce the problems of the universe to schematic diagrams are faintly ridiculous. His revolutionary forcefulness may explain why many of his disciples are to be found in the Mujahadin al Khalk, the Fighters of the People, a left-wing urban guerrilla group which now has a Marxist–Leninist faction which somehow still remains Islamic. Dr Shariati was, in the best sense of the word, an agitator and inescapably he was picked up by Savak, the Shah's notorious secret police; his death in 1975, when he was about fifty years old, was partly due to the treatment he received at their hands. He would seem to have favoured an Islamic order rather than an Islamic state, and was interested more in the religious and moral foundations for such an order than in the details of its political structure.

Any study of modern militant Islam cannot leave out the Libyan regime of Colonel Gaddafi. But can one take it seriously? If one pares away the two 'universal theories' that Gaddafi has adjoined to his straightforward Islamic reforms then those reforms may be taken as seriously as in any other country. In 1972 after prolonged public debate the Sharia was accepted as the law of the land, in its most literal interpretation; the payment of zakat, obligatory alms, was introduced and riba, usury, was to be examined by a committee. All this was a serious change for Libya, but nothing unusual. However, the colonel went on to make Islam the basis for what he called a 'new universal theory' of Islam, which merely means that anyone who is a monotheist is a Muslim. Islam was also made the basis for his 'third international theory' – though this by now may have changed, for in the latest edition of his *Green Book* (a little 'green book' on democracy, and a littler 'green book' on economics) the word 'Islam' does not occur, even in the context that all law must be based on religion. What this theory amounts to and what connection it has with Islam is altogether obscure, for like the little red book of Mao, the green books are a collection of portentous platitudes. Evidently the colonel has not taken to heart the words of advice from his idol, Nasser, who said, 'Don't try to invent electricity, it has been done already.'[30]

A small group of 'rethinkers' was emerging in the other two north African countries in the 1950s and '60s proceeding much along the same lines as the group around Allal al Fassi. Men such as Malek Bennabi in Algeria and, in Tunisia, those in the ministry of education who drew up the programme for religious instruction in the secondary schools, as well as the writer Mohammed Taalbi.

These 'rethinking' movements not only have similar goals but have resemblances in their structure, organization and leadership. Incidentally, the Jamaat and the Muslim Brothers have maintained steady contact with each other and there have been some links between the brotherhood and the movement in Iran. Their leaders are all laymen: an academic, an educator, a school teacher, a journalist, an engineer; in fact Natsir seems to be the only professional politician among them. The level of the leadership cadres is rising: when the brotherhood was rounded up, after the attempted assassination of Nasser, it was found to contain Egypt's leading mathematician, middle-ranking army officers, successful businessmen and university teachers. The groups around Allal al Fassi and Mehdi Bazargan are studded with doctors of philosophy from the universities of France and the United States. The membership too is slowly rising in the social scale. The Masjumi had, and has, a mass following and comprises all classes, but the brotherhood and Jamaat were essentially lower-middle-class movements. The lower middle class is not the most admirable state of society, for it seems to have a fatal weakness for authoritarian and totalitarian movements, from Japan to Germany, from Britain to the United States and it was doubtless the certitude of the Jamaat and brotherhood that attracted them. Another main constituent of membership has been students of high school and university. This membership implies that the movements are essentially urban: the peasants are with the ulema.

It is a disciplined, devoted and obedient membership, firmly organized in a cellular pattern. It is also highly motivated, because propaganda within and outside the movement has always been given great importance. The emphasis placed on education once again underlines the reaching out to the younger generation.

As a whole, in their countries of origin these movements are respected for their integrity, feared for their singlemindedness and grudgingly admired for their honesty in a context of endemic national corruption. But they are very seldom liked.

It should not be thought that because of their education the leadership of these militant movements consists of pleasant liberal gentlemen. They are tough, realistic operators who have not shrunk from using violence and will not do so again. Perhaps it is the repression to which they have all been subjected that has toughened them. Their worst fault is a narrow intolerance of other ideas: even the calm, mild-mannered, soft-spoken Natsir is quite unyielding when it comes to his party's programme. Because of their tactical clumsiness they have not been successful politically; if the Bazargan group and the Jamaat are near the centre of power now it is because other people put them there, rather than by their own efforts. They have done foolish and cruel things, so that their teaching is very much of the order of *do as I tell you but don't do as I do*. Unworthy vessels? Yes, to some extent, but still striving towards something bigger and better than themselves. Although, as we have said, the leaders of the rethinkers are laymen, perhaps we should see them as being in the mould of the flawed priests of Graham Greene.

6

An explanation has to be given of the striking difference between the political role of the ulema in Sunni countries and that of the men of religion in Iran. We have seen that even in those countries, such as Indonesia and Pakistan, where the Sunni ulema are organized and active in politics they are never dynamically so and, almost deliberately, hang back cautiously from any position of leadership; they have seldom if ever taken the initiative. Such has never been the case in Iran, where the Shiah ulema have always been the dynamic initiating leaders in every national crisis.

Visual evidence of the difference between Sunni and Shiah social practice (irrelevant to the point under discussion) was presented in the Independence Day of Algeria and the day of Ayatollah Khomeini's return to Tehran. On the former the streets of Algeria were full of the cover-all robes of Algerian women – white from top to toe. In Tehran the streets were dense with the all black cover-all chador.

Almost four centuries of history give an explanation. Since 1502 Imamate Shiism has been the official religion of the Persian state, and as the established faith it inevitably became structured and hierarchical, like any other state organ. However, it has never, and this is an important variation, been an official part of the governmental structure. It was a part of the establishment but never became an established Church. A national faith in the Shiah form which differentiated Iran from all its Sunni neighbours isolated her, but provided a good basis for the development of nationalism in the nineteenth century.

There are also several socio-religious reasons for the difference. The Shiah believer gives greater authority to his ulema than the Sunni have done to theirs. This comes about because of the basic Shiah respect for whoever is believed to have an element of *baraka*, personal spiritual power, which all Shiah ulema have, graduated according to their level in the hierarchy. The Shiah ulema are more centrally organized than their Sunni counterparts. Because of this they have been more effective in maintaining the solidarity of their organization and its independence from governmental control. The Shiah ulema have also not been so strongly challenged in their authority by the Iranian government as the Sunni men of religion have been. This was due to the strange circumstance that the main centres of the Shiah faith, the shrines at Najaf and Kerbela, are outside Iran; so whenever leading ulema were threatened by authority in Iran they simply moved over the border into Iraq, as Ayatollah Khomeini did and as many ulema did in the time of the last Shah's father, Reza Khan. Because of Iran's insularity the Shiah ulema were also relatively less challenged by the forces of modernity. Iran until recently was more backward than its Arab neighbours and so was less secularized. The various modernist Islamic movements in the rest of the Islamic world expressed themselves in Sunni terms because the rest of the Islamic world is Sunni. And modernism was conveyed through foreign languages which were much less widely known in Iran than in the Arab countries.

The nature of the Shiah hierarchy in itself ensured that the Shiah ulema kept in close touch with local believers. Promotion in the hierarchy was not ordained by any ecclesiastical authority but was produced by a slow-moving consensus of respect among the congregation of each mosque, which evaluated their local ulema according to their piety, their religious knowledge, their approachability and qualities of leadership.

Also the hierarchy could, literally, afford to be independent of the government as the mosques had ample funds of their own from the regular payment of zakat and income from religious endowments, or wakf, lands and property.

The political prestige of the ulema was enhanced because it became established tradition that ulema who were subservient to the government were spiritually inferior to those who maintained a position of distanced independence, for Iranians have always had a low opinion of their governments. This is why Ayatollah Khomeini, who refused to knuckle under to the Shah or to stop speaking out when the other senior Ayatollahs did keep silent, is now acknowledged to be the most superior, though not the most senior, ayatollah of them all. He earned his superiority.

Observers of the popular movement in Iran which, during the latter half of 1978, generated enough strength to uproot the Shah and his regime, were puzzled by one aspect of it: it was apparently very well organized and yet no organization as such was visible. The evidences of organization were only too clear – the disciplined control of vast emotional crowds, the thousands of banners inscribed with the same messages, the well orchestrated slogans, protest songs and poems; the leaflets, mimeographed sheets and cassettes bearing the exhortations of the then exiled Ayatollah Khomeini which were being distributed in the towns and cities of Iran within a matter of days, even hours, of their being issued from the Ayatollah's headquarters near Paris. The organization that made all this possible was invisible because it had been part of the human landscape of Iran for centuries and was taken for granted: it was the organization of the Shiah 'Church'. The framework of this structure is Iran's 180,000 mullahs with the even more numerous mosque officials and shrine attendants they have around them. This body of clerics is a unified grouping because, at some time or other, they all passed through the theological training schools in the holy city of Qom. The majority of them are simple village boys who after their training in Qom are sent back to their villages and remain there as the centre of village life for the rest of their careers: the humble nuts and bolts of the strong country-wide Shiah organization. (One source of Ayatollah Khomeini's popularity and power is that he still speaks with his original peasant accent.) The Shiah organization is strong because of the respect given to its members by the ordinary Iranian Shiah: the village cleric will not remain long in position if he cannot be trusted enough to receive the various and sizeable taxes that Shiahs pay into their community fund; it was this fund which provided the financial sinews of the revolution. To rise in the Shiah hierarchy the Shiah cleric has to have the qualifications of leadership, learning, piety and poverty, and this last is especially essential for the highest grade of all, the Ayatollahs who embody the power of renunciation. Hence it was no great problem for the Shiah organization to put its own armed militia on to the streets of Iran's cities to fight and then take over from the disintegrating army of the Shah. This force was often led into combat by men of religion carrying guns. It was also only too easy for it to set up the Khomeini committees or *komitehs* that became the really effective government of Iran after the Shah's exit. In the long run, however, the militia and the komitehs are likely to prove more a curse than a blessing for the cause of militant Islam in Iran because they are too intolerant, vengeful and unaware of the larger issues of modern life.

We can distinguish four groups among those Muslims who have responded to the many-sided challenge of the West. Two are religious: the ulema, and the brotherhoods and holy men; and two are lay: the religious-minded reformers and modernizers, and the non-religious or anti-religious secular nationalist Westernizers. We have dealt directly with the first three groups and indirectly with the fourth, because the exploiters of Islam have all come from that group; but it is important to note that the exploiters are a very small part of the nationalist Westernizers. These have not figured prominently so far in this account because they came to the forefront only just before and after the success of the nationalist movements (of which they were not the sole leaders). But after independence the struggle between the nationalists and the other three groups, and of these three groups with them and with each other, furnish practically the whole domestic history of the Muslim countries in the past few decades.

The depth of some of the cleavages can seem really alarming to the onlooker, especially to a non-Muslim onlooker. One such wrote in 1960: 'Unless somehow there is a fusion or synthesis between the two outlooks [of the Westernizers and the scholar-jurists, the ulema] the Islamic world as we have known it will cease to exist.'[31] Twenty years have passed and there are no signs that such a degree of alarm and despondency is at all justified. Even among the smaller group of rethinkers, who should be hanging together lest they hang separately, there is in some quarters ferocious antagonism. Witness these words of Colonel Gaddafi: 'I do not think that the Muslim Brothers represent a Muslim philosophy in the true sense of the word . . . they are against socialism, against Arab unity, against Arab nationalism: in so far as they preach Islamic unity they cannot but oppose Arab unity . . . both they and the Islamic Liberation Party (of Sheikh Nabhani) are mere agents of the West . . .' and so on, leading to accusations of payment by the CIA and threats of imprisonment against members of the two organizations. Gaddafi could claim that they were foreign organizations anyway, coming from Egypt and Jordan respectively, but even when wholly within their own countries the four groups, on their own or in various permutations and combinations, vigorously oppose each other.

However shifting, and sometimes shifty, the alliances, there are two groups which are invariably opposed to each other – the religious reformers and the nationalist Westernizers; there is much less antagonism between the ulema and the brotherhoods, perhaps because they do retain the connecting link of Islam.

This is the pattern of opposition and alliance in the post-independence period of these Muslim countries:

Indonesia a struggle between reformers and nationalists, with the latter allied to the ulema.

Pakistan antagonism between the ulema and the reformers, and also between the reformers and the Westernizers; with the Westernizers allied to the brotherhoods in the time of Ayub Khan, and allied to the ulema during the Bhutto period.

Turkey the struggle was at first between the ulema and the Westernizers (Kemalist variety) and then between the brotherhoods and the Westernizers; more recently the ulema, brotherhoods and pseudo-reformers have joined against the secular Westernizers.

Egypt ulemas and Westernizers have joined to combat the reformers; while the reformers have, occasionally, allied themselves with the tarikas, as the Muslim Brothers did.

Iran the ulema, brotherhoods and reformers have been and are in alliance against the Westernizers.

Morocco the reformers, in partial alliance with the ulema (through Allal al Fassi) oppose the Westernizers; partially allied to the brotherhoods.

Algeria a curious situation here, since the purely secular Westernizer is officially not supposed to exist because the one-party state is committed to an Islamic society; but in the recent past the ulema and the reformers were hostile to the brotherhoods.

Sudan the reformers, closely allied to the brotherhoods struggle against the Westernizers, not so closely allied to the ulema.

No peace in the House of Islam. All these crisscrossing antagonisms came to the surface after independence, almost giving the impression that things were better under foreign domination; but that is hardly a judgement that anyone would agree with.

There was one single cause for these conflicts – Islam, or rather Islam's place in the society of the newly independent countries. There is no escaping this issue in Muslim countries, because of the very nature of Islam itself. If no decision is taken about the part that Islam is to play in a Muslim society, or if it is decided to exclude Islam from that society and to make it merely a matter of personal piety as was the case in Turkey, then Islam becomes a permanent irritant, an indigestible substance that blocks the normal functioning of the body politic.

As between the ulema and the reformers the tussle is not so much over the place of Islam in a Muslim society but more over what sort of Islam it should be and who should be the mediators and interpreters of Islam to the rest of society. For the reformers the ulema call of 'back to the Koran' is not enough, because there are wide areas of modern life for which the Koran does not legislate. In such areas there has to be an application of ijtihad, independent judgement, on the basis of Koranic principles. Here the ulema and the reformers are at odds again as to the formulation of those principles and also as to whether they should be rigidly proximate to the Koran or flexibly derivative. The biggest dispute concerning ijtihad is over who should exercise it: the ulema naturally argue that it is only the fully qualified and learned scholar-jurists, namely the ulema themselves, who can be given the responsibility for ijtihad; whereas the reformers say that qualified laymen like themselves can join with the ulema in making independent judgements. Also, the reformers say, weight should be given to ijma, the consensus of the community; this is not unformed and uninformed public opinion but the seriously developed ideas of religious laymen – like the members of the brotherhood and Jamaat, or the party councils of the Masjumi or the Iran Liberation Movement. What the ulema object to, equally, are both the new ideas that the modernizing reformers wish to bring into Islam and the fact that these outsiders, and amateurs at that, are trying to intrude on the domain of the professionals.

The ulema's case against the modernist reformers is well made for them by Gibb in *Modern Trends in Islam*. In the first place, he says, outside Egypt conservative Islam is everywhere dominant in the Arab lands: 'There is little modernism outside the larger cities in Syria and Iraq or among the Muslims of Northwest Africa.' Therefore it is unrepresentative. Secondly, it is astonishing that the claim should be made 'that a small, self-constituted minority shall remodel the social institutions of one seventh of the human race . . . No wonder the religious leaders ask on what authority they propose to do this!' Gibb predicts that when Islam finds the solutions to its contemporary problems, 'we may be sure that the principles applied . . . will be practical and realistic and far removed from the intellectual confusions and the paralysing romanticism which cloud the minds of the modernists of today.'[32] Exactly five years after Gibb pronounced those words a 'confused' and 'romantic' modernist was prime minister of Indonesia, the largest Muslim state in the world, another modernist has been prime minister of the Sudan, one is prime minister of Iran today, and a very devout modernist, President Boumedienne, led Algeria for well over ten years. (This shows that *Modern Trends in Islam* was barely modern even when it was written. Today it is still of great but antiquarian interest.)

These very political successes of the modernists have brought them into a bitter head-on clash with the secular Westernizing nationalists. Here too there is an element of professional versus amateur. The professional politicians of the Wafd Party in Egypt, of the National Front in Iran, the Muslim League in Pakistan, the National Party in Indonesia, are at one in claiming that politics is for the politicians and not for former professors or engineers or journalists. But this clash is based on a very important issue that does not really permit of compromise: does or does not Islam have a place in Muslim society? On this issue the ulema and the reformer dwell in the same universe of discourse, but the reformer and the Westernizer live in different mental and spiritual worlds.

The case against militant politicized Islam has been best put by Sukarno, who really considered the problem seriously and over a period of years. He had actually become a member of the Muhammadiya reform movement and had accepted, and himself repeated, their claims that 'Islam is progress,' 'Islam insists on scientific research,' and so on. But in the end he could not believe that the small group of reformers would be able to drag the mass of ulema, with their slogan of 'back to the Koran', forward into the modern age: he feared that it was rather the ulema who would pull the reformers back.[33] This too has been the opinion, or the fear, of Westernized politicians in Pakistan, Egypt, Turkey and Tunisia. Yet in no Muslim country have the ulemas been able to influence the reformers nor, for that matter, have the reformers been able to influence the ulemas. Their antagonism has kept them apart and each side has stood firm and unchanging in its position.

The real and most serious grievance of the men of religion, the ulemas and the brotherhoods, and of the religious-minded reformers, is this: while for a century and a half the battle against the foreign rulers was almost exclusively inspired by Islam, and very largely led and organized by Islamic personalities and groups, the departing imperialists handed over power not to the Islamic elements, but to their Westernized trainees in the secular national parties. This, they feel, was a deliberate act of collusion between the Westerners and their mental and cultural heirs, the Westernized, alienated, local politicians. The Islamic groups feel that through this political sleight of hand they have been cheated of the prize they earned by their long struggle.

The nationalists reply that in the social and political vacuum created by the departure of the colonialists the Western-trained intellectuals and administrators were, at the crucial hour, the only sufficiently knowledgeable and experienced group on whom political power could devolve, and particularly because in many countries the colonialists got out in a hurry. The nationalists also argue that they took a prominent part in the various nationalist movements for twenty or thirty years, so that they too had earned the prize of power.

Continuing the argument the religious groups, especially the reformers, say that for all their much vaunted education and experience the new ruling class of Westernized nationalists –

alienated, rootless and cosmopolitan and therefore out of touch with the real needs and feelings of their people – has failed in its stewardship of the newly independent countries. They have not been able to solve any of the basic problems of Indonesia, Pakistan, Iran, Egypt or Turkey. Could the Islamic groups have done worse? When their material failure finally produces a failure of nerve all that the Westernized civilian politicians do is to make way for Westernized military politicians, who sometimes hand power back to the civilians in a game of political musical chairs.

The bitter clash (and bitter is the only word to describe it) is, in truth, the major internal political problem facing the Muslim world today. It is there or just beneath the surface in Indonesia, Pakistan, Iran, Turkey, Egypt, the Sudan, Morocco, and it is coming to the surface in Tunisia. It is most conspicuous in Pakistan and there it has been best articulated. One of the soldier-rulers of Pakistan has this to say of it: 'Our society is torn by a number of schisms; the most fundamental is the one which separates the educated classes from the traditional groups . . .' Understanding can only 'come about through a proper interpretation of Islamic principles and their application to the present-day problems. Unless this happens the gulf will grow which may eventually isolate the traditional groups from the modern educated classes and alienate the latter from Islam. . . All that was material, temporal, and secular was identified with the educated and all that was religious and spiritual became the monopoly of the ulema . . . the educated regarded the ulema as relics of the past and the ulema treated the educated as heretics and unworthy.'[34] Ayub Khan would not have seen the schism in quite such stark terms if he had not, like Sukarno, lumped the modernizing religious reformers like the Jamaat along with the ulema, although the difference between them has been very obvious in Pakistani politics. Yet he makes quite clear the alienation of 'the educated'.

One of these 'educated', the well known educator and historian, Dr I. H. Qureshi, a former minister of education in Pakistan and vice-chancellor of Karachi University, has these bitter words to say against the Westernized 'élite groups': these groups 'impose systems of education, economy, social institutions and mores to perpetuate the stranglehold that they have established over the entire area of national life. All this is done in the name of progress which is identified with Westernization. The Muslim peoples cannot come into their own until they dethrone these élite groups which are the creators of all their misery and have led their nations into a deep psychosis of an inferiority complex that paralyses their thought and actions alike. The élite suffer from their inferiority complex even more deeply than their victims.' The only hope, he says is 'to revive the sense of national identity and the uniqueness of Islam'. He concludes with an attack on some 'dictators' who 'with the name of Islam on their lips . . . destroy Islam in the name of Islam'[35] – a reference presumably to those leaders whom we have called 'exploiters'.

We have quoted these Pakistani statements at some length because they come at first hand from the protagonists themselves who are or have been directly involved on what has become militant Islam's new battlefield – an internal struggle this time, all the more bitter for being a civil war.

To judge by recent events in Iran and Turkey, the religious modernizers seem to have time on their side. And according to Gibb of all people, they have the socio-cultural tide running in their favour too. Writing in his *Studies in the Civilization of Islam*, after at least some of the Muslim countries had become independent, Gibb (much more discerning now) made the point that there were two currents in the Muslim world: that of the puritan reformers and the other in the military class and the new urban middle classes who are divorced from Muslim tradition and through whom 'the process of inner drying up, already far advanced in the West', began to spread to the Muslim world. Gibb evidently found the Westernized class even more deplorable than the modernist reformers and he foresaw the clash between the masses and this class. He thought he saw hopeful signs in groups in between the two. One group was the technocrats; the other was a new generation of leaders of the community and of social thought who came 'not from the old ruling classes but from strata which remained Muslim, in the strict sense, up to today'. Could he possibly, in his new wisdom, have been referring to those whom we call 'rethinkers'?

If as Dr Qureshi says the only hope for the Muslim world is for the Westernized élite to be dethroned, something will have to be put in their place. If it is to be an Islamic state or an Islamic order the time has come for us to examine the ideas militant Islam has on what the new dispensation should be like.

6 The modern Islamic state or Islamic order

If militant Islam is nothing new the militant Islamic state is not new either. Whenever after 1800 Muslims could break away from imperialist control they established such states – in Algeria under Abdel Qadir, in Morocco under Abdel Krim, in Somaliland under Muhammad Abdullah, in Western Sumatra, as late as 1949, under the Dar al Islam movement, and in the Sudan under the Mahdi. The first four 'states' were either too small or too short-lived to tell us much about the nature of an Islamic state, except that we know that they were all based on the Sharia. But a great deal is known about the Mahdist state in the Sudan which the main work on the subject describes as 'a powerful and militant Islamic state'.[1] Though the Sudan a century ago may not seem to have much relevance to our modern world there are certain resemblances between the Mahdist state and contemporary ones: it suffered from an excessive bureaucracy,[2] excessive taxation including supertax, and an enforced equality between rich and poor.[3] It was also akin in many ways to the killjoy regime that Ayatollah Khomeini is attempting to enforce in Iran. To ensure the renunciation of earthly vanities the state forbade intoxicants (80 lashes for infringement), tobacco (100 lashes), amulets, magic, music, processions, marriage and circumcision feasts, mourning and the visiting of tombs: 'Put aside everything that has the slightest resemblance to the manners of the Turks and infidels – dresses, drums and bugles.'[4] All this recalls the similar killjoy instructions, twenty-one in all, that Cromwell gave to his major-generals in 1655[5], and the even more severe puritanism of Calvin's republic of Geneva.

The difference between the Islamic state and an Islamic order has already been referred to: in the former, politics and religion are parts of the single totality of Islam, while in the latter politics are derivative from the spirit of Islam. Thus, the former is more strictly, more truly Islamic.

In their various projects to establish one or the other the Islamic rethinkers, lay and religious (for we will be taking the Khomeini movement within our purview), seem to follow two guiding principles: in non-religious matters everything may be deemed permissible unless expressly prohibited, which gives scope to ijtihad and ijma; in religious matters everything is prohibited unless expressly permitted, and here there is no scope for interpretation.

The political nature of the Islamic state or order is naturally of primary interest. When engaged in the practical task of drawing up a new constitution for Pakistan that 'would be in consonance with the teachings and history of Islam' Ayub Khan asked his experts to study Islamic history and the constitutions of other Muslim countries: 'Two things emerged clearly from this study: there was no place for kingship in Islam and succession could not be on a hereditary basis. The community as a whole must have the right to choose its leader and the right to remove him.'[6] (This means that all Muslim monarchies, whatever their pretentions to religiosity, have been totally un-Islamic.) On these two fundamentals there is indeed agreement among our political reformers, but on every other aspect of Islamic polity there are differences of substance and of emphasis, as is evident from the following survey of the political ideas of the various groups.

So far, then, two very important constituent elements of the Islamic state have been established: it must be a republic, and it cannot be a dictatorship, for the head of state is removable by the people.

Natsir, speaking for the Indonesian Masjumi, favours the Islamic state, for there has to be a state to order society. The title of the Islamic head of state is not important, far more important is the right the people have to remove him for wrong doing, by force if necessary. There should be no one-man rule; the leader must consult 'those people whom it is proper to consult', and the system of consultation is left to the people concerned: it could be consultation with a few or with a parliament containing various parties, though Natsir believes that the Western parliamentary system is not especially suited to other areas. He asks: 'Is Islam a democracy?' and answers: 'Islam is not one-hundred-per-cent democracy, neither is it one-hundred-per-cent autocracy. Islam is . . . Islam.' Rule by armed groups, Natsir has said, would be disastrous for Indonesia. An Islamic state will enforce the full range of Koranic prohibitions – intoxicants, gambling, theft, prostitution, superstition and polytheism.[7] In this way Natsir constructs a framework which leaves the details somewhat vague – a very Indonesian way of proceeding.

It might be expected that the political ideas of the Muslim Brotherhood would be much more precise, but they are not very much more so. One favourite slogan of the brotherhood is, 'The Koran is our constitution,' which does not take one very far. For them the essential principle is the centrality of the Sharia. On specifics the brotherhood says that an Islamic government operates on the concept of consultation, *shura*, and that the executive ruler is bound by the teachings of Islam and the will of the people. The political programme of the brotherhood is clearly for an Islamic state. The state is seen as only one part of a larger Islamic order which is the ordering of the whole way of life of an entire people according to Islam. The title of the ruler is unimportant – Khalifa, imam, king, governor – they have all been used in the Koran. Hassan al Banna favoured the American 'executive' pattern of authority over that of the 'ministerial' British variety. The tenure of office of the leader may be for life if the umma, the people, deems him fit. The umma is the sole source of authority and bowing to its will is a religious obligation. The election of the leader should be either directly by the people or by the consultative assembly. In this assembly, despite its name, lies the real power of the state, and its members should be elected by all the people. There need not necessarily be political parties in the assembly; indeed preferably not, for political groupings of any sort are divisive. The state leader, besides being sane and healthy must also be knowledgeable in Muslim jurisprudence (which drastically limits the choice). So, too, should be the representatives elected to the assembly, though heads of various organizations should also be eligible. Specialists and technicians may also be added. Their decisions should be by consensus. In the Islamic state-structure propounded by the brotherhood the division of powers would be as follows: all executive power in the hands of the ruler; legislative power shared by the ruler and the assembly, for the assembly does not initiate legislation; judicial power held by absolutely independent judges; financial power with officials nominated by the ruler but responsible to the community; and the power of 'control and reform' belonging to the community at large through the assembly.

The brotherhood stressed that no government established by force can be accepted, for consultation is mandatory according to Sura 42 verse 35 of the Koran. Hence military regimes produced by *coups* are un-Islamic. The Islamic state should have strong armed forces based on compulsory military service and on its own armament industries.

According to the Muslim Brothers every citizen is guaranteed the freedoms of thought, worship, expression, education and possession. The brotherhood is well aware that one of Egypt's major political problems is its enormous lazy, inefficient bureaucracy – the coffee slurpers of Cairo. This problem should be tackled by infusing them with 'an Islamic spirit'; by seeing that they do not stay up late at night; by employing more Azhar graduates; by eliminating favouritism; and improving the salaries of lower-grade officials (from whom the brotherhood drew many of its members).[8] These are singularly superficial solutions for a problem Egypt has faced and been defeated by since the age of the Pharaohs.

The brotherhood's dislike for the multi-party system is shared by another rethinker, Sadiq al Mahdi of the Sudan.[9] In both cases the dislike seems prompted more by a rejection of party strife in Egypt and the Sudan than by any fundamental incompatibility between the party system and the Islamic spirit.

The Sudanese leader, favouring an Islamic order, argues against a single type of constitution for an Islamic state because it would not fit Islamic countries that are at various stages of political development: 'The precise constitutional systems for particular states can be separately formulated.'[10]

Flatly contrary to this idea is that of Maulana Abdul al Maududi of the Jamaat in Pakistan. He not only favours an Islamic state, but one which is 'universal and all-embracing . . . considered from this aspect the Islamic state bears a kind of resemblance to the fascist and communist states . . . it is an ideological state ... such a state should be run only by those who believe in the ideology on which it is based and in the Divine law which it is assigned to administer.' That was written in 1939[11] and he seems to have changed his ideas since then. Indeed one difficulty in explaining Maududi's ideas is that they change even on important matters, and the changes are not unconnected with the imperatives and pressures of Pakistani domestic politics. Also Maududi has written far too prolifically for consistency to be maintained. In concordance with the ideas of the brotherhood Maududi says that the Islamic state should be ruled by an Amir (or with any other title) who should be elected directly by the people, and should hold full executive power. While he is obliged to listen to the consultative assembly he need not accept its opinion, though every effort should be made to reach a consensus. This assembly itself should be elected, *by* the generality, but not *from* the generality; instead, only from those competent 'to bind and loose' – a competency, intelligence, honesty bar should apply to prospective candidates. The judiciary should be completely independent. Maududi for some years quoted suras from the Koran which stigmatized those who sought office, and members of the Jamaat were not allowed to stand for elections; but, as we have seen, after the establishment of Pakistan they aspired to office by standing for elections. As to the purposes of the Islamic state, it is to establish virtue and eradicate vice, therefore 'A state in which adultery, drinking, gambling, obscene literature, indecent films, vulgar songs, immoral display of beauty, mingling of promiscuous men and women, co-education etc. flourish without let or hindrance cannot be called an Islamic state ... the above mentioned objective is the primary duty of the state.'[12]

Perhaps the most individual political idea of Maududi is that there should be a body of ulema to see that no proposed law should be repugnant to the Koran and the Sunnah. This has been partly implemented under the latest reforms made by General Zia al Haq.

Another distinctive feature in Maududi's political programme is its emphasis on élitism. Perhaps because he has always restricted the membership of the Jamaat – which is probably one reason why it has received such little support from the Pakistani electorate – Maududi, making a virtue of necessity, has given great importance to leadership being confined to an intellectual élite. But this seems rather like a move to remove the Westernized élite, who are 'responsible for all Pakistan's ills', by another not so very different leadership group. It is to Maududi's credit that although the Jamaat has fared consistently poorly in elections he still believes that the changes needed to bring an Islamic state into existence can come through democratic elections. There are, however, some Jamaat supporters who say that the party made 'a sad mistake' in not insisting on an educational qualification being imposed on voters.[13]

The Islamic Liberation Party wants to see an Islamic state devoid of parties, and with the full range of canonical punishments.

Colonel Gaddafi does not want political parties either, nor a state of any sort at all. For under his plan for democracy, according to the first part of the (little) *Green Book*, the whole state structure is to dissolve into a direct participatory form of democracy with every aspect of life being managed by committees. (It was announced in March 1979 that this dissolution had actually come about.) Whatever its other merits – it may work in a country with as small a population as Libya has – this scheme is not Islamic; though somewhere along the line there is to be a committee to see to it that the Koranic punishments are to be enforced.

The political programme of Allal al Fassi tends more towards an Islamic order than to an Islamic state. There will of course be a state, and he says its law should be the Sharia, but at the same time he wants the community, in freedom under God, to choose its institutions and form of government. He believes that the best form of government is multi-party parliamentary democracy, but agrees with Natsir that there should be an indigenous and Islamic variety, different, in some as yet unspecified way, from the British and French systems; there should not have to be an upper and lower house, for instance. Consultation is the key principle; its exact form can always be worked out. An independent judiciary is for al Fassi of paramount importance. Like Maududi, al Fassi is an élitist: 'To direct a nation, there must be an aristocracy of thought.'[14] He is opposed to 'priestly' authority and predominance.

In this opposition to the intervention of the ulema in politics, al Fassi is partially at odds with Maududi and wholly at odds with Ayatollah Khomeini whose book on the Islamic state is called *Velayat-e Faqih* or 'The Government of the Theologians' – nothing could be clearer than that.

Expressing a strictly Shiah point of view Khomeini stands for a Sharia-based Islamic state which will be republican. There will be a separate judiciary versus executive but the legislative branch will not initiate laws because they are already there in the Koran. The legislature will have two houses: the first will be an assembly of Fatvas (a *fatva* or *fatwa* is a religious-legal decree) composed of *mujtahids* (learned ulema) and specialists in Islamic jurisprudence; the second chamber will be an 'Islamic consultative assembly' consisting of men of piety, experts, and representatives of the Islamic community and of the religious minorities. According to Khomeini, the Islamic ruler or governor must be learned in Islamic law, and he must be just. Such is the importance of the law that even the ruler must seek the guidance of the theologians: 'Thus the real governors are the theologians themselves, and thus government must rightfully belong to the theologians, not those who, due to their ignorance of the law, must follow their guidance.' They inherit from the Prophet and the imams not only the tradition of learning but they also 'inherit the right to government over the people . . . it is they who must exercise supervision over all the executive, administrative and planning affairs of the country.' This assertion of the total, charismatic right of the ulema and ayatollahs is wholly Shiah: the Sunni ulema may very much want the same thing in their hearts, but it is two centuries since they have publicly asserted any such claim. Thus the Shia Islamic state is a 'hierocracy'. As to the actual ruler he must have the qualities of learning and justice that belong to the theologians, and therefore most probably should come from their ranks. Though no Sunni Muslim country will accept Khomeini's exaltation of the ayatollahs there is a certain logical consistency in his argument – if the Sharia is to be the foundation of the state then those who are knowledgable in the Sharia, almost exclusively the ulema, should have pre-eminence in the state. However, many of the lay religious reformers have also made themselves expert in the Sharia, such as Natsir, Maududi and al Fassi. As far as the administration of the Islamic state is concerned, Khomeini is insistent on one thing – a small bureau-cracy; but in this he is being naïve. In the Khomeini Islamic state there will be only one party, the party of the righteous. Although his spokesmen say that other parties will be allowed they add that no party will be allowed that may call 'for what is against the interests of religion', which can be interpreted to include anything and everything.[15]

This is one of the main points of difference between the Khomeini movement and Bazargan's Iran Liberation Movement. It too wants an Islamic state firmly based on the Sharia but the ulema will be only one element in the ruling group and other parties will be allowed, even the communists, provided they limit themselves to propagating their views and not trying to implement them by subversion. Both the Khomeini and the Bazargan movements accept the Koranic punishments.

All these various rethinking groups, and the Khomeini movement which stands on its own, are at one on foreign policy – this has to be non-aligned between the Eastern and Western blocs. And it should be positive non-alignment, for as Sheikh Takieddin Nabhani said, 'We are not just sandbags to strengthen the positions of either East or West.'

As to relationships within the Muslim world these should of course be as close and cooperative as possible. Sheikh Nabhani actually asked for a caliphal system that would provide one overall government for the whole Muslim world, and the brotherhood said that a revived caliphate might be something to consider, but later on. None of the other groups seem to have been much attracted by the idea of a caliphate, which is in any case only a very remote possibility.

The Khomeini movement is one, at least, that distinguishes clearly between Islamic nations or peoples and Islamic govern-ments with whom Iran's relations are being reconsidered, 'since some of them can hardly be called Islamic. They have completely given themselves up to the Western powers. Don't you see Sadat? Have you ever thought about Saudi Arabia? It is indeed shameful.'[16]

From these diverse views we can derive certain common elements in the political structure of the Islamic state. It will be a republican state with all executive power in the hands of an elected leader, who will in effect be 'a just despot'. When he ceases to be just, the leader must be removed, by force if necessary. But military regimes, or any regime imposed by force, is un-Islamic. The leader will be obliged to consult with an elected assembly that will have certain limited legislative powers. The leader should be elected by the entire community but the assembly may be elected on a limited franchise. The majority opinion would seem to be that a multi-party system is undesirable. Even those like al Fassi and Sadiq al Mahdi who prefer an Islamic order to an Islamic state and who opt for parliamentary democracy, if that be the desire of the people, insist that this system must be Islamized and not a mere imitation of Western models. There is unanimous agreement that the judiciary must be independent and that the legal basis of the state has to be the Sharia. It is also the majority opinion that even though the state is Islamic the Islamic men of religion have no special position or powers in its political ordering.

Thus, while there are quite a few variations on the three or four set themes of the political side of the Islamic state or order there is unanimity on what its economic policy should be in general terms although much disagreement on the specific terms. As in foreign policy, Islam takes a strictly middle position in its economic ordering, between Western capitalism and Eastern communism. One conservative middle-of-the-road Muslim commentator sums up the Islamic economic doctrine, quite justly, in these terms: 'Islam respects individual ownership, but within limits and so is not communistic. It differs from capitalism in three ways: (1) it fights against the accumulation of wealth and the retaining of it in the hands of a minority; (2) Islamic legislation conserves the funds of nations and individuals; (3) charity is part of worship.'[17] According to this author Koranic sanction can be produced to show that no less than four fifths of annual profit should go to the Islamic state.

From Natsir in the East to Allal al Fassi in the West there is agreement that in Islam there should not be very rich nor very poor, nor even rich or poor; that there should not be riba, usury; and that zakat, the alms tax or tithe, is the Islamic way to achieve economic equality.

What Islam really wants is just, equitable economic order, a welfare state on the best Scandinavian model: no more, no less.[18]

There has been much fashionable talk in the past two decades of 'Islamic socialism'. The actual words can be traced back a century to Afghani, and it was much on the lips of those 'exploiters', Jinnah and Bhutto, especially the latter who did very little to implement it. There has also been a great deal of discussion, serious this time, of Islamic socialism in Algeria, especially in the first few years after independence. Algerian newspapers then presented Muhammad himself as the advocate of 'a revolution of the poor against the rich', who sent the feudalists of Mecca 'through a Turkish bath'. The words of one Hadith, 'Men are associated in three elements: water, fodder and fire,' were taken as evidence that Islam provided for the nationalization of certain goods. [19] But after Boumedienne took over, such revolutionary zeal was abated and Algeria settled down to its present left-of-centre state socialism within a strongly Islamic ambience.

In any discussion of Islamic socialism the name of Abu Dharr almost invariably appears. He was one of the Companions of the Prophet and statements have been attributed to him according to which everyone ought to spend on the service of God, or in charity, the whole of his wealth or income beyond the minimum needed for subsistence. For his pains he is said to have been banished to a remote locality as a danger to society. On this rather shaky basis Abu Dharr has been elevated in Algeria to the position of 'the father of socialism' and even the brotherhood described his reaction as being 'in the true spirit of Islam'. Such are the words and the idealism, but the true exemplar in this, as in everything else, is not Abu Dharr but Muhammad who, until he fled from Mecca, was a moderately prosperous businessman. Islam is too realistic and rational to be anything beyond somewhat left-of-centre in its economic policy.

Maududi is very conservative and positively right-wing in his interpretation of Islamic economics. It is his deduction that Islam disallows the nationalization of industries by the government except in extraordinary circumstances, and that the principle of collective ownership of the means of production is contrary to the Islamic concept of social justice. In this context it is significant that when General Zia al Haq, who is much influenced by the Jamaat, announced his Islamic legal reforms in February 1979 he also issued a decree that industrial property would not be nationalized without compensation. Maududi also contended that Islam was against the state ownership of land, nor need there be any restriction on the extent of land ownership.[20] This last is the exact opposite of the position of Allal al Fassi and his Istiqlal Party who, in January 1970, issued the call, 'The land to those who till it', and asked the Moroccan government to fulfil the following programme: prohibition of landowning by non-agriculturalists; encouragement of smallholders to join cooperatives; all key sectors of the economy, especially heavy industry and mining, to be taken into public ownership or control.[21] Even more radical is the economic policy of the Society of Muslim Brothers. It demanded the nationalization of all the natural resources of the country; foreign capital and control should be abolished; there should be a ceiling on land ownership and national lands should be distributed to small owners and the landless; there should be comprehensive social security for all workers, both industrial and agricultural; and membership of trade unions should be compulsory. The brotherhood also favoured industrialization, especially of those industries using local raw materials, as well as handicrafts.[22] The Islamic Liberation Party was so enthusiastic for the creation of heavy industry in Egypt that it criticized Nasser for giving priority to the Aswan high dam project because it felt that the electricity produced by the dam was going to be used mainly for new light industries. In Iran the Bazargan group, as well as the Khomeini movement, both favour sweeping measures of nationalization and land reforms. Like the brotherhood they both advocate the nationalization of the banking system. An economic adviser to the Ayatollah has even spoken of workers' management of industries, through what will be called imam committees.[23]

The two specifics on which there are agreement are the abolition of riba, usury, and the imposition of zakat, the alms tax, although there are some differences of interpretation. Some difficulty has been left in defining the difference between usury and interest, and between interest paid by or to a person and interest paid by or to a government, bank or industry. The brotherhood is for the abolition of all forms of interest, and believes that the government should begin by rejecting interest charges in all its own operations. Allal al Fassi adopted the decision made earlier by Abduh which allows moderate interest to be taken on non-loan capital on deposit, but forbids interest on credit. Concealed interest is allowed, or tolerated, in time of need.[24] Maududi was against interest in all its forms, as are both the groups in Iran; but Maududi would allow limited foreign loans on interest if these became unavoidable.[25] The young Iranian economists admit that the abolition of interest will not be easy because it will mean creating a new sort of banking system; but they point out that there are already in existence many interest-free Islamic banks operating in several Muslim countries such as Saudi Arabia, Egypt and Jordan.[26]

For the Islamic reformers the strict imposition of zakat is the most effective means of bringing about economic equality. We have seen that the Pakistan government has introduced it in a comprehensive and well organized manner, probably under Jamaat influence. In line with his economic conservatism Maududi fixed the rate at $2\frac{1}{2}$ per cent, which would not bring in very much; the Pakistan government has accepted that rate on all money in banks or financial institutions, while it will be five per cent on agricultural land. Al Fassi would impose 'a tax of $2\frac{1}{2}$ per cent to 10 per cent on everything in excess of the strict minimum necessary for a decent life'.[27] For the brotherhood zakat was to be applied progressively, both on capital and on profit; in addition the head of state can at need assign levies or forced contributions on capital 'at a reasonable rate'. In this as in many another Islamic matter Shiah Islam has different regulations, and many more taxes, than Sunni Islam. Thus Khomeini argues that the Islamic state could draw ample funds, as the Shiah hierarchy has been doing, not only from the zakat, but from *khoms*, a twenty-per-cent tax on profit, *kharaj*, a land tax, and *jiziya*, a poll tax on non-Muslims, as a kind of compensation for release from military service.

From all this it is clear that a distinctively Islamic economic system can be put together. Forthcoming developments in Iran and Pakistan could show whether it will work and produce the desired results.

Apart from the Koranic punishments the two aspects of Islamic society that the non-Muslim world finds most difficult to understand or accept are Islam's acceptance of polygamy and of easy divorce on the initiative of the husband alone. Perhaps because personal law is the very heart of the Sharia the rethinkers have not really done much rethinking on these two matters. Even in Indonesia where, as in the rest of southeast Asia, women are free, equal and open in society, both the Masjumi and the Nahdatul Ulema merely accept the Koranic injunctions, which admittedly make polygamy a psychological impossibility (though this has not deterred the male sex). The same acceptance comes from the Jamaat, Khomeini (who is positively anti-feminist), the brotherhood and, partly, Allal al Fassi. The one reform suggested by al Fassi is bold enough – the official prohibition of polygamy – but he bases it on the Sharia and the Koran itself, in that the Koranic condition of granting equal justice to each wife is in present circumstances not generally possible. He also tries to mitigate the hardship imposed on women by the Islamic divorce system by suggesting the payment of alimony to the divorced wife. The brotherhood apologetically refers to the Hadith that says: 'Divorce is the most hateful to God of the lawful things.' But no amount of apologetics, no granting of equality to women in other spheres such as in politics which the Masjumi and al Fassi concede, can alter the fact that because of its marriage and divorce laws Islam puts woman in her personal status, which is the most important of all, into a position inferior to men.

This social timidity is the less understandable because two Muslim countries have not hesitated to alter the Sharia. In 1956 Tunisia forbade polygamy and divorce by repudiation and in 1961 Ayub Khan introduced changes which made both much more difficult, and gave the secular authorities the right to intervene to protect the interests of the wife.

It would be of interest here to quote the views of Kausar Niazi, a former leading member of the Jamaat who left it to become the Pakistani minister of information and later of religious affairs under Bhutto. Though a layman he is learned in Muslim jurisprudence, as befits a former member of the Jamaat. In one of his numerous publications, Niazi says that a woman can be an imam, that is, lead the prayers, as sanctioned by the Prophet; she can obtain from her husband the right to divorce; he quotes Abu Hanifah, the founder of one of the four Muslim law schools, to state that women can serve as the head of state; and that while women are obliged to provide sexual satisfaction to their husbands they cannot be compelled to cook, make beds, sweep, spin, weave etc; on this liberationist finding he quotes Abu Hanifah, Shafii (the founder of another law school) and Ibu Hazm. This shows that there is scope for rethinking Islamic provisions on matters of personal law within the four corners of orthodoxy.[28]

Modernizing Islam takes a pragmatic view of the problem of birth control. In general it accepts it as necessary where a country is overpopulated and as unnecessary if the country is underpopulated. The general belief is that the contraceptive method of *azl* or *coitus interruptus* was approved by the Prophet, used by some of his companions and accepted by most of the medieval jurists. On the other hand there are some Hadith which say the Prophet disapproved of this method. But it has been generally accepted by Islam, particularly after al Azhar, under pressure from Nasser, issued in 1966 a finding that birth control by this method was permissible. Indeed birth control has been debated by the Islamic jurists for many centuries.[29] The Muslim Brotherhood gave its approval and in doing so took up an untraditional position in Egypt where large families are regarded as desirable and a sign of God's bounty.

On the matter of purdah, or the veiling of women, the Jamaat Party and Khomeini (in the group of rethinkers) are the only ones who actually insist on it. The other groups merely say that women should dress modestly when they go out.

Since the Sharia is accepted as the bedrock of Islamic society it is worthy of note that some of the rethinkers have been consistent and thoroughgoing enough to say that the Sharia itself should come under scrutiny and perhaps be subject to revision. Sadiq al Mahdi has spoken in general terms of the need for a 'modern formulation of the Sharia' by 'scholars and universities' for 'only then can we expect a revival of the Islamic legislative reliability.'[30] But the brotherhood has gone into the matter in considerable detail. In the first place, it said, it should be decided what the Sharia consists of. It is generally assumed that it is composed of the Koran, the Hadith or 'traditions' of what the Prophet said or did, and the judgements of the four schools of Islamic law. The brotherhood would challenge the inclusion of the law schools, mainly because they are not very relevant for today. It would also challenge the authenticity of most of the Hadith, which many others do beside them. For instance al Azhar itself, as far back as 1941, approved a proposal to prepare a new collection of all 'sound' Traditions. If the brotherhood and other Muslim reformers press the point that the Sharia needs to be defined and revised they will be moving towards the most daring and drastic change that Islam has yet experienced. That would be a real rethinking of Islam in modern terms.

We conclude this survey of the Islamic state of order with a brief account of the reformists' attitude to one of Islam's most difficult problems – its attitude towards minorities in an Islamic state. It is brief because few can get round the hard fact that in an Islamic state, which is as Maududi correctly said an ideological state, only those people espousing the ideology can run the state. Our rethinkers go to great lengths to affirm that minorities will be given a respected position of their own, and that they will be equal before the law, with equal rights and duties (though Khomeini would deny them the duty of defending the Islamic state). Yet even the Koran makes some minorities – those three based on a holy book – more equal than others. What has happened to the Ahmadiyas in Pakistan, the Bahais in Iran and to a lesser extent the Copts in Egypt is not encouraging. There is no evading the quite obvious conclusion: that in an Islamic state non-Muslims cannot but be second-class citizens. If nothing can be done to change the fundamental inferiority of non-ideological minorities in an ideological state, the Muslim world – now more than ever interested in itself – has discovered a fact about itself that could mitigate such crudities as Khomeini's idea of a poll tax on non-Muslims. This fact is that around one quarter of the world's 750 million Muslims are minorities in non-Muslim countries – there are 3·5 million Muslims in Yugoslavia for instance. Sheer self-interest, the *quid pro quo*, would indicate that the Islamic state should deal at least justly with its non-Muslims if it expects similar treatment for its own co-religionist minorities. If the past, certainly, Muslim regimes have been tolerant of their minorities, as Jewish communities fleeing from Christian persecution have good reason to know. Militant Islam does not have to be intolerant Islam.

*

From considering the Islamic state or order in its various aspects we may conclude that the political and economic programmes of such a state or order are not incompatible with modern conditions. The weaknesses are most apparent in the domain of social affairs, where what is lacking is courage, and on the position of minorities, about which nothing can be done. On the legal side there are questionings – which is an excellent thing. There is enough here to justify the experiment of the militant push towards the Islamic state. That push will come, whatever the evaluation of the possible result. For all Muslim countries are led – doomed one might say – to do one of two things: to deny the essentials of Islam and opt for a secular state; or to go through the arduous struggle of trying to produce an Islamic state or an Islamic order. From that choice there is no escape.

Epilogue

There are many and varied aspects to militant Islam. Under Ayatollah Khomeini it appears harsh and stern; the variety presented by Allal al Fassi or Muhammad Natsir is open minded and flexible; with Sadiq al Mahdi it is flexible but impatient; the Jamaat's version in Pakistan is at once detailed and equivocal, while with the Muslim Brotherhood it appears well thought out and menacing. But beneath these variations there is always the same steely core. Partly this is explained by the fact that these movements have been hammered into hardness by repression. A more valid explanation is that these groupings, even though some of them may call themselves 'parties', are much more than mere political parties trying to implement a party programme. They are, rather, deliberately and self-consciously, engaged in the high and holy task of infusing the principles of a higher religion into workaday politics, economics and social affairs. And the steeliness of the core is all the tougher because the higher religion concerned happens to be Islam, which is quite uncompromising in the totality of its claims for authority over all aspects of the life of man. This steely hardness means that however fashionable militant Islam may seem to be at the moment of writing, in mid-1979, it is no mere fashion or passing fad. It has always been, and for a long while to come will remain, a permanent factor in the life of the Islamic world. Recent events in Iran and Pakistan in particular have merely enhanced the already existing steady pressure of militant Islam to rise to the surface of national life in all Muslim countries and then to take control of that national life. Hence the rest of the non-Muslim world is, to use a current vulgarism, 'stuck with' militant Islam and will have to learn to live with it.

Since it is to be with us for a while yet, it is appropriate to pose the question: whither militant Islam? In 1932, it will be recalled, the British Islamic scholar Gibb made the question, 'Whither Islam?' the title of a book in which he made some singularly inaccurate prophecies because he was, while seeming to be unaware of it, dealing with an Islamic world abnormally distorted by foreign domination. Nearly half a century later, the task of prophesying the future of Islamic militancy is made no easier by the fact that the Muslim nations are now independent, for freedom has laid them open to the impact of conflicting influences and forces from which they were insulated by the sheltering imperial systems. Nevertheless, despite the hazards and despite the daunting example of Gibb, answers must be attempted to that question – whither militant Islam?

The answers and the prophecies have to be made on three levels. The first, relating to the short term, concerns where and when militant Islam will come to power, and in which Muslim countries. The second and third are both longer term: the second issue is whether militant Islam has the answers to the challenges of modernity facing the Muslim countries; and if it has, and this is the third issue, what sort of militant Islam will endure and remain dynamic and challenging both before, but more especially after, it has taken power? In the first and second cases, Islam serves as the basis for political and economic programmes; in the third, Islam is the religion as such, the spiritual force informing militant Islam in all its motivations and manifestations.

Logically the second issue should have been the first to be decided: that is to say, it should first be clear whether militant Islam really has the answers to the problems of Muslim countries before it assumes power and responsibility. But life is untidy, and things have not worked out that way. Militant Islam is pushing for power, and has taken power in Iran, simply on the basis that it thinks it has the answers; and also, more realistically, it does not seem that any other grouping in Muslim countries has better answers, or even any real answers to the problems facing these countries. In these nations, as in many others of the Third World, all other alternative forms of governance have been tried and failed, especially in the all important economic sector. One-man rule, both monarchical and republican, has not produced the desired results; and it has been the same with one-party regimes; so too with multi-party systems, both democratic and parliamentary and undemocratic and non-parliamentary; the military men have tried their hand with little success, and in some cases have ordered themselves back to their barracks; equally unsuccessful have been the nonpolitical technocrats. Since all these alternatives have been used, and used up, what else is left? In a way the Muslim countries may count themselves lucky that they still have left the alternative of militant Islam, an alternative not available to the non-Muslim Third World countries.

Therefore, simply as the only other available alternative, *faute de mieux*, militant Islam is on the threshhold of political power in several Muslim countries, as we shall now see. This is very much the case in Indonesia even though General Suharto follows President Sukarno in practising towards Islam the policy first enunciated by the colonialist Snouck Hurgronje – that is, to tolerate Islam as a religion but to curb it as a political force. This division, fundamentally incompatible with the essential nature of Islam, has not worked and even in the rigged election of 1977 the religious parties polled thirty per cent of the vote. Masjumi, in particular, has been suppressed because it is more dangerous than the pliant Nahdatul Ulema. Though it has been forced to change its name twice and to merge with the Nahdatul and other religious parties, its appeal, force and distinctive personality remain intact: its numerical strength has declined only because of official pressure. An organized mass party like Masjumi with a clear, popular ideology and an able and experienced leadership, could be eliminated from the Indonesian political scene only by the sort of holocaust that decimated the Indonesian Communist Party, and that is most unlikely. The Masjumi has only to bide its time – time that is inexorably running out for the corrupt and inefficient military regime.

The future of militant Islam in Pakistan is not anything like as certain as it is in Indonesia: because although it has achieved organization and a well developed programme in the Jamaat, it lacks a broad popular base. This paradox has baffled the Jamaat itself, since it is generally agreed that the prevailing popular sentiment in Pakistan is for a form of government that is in accord with the Islamic way of life: that was and remains Pakistan's *raison d'être*. Could it be that the specific formulation

of militant Islam provided by the Jamaat is in some way faulty
and unappealing? Or is it that the personality of Maududi himself does not inspire confidence? It is difficult to see why either
proposition should be true, and yet the mystery of the Jamaat's
unpopularity remains. Despite this, and simply because of
General Zia's links with the Jamaat, militant Islam has achieved
some spectacular if superficial successes, through the general's
recent legal reforms, such as the introduction of the canonical
punishments; in fact the reorganization of the zakat system is
likely to be of more enduring value. Because of this close association with one particular political figure the cause of
militant Islam in Pakistan is bound to suffer if that figure
disappears from the political scene. Nevertheless what has been
accomplished so far cannot be undone, or not entirely; it may
be ignored but not for very long because of the strong prevailing
Islamic sentiment of the Pakistani people. In Pakistan militant
Islam needs to find a comprehensive and organized expression of
that sentiment, which would not be associated with just one leader,
like General Zia, or with one small grouping, like the Jamaat, or
with one professional caste, like the ulema. This should not be
too difficult because that sentiment is strong and widespread
and has already gained a large measure of public articulation.
Because of this one can say with a fair degree of confidence that
no future ruler of Pakistan can ever again be a secular civilian
politician like Liaquat Ali Khan or a secular soldier like Iskander
Mirza, nor even a semi-secular soldier like Ayub Khan and least
of all a civilian politician of the Bhutto stripe, cleverly but
obviously using Islam for his own political ends.

In Iran, as in Pakistan and for the same reason, the political
future of militant Islam is not as assured as it is in Indonesia and
Egypt, even though in the former countries it wields political
power and in the latter it is in oppressed opposition. The point of
similarity between Iran and Pakistan is that in both countries
militant Islam is too closely identified with a single very controversial political figure – General Zia and Ayatollah Khomeini.
There the similarity between the two leaders ends and the dis-
similarity begins. For while General Zia has listened to the
advice of the modernist Islamic reformers inside and outside
the Jamaat, the Ayatollah has done the opposite: having brought
in the leader of the Islamic reformist group, Mehdi Bazargan,

as his prime minister he has thereafter ignored him. The obscurantist and vengeful policies the Ayatollah has been following align him with the ulema groups in Indonesia, Pakistan and Egypt rather than with those of modernizing reform. General Zia is well aware of the complexities of the modern world, he knows that there is a 'big world' outside Pakistan; Ayatollah Khomeini, with his tirades against Western civilization in its entirety, seems unaware of anything beyond the confines of the holy city of Qom and his small, remote and backward village of Khomein. It is personalities and policies like those of the Ayatollah that give a bad name not just to militant Islam but to Islam as a whole. He is, in fact, a perfect example of the operation of the 'Peter Principle', by which people with some ability must necessarily, because of their ambition, be promoted beyond their capacity.[1] A splendid leader of the anti-Shah movement, he is quite beyond his depth as the self-appointed ruler of a state like Iran, which because of its oil and oil wealth has to be part of the modern world. If Khomeini remains the ruler of Iran to the extent that he is in mid-1979, his regime, because it is based on the organization of the Shiah divines rather than on non-clerical groups like those of Bazargan, will become an intolerant Shiah despotism; this in the long run will generate as much fear and hatred and opposition as did the regime of the Shah. Iran, like Pakistan, cannot ever again go back to a purely secular government, but what one hopes for it in the nearer future is that the Khomeini komitehs are replaced by a combined group formed of the more intelligent and broad-minded Ayatollahs, such as Telegani and Shariat Medari, and by the Bazargan party.

One problem that the Islamic regimes in Iran and Pakistan have already begun to run into is that by introducing funda-mentalist Shiah and Sunni reforms they have alarmed and antagonized their respective Sunni and Shiah minorities. This is a far more serious problem in Iran than it is in Pakistan, because in Iran the Sunnis are very nearly half the population of the country and are different both racially and/or linguistically from the Farsi-speaking Shiahs on the central plateau which the Sunnis surround: the Kurds and Turkomans have already risen in arms against what they see as Tehran's Shiah domination. Unless the Ayatollah can moderate his Shiah fervour and his preference for working through the organization of Shiah clerics, Iran will split apart along the lines of communal-territorial division. In Pakistan, where the Shiahs claim to be a quarter of the population, they are at least not concentrated territorially, but their opposition to the new reforms, especially the payment of zakat to the predominantly Sunni government rather than to their Shiah community organization, could impose great strains on Pakistan's already rather fragile state structure.

In between Iran and Pakistan, in Afghanistan, Islam is quite literally up in arms and is not merely on the threshhold of power but is rapping on the state's front door with the gun butt. However, this is not militant or reformist Islam but its opposite – the wholly orthodox and traditional Islam of the mountain tribes-men, led by their mullahs, who are fighting the secular pro-grammes of the communist government in Kabul. They are only likely to win, if at all, in the very long run, because Afghani-stan's communist rulers are not Amanallahs – the Westernizing king overthrown by tribesmen in 1929. Any such problematical success will only make the point that in a Muslim country it is difficult, if not impossible, to brutally and abruptly sever the Islamic roots of a devout people: a point that has already been made in Turkey.

In Turkey itself Islam has proved itself as a permanent and irreducible element in the nation's life. Yet the prospects for militant modernizing Islam in that country are not especially bright. This is because the political parties, those of Erbakan and Turkes, who speak in the name of Islam, are merely using the religion for essentially political and non-religious purposes. There may be some genuinely reformist thinkers in Erbakan's National Salvation Party but they do not seem enough to leaven the lump. In any case, despite their crude appeals to popular Islamic feeling neither party has as yet been able to rally wide-spread support, which is to the credit of Turkish Islam. If the Ecevit government is eventually replaced by another coalition led by the Democrat Party under Demirel, with the Erbakan and Turkes groups as very junior partners, there may be a few more superficial changes of an Islamic nature. But if, as is more likely, the Turkish armed forces tire once again of the self-seeking game of the politicians and retake power then, in the name of the secular Kemalist 'revolution', they will apply the brakes to any movement towards Islamic politics, genuine or otherwise. It is Turkey's misfortune that although it is a profoundly Muslim country it has not yet produced the serious and intelligent movement of Islamic modernism that it warrants.

It would be a sad day for Islam if ever militant politicized Islam manifested itself in Iraq, Syria or Lebanon; because, for reasons mentioned earlier, the potential communal splits of Pakistan and Iran would rapidly become for them realities resulting in their partition. Militant Islam plays no part on the political scene in Iraq and Syria because the Baath Socialist Party regimes in both countries will not tolerate any such competition or opposition. But this ban is in line with the already established national policy which was to mute the political role of religion because of the multiplicity of sects. This is a wise policy which should be maintained, whether by consent or coercion.

For much the same reason, the need for national unity, the Palestine Liberation Organization, so long as it remains the body representative of the Palestine national movement, will not allow militant Islam to have any role in that movement. It can hardly do so when its ultimate objective is a democratic *secular* state embracing all of Palestine and comprising its Jewish, Christian and Muslim citizens.

We now come to the most curious case of Saudi Arabia. Curious it certainly is, for in this mother country of Islam, militant Islam is there, has been there for half a century or more and yet, really and truly, it is not and never has been there. This contradiction exists because, on the one hand, the Saudi state has been and is a fully Islamic state, the Koran is its constitution, it is claimed, and its law is the Sharia, including all of the controversial canonical punishments; yet on the other hand the very form of the state, a monarchy that is hereditary within a single family, is most definitely un-Islamic, while the notorious personal behaviour of many members of the ruling family has been an abomination to the letter and spirit of the Koran: the Saudi princes have made 'Arab' a byword for 'extravagant licentiousness'. It is this contradiction between Islamic form and anti-Islamic practice that has made the Saudi regime the target of fierce criticism from many if not most Islamic reformers, especially the Muslim Brotherhood in the past and, more recently, from both the Khomeini and Bazargan groups in Iran. What, then, are the future prospects for real reformist militant Islam in the heartland of Islam? None whatsoever under the present regime: for while the Saudi government may perhaps give its support to reformist groups, like the brotherhood or Jamaat in other Muslim countries, they are not tolerated in the Saudi kingdom: and for the obvious reason that they are the regime's most dangerous enemies since they would attack it from within the ambit of Islam which is the foundation on which that regime has chosen to base itself.

It is a widespread and well based assumption that the regime of the House of Saud cannot long endure, neither in its present form nor in any improved model; and that events in Iran have considerably shortened its life expectancy. It can only be replaced by a military regime. What are likely to be the prospects for militant Islam under any such alternative regime? Not necessarily good, because it would suffer from the fact that the new Saudi rulers would be motivated by revulsion against the principles and practice of the present rulers, especially their religiosity; and this revulsion may not be discriminating between Islam good, Islam bad or Islam indifferent. However, because of the overwhelming Islamic atmosphere in Saudi Arabia it is wholly unlikely, impossible even, that the prospective military rulers of that country should be non-Islamic or anti-Islamic soldiers as is presently the case in Afghanistan. They probably could not be as non-Islamic as was Turkey's military chief, Kemal Atatürk, but they very well could be military rulers on the Nasser model, respectful towards religion, but keeping it in its place – on the sidelines of national life. Of course a compromise may be achieved if the new military rulers are men personally devout, like General Zia in Pakistan, but when well-established regimes are violently overthrown compromise arrangements or personalities are not the usual outcome. And as Saudi Arabia will go, so also will go the emirates around the periphery of the Arabian Peninsula.

In Egypt the future prospects of militant Islam, represented by the Muslim Brotherhood, are at least as good if not better than they are in Indonesia. That is to say the brotherhood, as the only possible alternative, has merely to bide its time, time which is running out fast for the present ruler Anwar Sadat, and which is running out at a faster rate than it is for General Suharto in Indonesia (in any case nothing moves fast in Indonesia, the climate and the diet sees to that). One can speak with certainty of the eventual ousting of Sadat because it is clear that his regime, or any other of the same type, does not have the answer to Egypt's real problem, its increasingly acute economic situation, which cannot be alleviated by foreign aid, aid that will not be forthcoming in sufficiently large quantities anyway.

Under Saudi influence the Sadat regime for many years tolerated the existence and semipublic activities of the Muslim Brotherhood, even though it was still technically illegal, and this gave it the tremendous opportunity, which it seized, to reorganize and expand; it was even permitted to produce a publication which began as a monthly but then became a weekly with a steadily increasing circulation. In this publication the Sadat peace initiative was harshly criticized from the beginning. When in April 1979 Saudi Arabia and the other Arab states broke with Egypt, Sadat's policy towards the brotherhood changed from toleration to hostility and editions of the weekly began to be banned. However, this change was to the brotherhood's advantage because official toleration, despite the brotherhood's criticism of that policy, had made the movement suspect in many eyes. Pushed squarely into opposition the brotherhood's position as the only possible alternative regime has been clarified and highlighted – the army has been tried and found wanting, the left is small and fragmented, and the peripatetic mummies of the pre-Nasser Wafd Party certainly do not have the capacity to handle the monumental mess that is Egypt.

President Numeiry of the Sudan has chosen to link his fortunes closely with those of Sadat, so Sadat's exit would quickly bring about his own. Even if another army regime succeeds, which is by no means certain – for when the army's nerve broke before, it took itself out of politics – the officers will still need popular backing which they can get from three sources – the Communist Party, the local Muslim Brotherhood or the Umma Party of Sadik al Mahdi. They are hardly likely to choose the first alternative and will probably prefer the third. So in the Sudan, too, militant Islam has prospects that are reasonably good.

As regards north and northwest Africa it can be said that

militant Islam is already in power, in a certain sense, in the strange regime of Colonel Gaddafi. It is more intelligibly present in Algeria, but firmly incorporated, at a low and muted level, in that country's monolithic one party state. In Tunisia, in view of President Bourguiba's advanced age and ill-health it is not inappropriate to consider the nature of the successor regime. It is not likely to be a militantly Islamic one but certainly one in which Islam will have a larger role than it has under Bourguiba. Firstly, because at least one of the un-Islamic reforms he introduced, the official non-recognition of the fasting month of Ramadan, was known to be of his personal inspiration because Bourguiba thought fasting was not modern or efficient; and, secondly, there are in the Tunisian administration thoughtful Muslim reformers of the best sort, as witnessed by the quality of the programme of religious instruction in the Tunisian school system. In view of the numerous attempts to assassinate King Hassan of Morocco the successor regime in that country is of current interest. As in Tunisia it is bound to have a stronger Islamic coloration because the future rulers are unlikely to repeat the king's excessively sophisticated cosmopolitanism; because of the continuing influence of Allal al Fassi and his disciples; and because radical reformist Islamic groups, like the Muslim Brotherhood, are already said to be strong in those bastions of opposition forces, the university campuses. (When reference is made to the existence of the Muslim Brotherhood in countries outside Egypt, such as the Sudan, Libya and Morocco, it cannot be ascertained with certainty, because of their clandestine role, whether these groups are separate and indigenous organizations merely using the same name or whether they are local branches of a single organization with its headquarters in Egypt. If it is the latter possibility, and if the brotherhood has in fact become an active pan-Arab movement, then it must be accounted a truly formidable force.)

Of the Muslim countries of Black Africa all that is known for certain is that in Chad, as in Afghanistan, militant Islam, but evidently not reformist militant Islam, is battling for control of the state. But what the Islamic picture is in such other Muslim African states as Senegal, Gambia, Guinea, Mali and Niger is, alas, beyond our ken.

This survey of the prospects of militant Islam in countries

across the expanse of the Muslim world reveals that those prospects, on the whole, are good and getting better. Thus, militant Islam is in position, though in a somewhat secondary and passive role in Libya and Algeria. It already actively wields power, wholly or very substantially, in two large and important countries, Iran and Pakistan, even though in both it is the focus of controversy and challenge. It is very well placed to come to power in even larger and more important countries: in Egypt and the Sudan in the near future, and in Indonesia in the not too distant future. It seems certain to make gains in Tunisia and Morocco. It is in countries like Saudi Arabia and Turkey that its future seems most problematical. Just as the frontier of Islam, as a religion, is moving steadily outwards and southwards in Black Africa, so too the spiritual or ideological frontier of militant Islam progresses steadily towards the Islamic state. And just as Islam, historically, has been extremely tenacious in holding on to any new territory acquired, so too any gains made by militant Islam will almost certainly be for the most part irreversible: one cannot conceive of either Iran or Pakistan ever again becoming completely secular states. The onward march of militant Islam is that much more assured not only because of the lack of an alternative but also because there are signs of a possible accommodation with its chief opponent.

That opponent is Westernizing nationalism, also the main antagonist of communism, which it has successfully rebuffed in Afro-Asia. Will it be as successful in halting the advance of militant Islam in Indonesia, Turkey or Egypt? There is the fact that, so far, the Westernizing nationalists, both the civilian politicians and the military men, have not succeeded in solving the fundamental, essentially economic, problems of their countries. Perhaps because of this observable failure we see civilian Westernizing nationalists, especially in Iran but also in Pakistan and to some extent in Turkey, moving back to their roots. The same is true of some of the Westernized military men – General Zia in Pakistan, General Nasution in Indonesia, Colonel Boumedienne in Algeria. On the other hand many of the religious reformers accept the importance of controlled Westernization – men like Ayatollah Telegani in Iran, Sadik Mahdi in the Sudan, and Natsir in Indonesia.

Apart from these evidences of mutual rapprochement the

religious reformers must set about trying to reach a serious and long-term accommodation because nationalism as a political emotion is still an immensely strong force in Afro-Asia, perhaps even of equal strength to Islam. The time does not yet seem ripe for supranational or anti-national Islamic political structures – on the basis of the caliphate, or of pan Islam or of the world-wide umma, the Muslim community. A good example of the exalted but rather utopian thinking on the umma theme is given in 'The Challenge of Islam':[2] 'The Muslim world must organize itself under the aegis of a Treaty of Mecca . . . it should be (easy) for the Muslim nations to submit to the supranational authority of the umma. The proposed Treaty of Mecca should establish an umma court of international justice, an umma council of education and cultural affairs, an umma currency and an umma bank of trade, investment and development. The Muslim world needs a press. The Jews have a press, the Chris-tians have a press, the Socialists have a press, the Communists have a press. The Muslim world has newspapers but no press.' But, as a first step, should not Mecca itself be ruled by a regime somewhat nearer the Islamic ideal than is the present one there?

So also Islamic nationalists need not push their nationalism towards exclusive chauvinism but, as an initial relaxation of nationalism, move towards regional arrangements: for which north Africa is an ideal testing ground and for which Colonel Gaddafi has been pressing. The whole Arabian Peninsula is a single geo-politico-economic unit, and should become so in practice. And Indonesia and Malaysia have more things in common than language and religion.

What has been objectionable to reformist Islam about nationalism has not only been its narrowness and divisiveness but its Western characteristics and the secular irreligiousness of its Westernized exponents. Both these objectionable features are being indigenized and diluted. Also, several of the reformist movements – the brotherhood, Masjumi and the Jamaat – have strongly advocated that type of nationalism called love of country or patriotism, so that on every side the lines of opposi-tion between Islam and nationalism are being blurred. Indeed a form of Islamic patriotism could become a median position between strict nationalism and supranational all-umma uto-pianism.

We now come to the crucial question in this assessment of the future possibilities of militant Islam, the primary question which has been pushed into second place by the headlong pace of developments in the Muslim world: does militant Islam have the answers to the political, economic and social problems of the Muslim countries?

Its political answer, as given in the form of the ideal constitution of the Islamic state is to place all, or almost all executive power in the hands of a single man, a modern caliph, and having democratically given him despotic powers to hope that he will be and remain 'a just despot'. This seems like asking too much from human nature, for it is a historical fact that 'power corrupts . . .' which is probably why there have not been all that many 'just despots' in Islamic or even in world history. Apart from the first four caliphs one can list the Emperors Ashoka, Marcus Aurelius, Suleiman the Magnificent, and Akhbar, also Salahadin and in more recent times De Gaulle, Tito and Nasser. Other names could, possibly, be added to this list but not all that many. If in the ideal Islamic constitution the legislature is decidedly inferior to the executive, the judiciary is supposed to be independent and therefore equal to the executive. But for how long will an almost all-powerful despot, however just, tolerate an independent judiciary? So militant Islam's answer to the terrible problem of power is not so much a solution, more a calculated risk. One thing is certain – the man of religion with the gun can and should never be anything more than a transitory phenomenon.

The real test of militant Islam's relevance or competence will be its handling of the economic problems of the Muslim countries. Here it is on surer ground than in the political sphere. It is, by now, well known what these problems are, and that they are common to all Afro-Asian countries; thus the Islamic solutions to them have also been extensively studied, almost too much so. A research report on *Contemporary Literature on Islamic Economics*, with chapter headings such as 'The Economic Philosophy of Islam', 'The Economic System of Islam', 'Economic Analysis in an Islamic Framework' and so on, lists no less than 700 works.[3] So there is no dearth of Islamic ideas on economic problems. There is still less of a dearth of money, because the oil-rich Muslim states have shown a commendable readiness to share their wealth with their less fortunate Muslim brethren. What is needed, and so far has been in very short supply in rich countries like Indonesia, Iran and Saudi Arabia, is character: drive linked to dedication and honesty. These qualities the Islamic reformist groups are well able to supply; for even in lax societies like Indonesia and Egypt it is agreed that the members of these movements are noteworthy for possessing just such qualities of character. This is why they have been both envied and feared.

As a solver of social problems the Islamic state begins with two initial disadvantages. Governments based on or closely associated with religions are automatically associated with the right of the political spectrum; hence, despite active wooing, the failure of the Jamaat and the brotherhood to make much headway with the trade unions in Pakistan and Egypt. But perhaps Algeria for the Sunnis and Ayatollah Telegani of Iran for the Shiahs have done something to shift the image of political Islam towards the left. This is important because the basic trend in Afro-Asia is towards the left, and it is also industrializing with trade unions becoming more powerful.

The second disadvantage is massive: the fact that Islam puts one half of the human race, women, into a subordinate position to the male half – no amount of apologetics about respect for women, protection of their just rights and so forth can get around this basic and unjust discrimination. It is firmly embedded in Islamic practice because it is there in the Koran, as are the canonical punishments.

This brings us to a consideration of what sort of Islam can provide the enduring basis for militant Islam, both before and after it comes to power in a Muslim country. As such a basis Islam will constantly run into problems and contradictions and self-contradictions if it clings to two dogmas – an old one, that every single word in the Koran is of divine inspiration, and a newer one, that Muhammad is the most perfect human exemplar and is above all or any criticism. Militant reformist Islam can be solidly based only on a reformed Islam. Because, so far, new unorthodox Islamic thinking on political, economic and social problems has gone along with a touching but inconsistent loyalty to orthodox theology, militant Islam has tended to fall between two stools. Any real reconstruction of religious thought in Islam needs to be based on the principle that the area of unquestioned revealed truth needs to be narrowed, but not diluted.

The omens for this sort of radical religious reform are both bad and good. The bad omens were the way in which two previous attempts in rethinking the Koran itself were stamped upon. The first attempt was made in 1925 in a book by the Egyptian scholar Ali Abdel Razzek, in which he asserted that 'There are no such things as Islamic political principles,' and that Muhammad's mission was purely prophetic and religious and therefore that the spiritual parts of the Koran had eternal validity but not those dealing with mundane matters. The book raised a tempest of protestation: it was formally denounced by a council of ulema of al Azhar and the author declared unfit to hold any public office.[4] The second attempt came in the 1940s when another Egyptian, the professor of literature Muhammad Khalafallah made the much more modest suggestion, and a fairly obvious one, that the narrative portions of the Koran, the story of Noah for example, were not necessarily of divine inspiration. This raised yet another storm, followed by the withdrawal of the book.

The favourable omens for the modernist rethinking of Islam as a religion are that both Sunni and Shiah religious authorities have officially called for the revision of the corpus of the Hadith or prophetic traditions: al Azhar in the case of the Sunnis and Ayatollah Burujurdi, the previous *marja i taqlid* or chief religious authority of the Shiah world. But tinkering with the Hadith does not take one very far: the whole body of the Sharia has to be scrutinized and the Koran itself has to be looked at reverently but critically through modern eyes, in the same way in which devout Christian theologians, religious and lay, have been looking at the New Testament for the past hundred years. Muslim reformers have been looking for a Luther ever since the time of Afghani; they should also be looking for a Barth, a Niebuhr, a Temple and a Mauriac.

What are needed are statements like the following. The first is from Sayed Amir Ali, the author of *The Spirit of Islam*: 'It is earnestly to be hoped that before long a general synod of Muslim doctors will authoritatively declare that polygamy, like slavery, is abhorrent to the laws of Islam.'[5] The second is a statement of faith by the well known scholar of Muslim law, A. A. A. Fyzee.[6] Fyzee begins by asserting that in any rethinking of Islam the distinction must be made between universal moral ideals like kindness, honesty and loyalty, and prohibitions peculiar to Islam such as eating pork, drinking alchohol, the giving and receiving of interest, which are no longer applicable today; since ethics are personal, attempts to enforce them through the Sharia are unnecessary; Muslim law is suitable only for seventh-century Bedouins; it is inapplicable to Eskimos, Bushmen or even Bengalis; the Koran is responsible for the subjection of women in the Muslim world; the Koran is the word of God but its descriptions of heaven and hell are mere poetic imagery; the suras of the Koran enunciated in Mecca can be accepted as being divinely inspired but not all those given at Medina; and rituals like observing the fast of Ramadan and the five daily prayers, depending on outward observance, retard inner spiritual development. It may seem, even to Islamic reformists, that Fyzee goes too far in his iconoclasm; but what really militates against his views, and those of Amir Ali, being taken seriously is that both men were Shiahs and from the Indian sub-continent. It is only when such views are propounded, if simply as a basis for serious discussion, by devout and thoughtful Sunnis from the Islamic heartland, it is only then that it could be said that the real rethinking of Islam in modern terms has begun.

The gates of ijtihad, of independent judgement, need to be flung wide open. Till that happens and Muslim thinkers begin to think the unthinkable, and to publish their unthinkable thoughts, they will continue to spend far too much time, as they do at present, putting forward unconvincing apologies for Islam on such issues as the position of women and the canonical punishments. Islam has bigger and better tasks ahead of it: Toynbee has indicated two tasks for which he believed Islam was peculiarly fitted – the solution of the problems of racial discrimination and of alchoholism. But Islam would do better to devote itself to such tasks, after it has done the essential rethinking of its essential nature, and the reformation of thought, rather than indulging in flexing its military muscle as when in January 1979 it was announced that forty-one Islamic nations had spent $40 billion on their defence forces, had 3·5 million men under arms, and owned more tanks and aircraft than NATO excluding the USA; and that all this military might could be pooled in a single Islamic armoury. But there is not going to be another Poitiers or another Vienna.

Such boastings can best be excused as expressions of youthful vigour. And indeed it is this very vigour of Islam, its youthful militancy, the generation gap between it and an ageing Christianity, that is itself productive of misunderstanding. The original essay in the *Economist* from which this book has stemmed was productive of several letters in which Islam was advised to be as relaxed and tolerant as Christianity or as the post-Christian West. Similarly, Buddhist visitors to fourteenth and fifteenth century Europe, viewing with the heavy lidded wisdom of the immemorial East the militant activities of the Fathers of the Reformation might have advised Wycliffe, Hus and Luther to be more relaxed and tolerant, not to be so sure of their beliefs, and not to split the seamless robe of Christendom with their agitational sermonizing. But militant Islam *is* certain of the truth of its beliefs, and it believes that it *does* really know the truth. Like its militant Protestant predecessors it is not going to relax or to be particularly tolerant. And it will not cease from mental and spiritual and material strife till those beliefs govern the destinies of every Muslim country.

March–May 1979
Oxford and Nicosia

Notes

Prologue

1 N. A. Daniel: *Islam and the West. The Making of an Image*, University Press, Edinburgh, 1962.
2 Sadeh al Mahdi: 'The Concept of an Islamic State', p 119 in *The Challenge of Islam*, edited by A. Ganhar, Islamic Council of Europe, London, 1978.
3 See 'The Geographical Setting' by X. De Planhol in volume 2 of *The Cambridge History of Islam*, University Press, Cambridge, 1970. Also, the same authors' *Les Fondements Géographiques de l'Histoire de l'Islam*, Flammarion, Paris, 1968.

Chapter 1

1 'Islam: Basic Principles and Characteristics' by Khurshid Ahmad, p 37 in *Islam, Its Meaning and Message*, edited by K. Ahmad, Islamic Council of Europe, London, 1976.
2 Press conference in Cairo, April 1972.
3 Lahore, February 1974.
4 Abul al Maududi: 'What Islam Stands For', p 4, in *The Challenge of Islam*.
5 Fazlur Rahman: *Islam*, Weidenfeld and Nicolson, London, 1966, pages 33 *et seq*.
6 In one curiously prophetic Hadith concerning the signs of the Day of Judgment, Muhammad is recorded as saying: 'You will see the barefooted, naked destitute herdsmen competing in constructing lofty buildings.' Is this a prediction of the present building boom in the oil-rich Gulf States and Saudi Arabia? From An Nawawi's *Forty Hadith*, Koran Publishing House, Damascus, 1976, p 32.
7 The word *Sharia* originally meant 'the path or road leading to the water'. As applied to a sacrosanct legal system this could be taken to mean something like 'a way to the very source of life'. See Fazlur Rahman *op cit*.
8 W. Montgomery Watt: 'Islamic Political Thought', *Islamic Surveys*, number 6, University Press, Edinburgh, 1968.
9 This point is made with the proviso that nobody seems to know

what was the original doctrine in Buddhism. See Mrs C. Rhys
Davids: *Buddhism*, Home University Library, London, and *What
Is The Original Doctrine in Buddhism?*, London.
10 Reported in the *International Herald Tribune*, 23–4 December
1978.

Chapter 2

1 For an account of one black Muslim's development towards Islam
proper see the remarkable *Autobiography of Malcolm X*, Penguin,
London.

2 *Islam et Jeunesse en Turquie d'Aujourd'hui* by Sabine Dirks, pp 305
et seq. Librairie H. Champion, Paris, 1977.

3 S. M. H. Nainar: 'Basic Concepts of Javanese Culture and the
Preachers of Islam' in *Arabic and Islamic Studies in Honor of
H. A. R. Gibb*, edited by G. Makdisi, Brill, Leiden, 1965, p 506.

4 *Indonesian Political Thinking, 1945–1965*, edited by H. Feith and
L. Castles, Cornell, 1970, p 192.

5 W. S. Trimingham: *The Influence of Islam upon Africa*, Longmans,
London, 1962, p 2.

6 *Northern Africa: Islam and Modernization*, edited by M. Brett,
Cass, London, 1973, p 59.

7 Trimingham, *op cit*, pp 34 *et seq.*

8 O. Depont and X. Coppolani: *Les confréries religieuses musulmans*,
Algiers, 1897. As the publication dates of the following books
indicate, interest in the brotherhoods is quickening and may even
be becoming fashionable (in orientalist circles, that is): J. K.
Birge: *The Bektashi Order of Dervishes*, London and Hartford,
1937; J. W. McPherson: *The Moulids of Egypt*, Cairo, 1941; E. E.
Evans-Pritchard: *The Sanusi of Cyrenaica*, Oxford, 1949; J. M.
Abun-Nasr: *The Tijaniyya*, London, 1965; M. Berger: *Islam in
Egypt Today – social and political aspects of popular religion*,
London, 1970; M. D. Gilsenen: *Saint and Sufi in Modern Egypt*,
Oxford, 1978; F. de Jong: *Turuq and Turuq-Linked Institutions in
Nineteenth-Century Egypt*, Brill, Leiden, 1978.

9 'It was, indeed, Sufism, or Islamic mysticism, rather than Islamic
orthodoxy which for a long time held sway in Java and in parts of
Sumatra . . . ' from H. J. Benda: *The Crescent and the Rising Sun*,
W. Hoeve, The Hague, 1958.

10 There is now an adequate literature on African Islam provided,
single-handed, by J. Spencer Trimingham in his books on Islam
in the Sudan, east Africa and west Africa; also his summing up in
the volume mentioned in note 5 above. The first six chapters of
the book referred to in the note above are good detailed studies of
certain aspects. On Islam in Indonesia, which despite the fact that

Indonesia is the largest Muslim state, has been somewhat
neglected by Western Islamists, except the Dutch (whose writings
being in Dutch are virtually inaccessible) see:

W. Montgomery Watt: *Islam and the Integration of Society*,
Routledge and Kegan Paul, London, 1961, p 137.

11 H. A. R. Gibb: *Modern Trends in Islam*, University Press, Chicago,
1950, p 2.

Chapter 3

1 N. A. Daniel, *op cit*, p 79.
2 L. Levonian: *Studies in the Relationship between Islam and
Christianity*, Allen and Unwin, London, 1940, p 80. At the time of
writing *Militant Islam* the author was Dean of the Near East
School of Theology, Beirut.
3 Daniel, *op cit*, pp 251 *et seq*.
4 Daniel, *op cit*, p 263.
5 K. S. Latourette: *A History of the Expansion of Christianity*,
volume II, Harper, New York, 1938.
6 Daniel, *op cit*, p 121. Daniel describes this bizarre episode in full;
Latourette merely says: 'a group went to Morocco and there
suffered martyrdom.'
7 Latourette, *op cit*.
8 The information in the preceding paragraphs is drawn from *The
Modernist Muslim Movement in Indonesia* by D. Noer, OUP,
London, 1973, pp 22 *et seq* and pp 162 *et seq*.
9 Latourette, *op cit*, volume V, pp 291–2.
10 Latourette, *op cit*, volume VI, p 9 *et seq*. See also: N. A. Daniel:
Islam, Europe and Empire, University Press, Edinburgh, 1966,
pp 326 *et seq*; Stephen Neill: *Colonialism and Christian Missions*,
Lutterworth, London, 1966; J. Abun-Nasr: *A History of the
Maghrib*, CUP, Cambridge, 1971.
11 M. O. Beshir: *The Southern Sudan*, Hurst, London, 1968, p 35.
This valuable work is based entirely on official sources and I have
relied on it in this section.
12 Including J. Spencer Trimingham, then Secretary of the Church
Missionary Society in the Sudan.
13 Latourette, *op cit*, volume VII, pp 272–3.
14 *Op cit*, pp 469–72.
15 J. Riley-Smith: *What Were The Crusades?*, Macmillan, London,
1978, pp 19 *et seq*.
16 Stephen Neill, op *cit*, p 39.
17 Daniel: *Islam and the West*, p 265.
18 Splendidly portrayed in Lesley Blanche's *The Sabus of Paradise*.
See also: *Central Asia: a Century of Russian Rule*, edited by

E. Allworth, Columbia, London, 1967 and R. A. Pierce: *Russia in Central Asia, 1867–1917*, University of California, Berkeley, 1960, an extremely detailed survey.

19 *New Cambridge Modern History*, Cambridge, 1962, volume XI, p 609.
20 Watt: *Islam and the Integration of Society*, p 175.
21 Charles F. Gallagher: 'Language and Identity' in *State and Society in Independent North Africa*, edited by L. C. Brown, Middle East Institute, Washington, 1966, pp 76–7.
22 A. L. Tibawi: *Islamic Education*, Luzac, London, 1972. In this section I am much indebted to the work of this meticulous scholar.
23 Tibawi, *op cit*, p 172.
24 George McT. Kahin: *Nationalism and Revolution in Indonesia*, Cornell, New York, 1952, pp 29–35, 54–5.
25 Harry J. Benda: *The Crescent and the Rising Sun*, Van Hoeve, The Hague, 1958, p 74.
26 Harry J. Benda: *Continuity and Change in Southeast Asia*, by H. J. Benda, Yale, New Haven, 1972, p 97.
27 I had just begun writing this book when *Orientalism* by Edward W. Said (Pantheon Books, New York, Routledge and Kegan Paul, London) appeared. Mr Said refers critically to Gibb at some length and very briefly, in passing, to Hurgronje. His approach to these two scholars is rather different from mine since Mr Said is concerned with the over-arching concepts of Orientalism. His is an angry book, justifiably so, brilliant and learned.
28 C. Snouck Hurgronje: *Selected Works*, edited by G. H. Bosquet and J. Schact, Brill, Leiden, 1957, p 48.
29 C. Snouck Hurgronje: *Mohammedanism*, Putnam, New York, 1916, p 147.
30 Quoted on p 24 of Benda *The Crescent*.
31 Quoted on p 103 of *L'Islam dans le Miroir de l'Occident* by J. J. Waardenburg, Mouton, Paris, 1962.
32 *Op cit*, p 103.
33 *Op cit*, p 102.
34 *Op cit*, p 102.
35 Benda: *The Crescent*, p 26.
36 *Op cit*, p 26 and especially note number 56.
37 Waardenburg, *op cit*, p 127.
38 *Mohammedanism*, p 103 *et seq*.
39 Quoted in Waardenburg, *op cit*, p 101.
40 Benda: *Continuity*, p 89.
41 *Whither Islam?* edited by H. A. R. Gibb, Gollancz, London, 1932; see pp 88, 253, 258 *et seq*.

42 *Op cit*, p 97.

43 They also have a very firm grip of Middle Eastern studies in the universities of the United States. See *MERIP Report* 38, June 1975.

Chapter 4

1 *Cambridge History of Islam* volume 2, pp 400 *et seq.*

2 Any writer on Afghani, Abduh or Rida must be deeply indebted to the lucid and learned pages of Albert Hourani's *Arabic Thought in the Liberal Age*, OUP, London, 1962. See also Gibb: *Modern Trends*; W. Cantwell Smith: *Islam in Modern History*; and G. E. von Grunebaums: *Islam: Essays in the Nature and Growth of a Cultural Tradition*, American Anthropological Association, 1955.

3 *Cambridge History of Islam, op cit*, p 619.

4 Quoted in Daniel: *Islam, Europe and Empire*, p 333.

5 *The Cambridge History of Islam*, volume II, p 162.

6 See Abun-Nasr, *op cit* and Alastair Horne: *A Savage War of Peace.*

7 Daniel, *op cit*, p 337.

8 Allworth, *op cit*, pp 163–71.

9 Aziz Ahmad: 'Activism of the Ulema in Pakistan', p 257, in *Saints and Sufis*, edited by N. R. Keddie, Berkeley, 1972.

10 Wilfred Cantwell Smith: *Modern Islam in India*, pp 161 *et seq*, 195 *et seq.*

11 P. M. Holt: *The Mahdist State in the Sudan*, Oxford, 1958.

12 J. Spencer Trimingham: *Islam in the Sudan*, OUP, London, 1949, pp 158–9.

13 Abun Nasr, *op cit*, pp 377–92.

14 S. H. Longrigg: *Iraq, 1900 to 1950*, OUP, London, 1953, pp 122 *et seq*; and A. T. Wilson: *Loyalties, Mesopotamia*, OUP, London, 1931, pp 294–302.

15 *Op cit*, pp 364–6.

16 The information in the following paragraphs comes from the two volumes of Y. Porath: *The Emergence of the Palestinian–Arab National Movement: 1918–1929*, 1974, and *The Palestinian Arab National Movement: 1929–1973*, 1977; both published by Cass, London. A thorough piece of work, and a fair-minded one; a point to be appreciated, for the author is an Israeli.

17 Gibb: 'The Reaction in the Middle East Against Western Culture' in *Studies etc*, p 324.

18 B. Grant: *Indonesia*, University Press, Melbourne, 1964, pp 18–20.

19 In the preceding paragraphs use has been made of A. L. Tibawi, *op cit*; E. Rosenthal: *Islam in the Modern National State*, University Press, Cambridge, 1965; and *Man, State and Society in the*

Contemporary Maghrib, edited by I. W. Zartmann, Pall Mall, London, 1973, section 32.

20 Fazlur Rahman: 'Islam and the New Constitution of Pakistan', p 37 in *Contemporary Problems of Pakistan*, edited by J. H. Korson, Brill-Leiden, 1974.

21 N. Berkes: *The Development of Secularism in Turkey*, McGill, Montreal, 1964, pp 466 *et seq*, 501.

22 For Gokalp see *The Foundation of Turkish Nationalism*, by the late-lamented Uriel Heyd, London, 1950; and the selection of his works translated in *Turkish Nationalism and Western Civilization*, by N. Berkes, Allen and Unwin, London, 1959; a most useful collection: pp 143, 222, 272, 276, 279, 298–300. For the strange theory of Turkishness versus Islam see Heyd, *op cit*, p 103 and Halide Edib: *Turkey Faces West*, New Haven, 1930, pp 120–1.

23 'Said Nursi and the Risala-i-Nur' by Hamid Algar, in *Islamic Perspectives*, Islamic Foundation, London, 1978, pp 313 *et seq*; also Dirks: *Islam et Jeunesse*, pp 172–7.

24 Max W. Thornburg: *Turkey: an Economic Appraisal*, Twentieth Century Fund, New York, 1949, page vii.

Chapter 5

1 In addition to producing half a dozen songs that will last as long as the hundreds produced by Schubert.

2 Sadiq al Mahdi: 'The Concept of an Islamic State', p 130, *op cit*.

3 Ismail R. Faruqi: 'Islam and Other Faiths' in *The Challenge of Islam*, p 98.

4 Mohammed Ayub Khan: *Friends Not Masters*, OUP, New York, 1967, p 197.

5 Richard P. Mitchell: *The Society of the Muslim Brothers*, OUP, London, 1969, p 264. There would be far fewer misunderstandings of militant Islam if this masterly and scholarly work on one of the most militant Islamic groups had received the attention it deserves.

6 Sura 34, verse 28; 36, 70; 61, 9.

7 Mitchell, *op cit*, p 264.

8 *Ibid*.

9 Altaf Gauhar: 'Islam and Secularism', p 305 in *The Challenge of Islam*.

10 *Indonesian Political Thinking, 1945–1965*, edited by H. Feith and L. Castles, Cornell, 1970, p 164.

11 *Op cit*, pp 200–1.

12 Z. A. Bhutto: *Thoughts On Some Aspects of Islam*, Ashraf, Lahore, 1976, p 52.

13 Penelope Mortimer in the *New Statesman*, London, volume 97,

number 2506, p 436. This journalist, witnessing communal prayers in Saudi Arabia, writes of it, 'Allah, presumably, had arrived' – a remark of such arrogant silliness as to convince a militant Muslim that the spirit of the arrogant missionary and the silly Crusader is still alive in England today, and that only a greater degree of punitive militancy will bring the West to understanding or at least politeness.

14 Daniel: *Islam, Europe and Empire*, p 385.
15 H. V. F. Winstone: *Gertrude Bell*, Cape, London, 1978, p 162.
16 Daniel, *op cit*, p 467.
17 E. Rosenthal: *Islam in the Modern National State*, CUP, Cambridge, 1965, pp 212–13.
18 Z. A. Bhutto, *op cit*, p 74.
19 'Islam in the new Egyptian Constitution', by J. P. O'Kane, pp 137–48, *Middle East Journal*, Spring, 1972.
20 L. Binder: *The Proofs of Islam*.
21 Ayub Khan, *op cit*, pp 198–207.
22 Information in the section is from Mitchell: *The Society of the Muslim Brothers*. Two earlier works in English on the subject are I. Husayni: *The Moslem Brethren*, Beirut, 1956; and J. Heyworth-Dunne: *Religious and Political Trends in Modern Egypt*, Washington, 1950. Mitchell's book supersedes these and other later works on the brotherhood.
23 The author is indebted for the information in this section and in the next chapter to Mr Mohammed Ali Abu Hamdeh of St Antony's College, Oxford.
24 Nissim Rejwan: 'In The Name of Allah', *New Outlook*, Tel Aviv, volume 8, number 7, pp 21 *et seq.*
25 Freeland Abbot: 'The Jamaat i Islami of Pakistan', *Middle East Journal*, volume II, number 1, pp 37–51.
26 E. Rosenthal, *op cit*, p 247. The most comprehensive work on the Jamaat is *The Jamaat i Islami of Pakistan*, by Kalim Bahadur, Progressive Books, Lahore, 1978. It is a work of uneven merit and the fact that the author is an Indian Muslim is often too evident. There are also three essays on Maududi in Part IV of *Islamic Perspectives*, *qv*. Very many of Maududi's publications have been published in English, mostly in Lahore. Also 'The Ideology of Maududi' by C. Adams in *South Asian Politics and Religion*, edited by D. Smith, Princeton, 1966.
27 See Kahin and Noer, *op cit*. Also B. J. Boland: *The Struggle of Islam in Modern Indonesia*, Nijhoff, The Hague, 1971.
28 Attilio Gaudio: *Allal al Fassi*, Moreau, Paris, 1972.
29 If the movement of militant Islam is misunderstood in the non-Muslim world because not enough is known about it, this is

partly its own fault in that it has not tried or bothered to explain itself to outsiders. But one must remember two things – the distraction of the struggle itself, and the fact that every branch of the movement has at one time or another been banned and has had to limit its publications to underground material meant only for the membership.

30 Watt: *Islam and the Integration of Society*, p 251.
31 Bianco, *op cit*, pp 94–7.
32 Gibb, *Modern Trends in Islam*, pp 54 and 104–5.
33 Boland, *op cit*, pp 123–34.
34 Ayub Khan, *op cit*, pages ix and 195.
35 I. A. Qureshi: 'Islam and the West – Past, Present and Future', pp 243–4 in *The Challenge of Islam*, qv.

Chapter 6

1 P. M. Holt: *The Mahdist State in the Sudan*, OUP, Oxford, 1958, p 100.
2 Holt, p 247.
3 Trimingham: *Islam in the Sudan, op cit*, 155.
4 *Op cit*, pp 156, 162.
5 C. Hill: *The World Turned Upside Down*, Penguin, London, 1976; and J. P. Kenyon: *The Stuart Constitution*, CUP, Cambridge, 1976, pp 336, 348.
6 Ayub Khan, *op cit*, p 204.
7 D. Noer, *op cit*, pp 287–91.
8 Mitchell, *op cit*, pp 245–50, 260–3.
9 *Le Monde*, 27.7.1977.
10 Sadiq el Mahdi, *op cit*, p 131.
11 A. A. Maududi: *The Islamic Law and Constitution*, Islamic Publications, Lahore, 1969, p 140.
12 *Op cit*, pp 246–61.
13 A. K. Brohi: 'Maududi, the Man, the Scholar, the Reformer', p 305 in *Islamic Perspectives, qv*.
14 Gaudio, *op cit*, p 105.
15 See excerpts from Khomeini's book and that of Ayatollah Nuri given in *Kayhan International*, Tehran, 29, 30, 31 January; 1 February 1979.
16 Haj Ahmad Agha Khomeini, the Ayatollah's son, in an interview in *Tehran Journal*, 29 January 1979.
17 A. F. Tabbarah: *The Spirit of Islam*, Beirut, 1978, p 293 *et seq*.
18 Maxime Rodinson: *Islam and Capitalism*, Penguin, London, 1974, pp 24, 224 *et seq*.
19 R. Vallin: 'Muslim Socialism in Algeria', pp 50–64 in Zartmann, *op cit*.

20 Kalim Bahadur, *op cit*, pp 177, 182.

21 Gaudio, *op cit*, pp 173, 179 *et seq*.

22 Mitchell, *op cit*, pp 250–3, 272–4.

23 Abdul Bani-Sadr in *Keyhan International*, 25 January 1979.

24 Rosenthal, *op cit*, p 165.

25 Kalim Bahadur, *op cit*, p 181.

26 For details on interest-free banking see 'How an Islam bank will do without usury', *Financial Times*, London, 22 March 1977, p 32.

27 Gaudio, *op cit*, p 121.

28 Kansar Niazi: *Modern Challenges to Muslim Families*, Ashraf, Lahore, 1976.

29 A. al Sharabassy: *Islam and Family Planning*, Cairo, 1969.

30 Sadiq al Mahdi, *op cit*, pp 130–1.

Epilogue

1 L. J. Peter and R. Hall: *The Peter Principle*, Pan Books, London, 1971. It is easier to observe the operation of this principle in military rather than civilian life: two recent examples of promotion beyond the level of competency are the US General Westmoreland in Vietnam and Field Marshal Montgomery in World War II.

2 'The Challenge of Islam', *op cit*, *Islam and Secularism*, by Altaf Gauhar, p 309.

3 M. N. Siddiqui: *Contemporary Literature on Islamic Economics*, The Islamic Foundation, Leicester, 1978.

4 Hourani, *op cit*, pp 183–92; a detailed and lucid analysis of the whole debate.

5 Quoted on p 97 of Gibb's *Modern Trends*.

6 I regret I cannot quote Fyzee's essay directly, but can only refer to it as quoted in *Islam versus the West*, by Mariam Jameela, Ashraf, Lahore, 1962, p 110 *et seq*. The author mentions that Fyzee's essay appeared in the *Islamic Review*, but gives no date of publication, and I have not been able to obtain a copy of the issue containing the essay. The author of several standard works on Indian Muslim jurisprudence, A. A. A. Fyzee served as Indian ambassador to Egypt, and when he wrote this essay was vice-chancellor of the University of Kashmir.

Index